"Theologically astute, musically adept, and practical, Paul Jones's *Singing and Making Music* is an important entry into the current discussion of public worship and music. For those serious about attaining a robust biblical understanding and practice of music as handmaiden to theology, Jones is a must-read. Constructively provocative, learned, and commonsensical, this volume is a treasure trove for pastors, church musicians and Christians who want to build a biblical theology of music and worship, as well as address the most pressing issues of today's 'worship wars' positively and pastorally."

J. Ligon Duncan III
Senior Minister, First Presbyterian Church, Jackson, MS
President, Alliance of Confessing Evangelicals

"We live in an age of worship wars and worship controversies. Beyond all this, many evangelical churches have simply lost any vision of true Christian worship. The authority of our scriptural foundation and the riches of the church's heritage are neglected in favor of superficial entertainment and endless innovations. Paul S. Jones offers a much-needed corrective in *Singing and Making Music.* A wonderfully skilled musician, Dr. Jones combines keen theological insights with fascinating historical background. This book arrives just in time and will help Christians to rethink worship—and to recover its authentic splendor."

R. Albert Mohler Jr.
President, The Southern Baptist Theological Seminary, Louisville, KY

"As Organist and Music Director of historic Tenth Presbyterian Church in Philadelphia, Dr. Jones is at the center of Philadelphia's arts community, halfway between Curtis Institute and the Kimmel Center, where the Philadelphia Orchestra has for generations shaped the musical education of our nation. For the last several years it has been my privilege to have worshiped at Tenth Church and Sunday after Sunday to have been inspired by the worship music he has so brilliantly directed. Both my wife and my daughter have sung in his choir, which almost makes him a member of the family! Such high academic qualifications and such refined artistic taste are rarely found together in one person. This book gives us insight into the genius of his Christian witness in one of the music centers of our nation."

Hughes Oliphant Old

Dean, Institute for Reformed Worship, Erskine Seminary
Lecturer, Princeton Theological Seminary

"Music and ministry are intimately woven together throughout the Scriptures. Paul Jones's well-written and timely book provides our Reformed and Presbyterian churches with a fresh and passionate guide to the spiritual fabric of musical sound and sound theology. Pastors, teachers, and musicians will grow in wisdom and worship as they reflect on this study of the praise of our sovereign God of redeeming grace through church music."

Peter A. Lillback

President, Westminster Theological Seminary
Senior Pastor, Proclamation Presbyterian Church, Bryn Mawr, PA

"The church in every generation needs to be reminded that true praise begins with God and his glory, and not man and his need. Paul Jones sounds this note loud and clear in what is a very helpful book."

Alistair Begg

Truth for Life; Senior Pastor, Parkside Church, Cleveland, OH

"This book calls us back to biblical worship with theological content as the priority in today's church."

Clayton Erb

Minister of Worship and Music, Grace Community Church,
Sun Valley, CA

Singing and Making Music

Issues in Church Music Today

PAUL S. JONES

Foreword by Eric J. Alexander

P.O. BOX 817 • PHILLIPSBURG • NEW JERSEY 08865-0817

Italics within Scripture quotations indicate emphasis added.

Page design and typesetting by Lakeside Design Plus

Printed in the United States of America

Library of Congress Cataloging-in-Publication Data

Jones, Paul S., 1969–

Singing and making music : issues in church music today / Paul S. Jones ; foreword by Eric J. Alexander.

p. cm.

Includes bibliographical references and index.

ISBN-13: 978-0-87552-617-1 (pbk).

ISBN-10: 0-87552-617-9 (pbk.)

1. Music in churches. 2. Church music. I. Title.

ML3001.J66 2006

264'.2—dc22

2005057514

To

my parents, Eric and Sharon Jones
who taught me to think, work, live, and love

with deep gratitude to

Samuel Hsu
and
James Montgomery Boice

The Lord is my strength and my song,
and he has become my salvation;
this is my God, and I will praise him,
my father's God, and I will exalt him.
—Exodus 15:2

Contents

Foreword

Singing and Making Music is a splendid collection of essays, covering a very wide field. It is one of the most relevant books on the ministry of music for twenty-first-century churches seeking to deal biblically with this subject. Because it emphasizes biblical principles and not just local methodology, it applies not just to large churches like Tenth Presbyterian in Philadelphia, where the author serves as organist and music director, but to all kinds of fellowships of God's people, large and small, urban, suburban, and rural.

Someone has described "any Tenth service" as "a cross section of racial, ethnic, socio-economic and age groups . . . students, young families and old, suits and dresses, jeans and T-shirts—all holding hymnbooks, standing side by side, singing all verses of a hymn." The point is that by upholding biblical principles and musical excellence, we should be teaching and exemplifying what is as universally relevant as Scripture itself.

Dr. Paul Jones ranks among the finest church musicians I have ever known. His gifts, standards, and skills as a soloist, accompanist, and conductor, and as a trainer and teacher of choirs, are remarkable. He excels in inspiring congregations and pupils alike to seek biblical and musical excellence in their whole approach to worship, which is one of the great passions of his life.

Dr. James Montgomery Boice, with whom Dr. Jones worked fruitfully in Tenth Church, told me after one service at which I had been present, "Paul is everything I ever prayed for in a music director." The harmony with which they served God in Tenth was a remarkable blessing to the congregation in the all-too-brief time before Boice's death. One lasting evidence of that partnership is the original hymns they mutually produced as author and composer. These hymns are distinguished by their biblical faithfulness, theological depth, and musical quality. They are illustrations of so many of the truths expounded in this book.

Paul Jones is not only highly trained and qualified as a professional musician, but also well read in the world of biblical theology and writings of the Reformers. It is this combination of musician and theologian that I think is the key to his wisdom in this outstanding material on the church's musical worship. The key phrase in all this is the one with which the preface to this book closes. It is often abbreviated to the letters "SDG"—representing the Latin words *soli Deo gloria* ("to God alone be glory"). This is what leads Dr. Jones to his basic convictions about church music (it should honor and exalt God, not merely entertain the congregation) and church worship (it should glorify God, not merely satisfy the worshipers).

I pray that God may prosper this book abundantly; cause it to be widely read, digested, and heeded within the Christian church; and thereby bring to himself a new revenue of glory in our generation.

Eric J. Alexander
St. Andrews, Scotland

Preface

Why another book about church music? Surely the shelves of Christian bookstores are already lined with volumes devoted to worship music and to various perspectives on the "worship wars" debate. Other authors have provided historical information on the development of church music over the centuries. With penetrating insight, the culture-watchers have sought to guide us through the maze of recent trends. So what need is there for another book?

First and simply, this volume exists because it contains ideas that every worshiper (pastor and layperson) and Christian musician (performer and academic) may benefit from reading, since it is entirely possible to live in the subculture of the evangelical church without encountering some of them. God's creation itself, through general revelation, informs wide-ranging aspects and principles of music. But more specifically, since the Bible is our infallible guide of Christian faith *and practice,* it contains sufficient instruction for us to understand the roles of music in the church. In considering these roles, I have sought to be practical, philosophical, and biblical. Thus, the volume in your hands is a collection of short essays organized into four categories that interact with the issues and people involved in the music of corporate worship, exploring what the Bible reveals. Any book that asserts ideas about church music will be provocative, but in so doing my goal is to speak clearly, not uncharitably. Engaging in church music ought to be a uniting, compelling, involving activity—not a divisive, troubling one.

Second, the book was written to be of aid to those pastors, church leaders, and musicians who desire help regarding the use of music in the church, particularly as this applies to worship. Decisions about church music need not be made on the basis of limited experience, personal preference, or expediency. This volume asks questions to provoke thought about what we do and why we do it, and it endeavors to provide basic information about music's relationship to the church. There are also things that one will not find in this book. It contains no list of acceptable and unacceptable repertoire. One will not encounter a subjective list of the names of good and bad contemporary composers. Throughout the book, however, assumptions about music in the church are challenged, and practical suggestions for change are offered.

Institutions of higher learning, particularly our seminaries, could be at the forefront of such change in church music. Fifty years ago, Frank E. Gaebelein suggested that "the theological seminaries might well give music a real place in the curriculum, for among Christian workers the pastor can least of all afford to remain musically illiterate."[1] Five hundred years ago, Martin Luther wrote, "We shouldn't ordain young men to the ministry unless they be well schooled in music."[2] While seminaries may offer a course touching on the history of Christian worship, courses dealing with basic music appreciation and hymnology should also be included. The music that a seminarian encounters in chapel should reflect the theology taught in the school, in text, musical substance, and character. It is important to have *a theology of worship music* based on Scripture.

Evangelical Bible colleges and liberal-arts schools share this fertile ground for change with the seminaries, with the steady supply of young music and theology students that they enjoy. Such institutions should be standard-bearers. But if the mission of these schools does not rise above equipping the next generation of musical and biblical leaders with what churches currently believe they require in pastors and musicians, this precious opportunity will be lost. Rather, as Gaebelein so clearly articulated five decades ago:

> The call is for Christian education to lead the way to higher things. But that call will not be fully answered until our schools, colleges, and seminaries espouse a philosophy of music befit-

> ting the Gospel. So long as the lower levels of an art so closely linked to man's emotions are cultivated at the expense of the best, we shall continue to have Christian leaders many of whom are deaf to the nobler elements of spiritual song. Evangelicalism is due for a musical reformation. The reformation will come only when Christian education, having set its face against the cheap in this greatest of the arts, seeks to develop in its students, response to a level of music worthy of the deep things of God.[3]

Christian schools at all levels should be preparing the next generation of well-educated leaders to correct the current disparity between faith and practice. Such schools need a high view of the arts. Academic vision starts at the top, with presidents, boards, and provosts, just as ecclesiastical vision begins with elders, sessions/boards, and pastors. Church and academic musicians must patiently seek to love, learn, and educate. Tough questions need to be asked. Do fiscal purposes regularly influence decision-making more than biblical purposes? Do tangible things rule over the intangible regardless of significance? At what point do programs and course offerings exist to attract students rather than to educate them appropriately? At what point does the music offered in worship become more about putting people in the pews than about God? And just how important are style, culture, and diversity to the musical choices we make? These are the kinds of difficult questions that we should be asking—questions that should lead to examination and systemic change, if necessary.

Third, these essays have been written in response to questions asked, situations encountered, and particular interests that have arisen from personal study. Above all, my desire, which I know others share, is to help shape music ministry by biblical standards for the glory of God. If man's chief end truly is *to glorify God and to enjoy him forever,* then this applies nowhere more clearly or more vitally than in worship, both personal and corporate. As a trained church musician or professor, one is asked to explain, and at times even to defend, the existence of our profession, standards, livelihood, curriculum, and "people" (staff, students, colleagues). We can thank God for these circumstances, though they are difficult, since they compel us to think, read, and respond. Such experiences have been seminal to several of the essays included in this volume.

Music, it seems, is omnipresent in church work, but worship music should not be treated as a common, utilitarian object, or manipulated to achieve unbiblical ends. The light of the Word of God must inform our practices, and where it speaks clearly, there is no debate. Where it makes inferences, we must consider the whole counsel of Scripture as well as the teaching of great theologians and musicians, and think deeply along with them.

What has become increasingly apparent is that no presupposition in the realm of church music can be adequately defended outside the authority of Scripture—not by arguments of reason, history, taste, philosophy, or culture, although those bases are all significant. So I have attempted to study the Bible with music in mind, to verify what Luther, Schütz, Bach, Mendelssohn, Stravinsky, and others had previously discovered and displayed—that God created music for a purpose, ordained the office/calling/role of church musician, filled the Bible with song, and showed us the nature of heaven's worship. The Lord God expects us to glorify him with excellent music that is written, played, and sung according to the principles that he has revealed in Scripture and in the cosmos. And there should be great joy in praising God through music! Musical praise is a wonderful individual and group response to Christ's creation and redemption of his people. Music's richness of expression and spiritual nature are among its greatest qualities.

That divine calling of the church musician and its practical outworking is what this humble and, it is hoped, useful collection is about. It will not provide all the answers. I pray that it will, however, cause an open-minded reader to think about the significance of worship music and to reconsider its place in our churches. And I sincerely hope that some phrase or idea might encourage a deeper search for the truth of God's Word as it relates to this wonderful gift of music, bestowed on us by God—for his own glory. S.D.G.

Paul Steven Jones
Philadelphia, Pennsylvania

Yes, if you call out for insight
and raise your voice for understanding,
if you seek it like silver
and search for it as for hidden treasures,
then you will understand the fear of the LORD
and find the knowledge of God.
For the LORD gives wisdom;
from his mouth come knowledge
and understanding. —Proverbs 2:3–6

Notes

1. Frank E. Gaebelein, *The Pattern of God's Truth* (New York: Oxford, 1954), 79.

2. Martin Luther, *Table Talk,* German ed. (Irmischer) 62, no. 2848 (Erlangen: Verlag von Hender & Zimmer, 1854): 308ff. See also Ewald M. Plass, *What Luther Says* (St. Louis: Concordia, 1959), 980.

3. Gaebelein, *Pattern of God's Truth,* 80–81.

Acknowledgments

Many people contributed to the production of this volume. Some asked thought-provoking questions, among them a number of students and colleagues. Some engaged me, directly or indirectly, in searching the Scriptures for answers. And a host of musical and biblical teachers over the years have so deeply influenced my thinking that I am unaware of where their teaching ends and my own thoughts begin.

Specifically, however, I wish to thank those who sacrificially assisted me as readers/editors, among them Professor RoseLee Bancroft, Professor Samuel Hsu, Mary Beth McGreevy, and Philip Graham Ryken. I would also like to thank Allan Fisher, for whose guidance I am grateful, as well as editors Karen Magnuson and Thom Notaro. Then there are those who helped with specific sections of the work, including music educator Melissa Strong and Professors Julius Bosco, William Edgar, Dan McCartney, Fred Putnam, and Leland Ryken. Gratitude also goes to my colleague Jeremy Strong, who prepared the musical scores included, and to hymn collaborator and esteemed friend Eric J. Alexander for writing the foreword.

I am particularly appreciative of Philip Ryken's encouragement as my pastor in the pursuit of this work, and to the session of Tenth Presbyterian Church, Philadelphia, Pennsylvania, for granting the study leave requisite to its production. It was James Montgomery Boice who first encouraged these written efforts by engaging me to speak to pastors, through our hymn collaboration, and by the efficacy of his powerful, biblical teaching. Truly, I am thankful to God to have had the privilege of knowing and working with all those mentioned above, and so many other teachers and friends who have influenced my life, thinking, and music.

PART ONE

Corporate Worship

Worship is more than an act in which we participate on Sundays; it is our very purpose for being. God created us to glorify him with our whole lives, which are to be, according to Romans 12:1, *living sacrifices.* In other words, all our activities, to some extent, should be acts of worship because they are to be done "as for the Lord" (Col. 3:23). Intentional worship should be a daily activity for the Christian, and a spirit of worship should encompass all we do.

Corporate worship—the gathering together of believers to worship God in the same time and place—is something both special and ordinary, or at least it should be. It is special in the sense that it is the unique activity of Christian people gathering to worship the one true and living God. It is ordinary in that it should be a way of life for us, not an occasional experience. While God is both the subject and object of our worship, corporate worship is an activity with many participants. Worship properly involves every Christian and every part of the Christian—his mental, physical, spiritual, and emotional being. Both pastor and people (including the musicians) are active participants.

Over the years, and particularly in the last few decades, our understanding of what worship should be has changed. If it is not the essence of worship that is different, at least one can state that its activities have been altered. For instance, evangelicals did not encounter movies, drama teams, skits, puppets, magicians, dance, or pop-music bands as regular aspects of worship before 1970. The danger here is that some worship practices are more about us than they are about God; at least they have the potential to distract us from God. Music, unfortunately, is an area in which worship anomalies frequently occur. Sometimes they enter our services innocently, seeming to be good, helpful, or relevant; but such incongruities almost always take us further from the truth.

The essays in this section seek to reexamine what the Bible teaches us about music in worship, with a desire to be biblically authentic. We begin with a concept derived from Scripture—that biblical music-making shares many of the same roles and goals as the teaching or pulpit ministry. This idea, while simple, may have radical implications for the individual believer or church that has not previously considered it. Indeed, the concept of the pastoral musician may be novel to some or at least atypical, and the partnership that pastors and music directors should share in their spiritual work (the gospel ministry) is more foreign an experience than one might think.

1
Sermon in Song: Sacred Music as Proclamation

My tongue will sing of your word,
for all your commandments are right. —Psalm 119:172

In the modern evangelical church, singing, praying, giving, and other congregational acts of worship are regarded at times as preamble to the sermon. Music, in particular, appears separate from elements of worship that seem to be more spiritual, such as praying and preaching. This worship dichotomy does not exist in Scripture, and our thinking is more biblical when we understand that musicians and preachers actually share in the ministry of the Word. Proclamation and interpretation of the Bible, and the edification and encouragement of the saints, with the ultimate goal of giving glory to God—these are also purposes of sacred music delineated in the Word of God and heralded by theologians and musicians throughout the history of the church.

Luther's View

Martin Luther (1483–1546) realized the significant role that music could play in the *spiritual growth* of the Christian. He declared, "Music and notes, which are wonderful gifts and creations of God, *do help gain a better understanding of the text*, especially when sung by a congregation and when sung earnestly"; and, "We have put this music to the living and holy Word of God *in order to sing, praise and honor it.* We want the beautiful art of music to be properly used to serve her dear Creator and his Christians. He is thereby praised and honored and *we are made better and stronger in faith* when his holy Word is impressed on our hearts by sweet music."[1] Paul Westermeyer, professor of church music at Luther Seminary, expands on these statements:

> Luther was not simply fond of music. Luther thought music has a theological reason for being: it is a gift of God, which comes from the "sphere of miraculous audible things," just like the Word of God. Music is unique in that it can carry words. Since words carry the Word of God, music and the Word of God are closely related . . . It almost seems as if Luther sees music in its own right as a parallel to preaching . . . But the weight falls on its association with the Word and words that carry the Word.[2]

With Johann Walter, Luther compiled and edited several hymn collections, and for many of these he wrote prefaces. One goal, Luther explained, was to properly educate the youth of his day:

> Therefore, I too, with the help of others, have brought together some sacred songs in order to make a good beginning and to give an incentive to those who can better carry on the Gospel and bring it to the people . . . And these songs were arranged in four parts for no other reason than that I wanted to attract the youth (who should and must be trained in music and other fine arts) away from love songs and carnal pieces and to give them something wholesome to learn instead . . . It is unfortunate that everyone else forgets to teach and train the poor young people; we must not be responsible for this too.[3]

Luther did not invent the notion that music and the proclamation of the gospel are related. He found its basis in Scripture (see "Biblical

Support" below). The Bible contains more than six hundred references to music, and we know from Scripture that singing is an eternal occupation. Singing should be a daily activity of the Christian. Luther believed that music should be composed to teach doctrine and to instruct young people—that by singing the Word of God, one's faith can be strengthened.

Bach's Example

Johann Sebastian Bach (1685–1750) has been called a musical preacher, and his church music can be properly termed "hermeneutical." (See chapters 25 and 26, "J. S. Bach and Musical Hermeneutics.") Georg Motz, a German contemporary of Bach, added his voice in support of this idea when he compared composers and preachers: "You only have to look at an honorable composition to detect exactly what you find in a good preacher. For he takes as much care to guide his listeners toward what is good as a musician stimulates his audience toward the same goal through different variations and motions."[4] In fact, Motz posits that music may be an especially evocative type of sermon:

> What is more, when such a composition is performed . . . you can also hear a charming and beautiful harmony, in which the great God grants His people on earth a foretaste of heavenly joy and the marvelous and sweet sound of the "*englische Kapelle*" (choir of angels), so that they can be reminded even better of the divine being . . .[5]

Motz maintained that good church music possesses the qualities of a good sermon. In his view, an excellent church-music composer is the equal of an excellent preacher. It may prove challenging to find many church-music composers of whom this is true, but in Bach's case the claim is justified.

Biblical Support

Within the context of proclamation, we expect to find elements of exhortation and admonition, of teaching and doctrine. Isaac Watts's position on this was clear. According to Horton Davies, in Watts's "belief in the didactic value of praise, as in his insistence upon intelligibility, his aim, like that of the Puritans, was edification."[6] What does the Bible teach about the instructive use of music? We know that a number of the psalms record the works of the Lord so that these might be passed on by oral tradition from priests to people and from parents to children.[7] Psalm 60 actually has the ascription "For Instruction." But clearly all the psalms were meant to be taught and sung. A New Testament statement is found in Colossians 3:16: "Let the word of Christ dwell in you richly, *teaching and admonishing* one another in all wisdom, singing psalms and hymns and spiritual songs, with thankfulness in your hearts to God." Music (singing in particular) is advocated for instructing and exhorting one another. The Bible is unambiguous in stating that sacred music has a spiritually educational purpose.

The idea that singing the Word of God will strengthen one's understanding of it has biblical support. Singing should, in fact, be a result of hearing and meditating on God's Word, as the psalmist said in the last section of Psalm 119, that great song of the Word: "My lips will pour forth praise, for you teach me your statutes. My tongue will sing of your word, for all your commandments are right . . . I long for your salvation, O LORD, and your law is my delight. Let my soul live and praise you, and let your rules help me" (vv. 171–72, 174–75). Psalm 119, which is also an extensive acrostic poem, earlier reads, "Your statutes have been my songs in the house of my sojourning" (v. 54). Since singing is a biblical response to God's Word, it follows that the singing of psalms, hymns, or other musical responses rightly follow the reading and preaching of Scripture in our worship.

In 1 Corinthians 15, Paul again articulates the gospel, which he had preached and proclaimed to his Corinthian brothers. The *euangelion,* or "good news," was the death, burial, and resurrection of Jesus Christ. Christ's resurrection power over death is celebrated, particularly at the end of the chapter: "Death is swallowed up in victory. O death, where is your victory? O death, where is your sting?" (vv. 54b–55). Here Paul quotes Isaiah 25:8, which is a *song of praise*, and Hosea 13:14, which delivers God's Word through the prophet. Intentionally or unintentionally, Paul relates song and the proclamation of the gospel, something he does again in Ephesians 5:19 and Colossians 3:16. Luther's commentary on 1 Corinthians 15 summarizes the Pauline conclusion in this manner:

> And now St. Paul appropriately concludes with a song which he sings: "Thanks and praise be to God, who gave us such a victory!" We can join in that song and in that way always celebrate Easter, praising and extolling God for a victory that was not won or achieved in battle by us . . . but we must . . . sing of this victory in Christ.[8]

And in his foreword to one of Johann Walter's hymnals, Luther wrote, "We may boast, as Moses does in his song in Exodus 15, that Christ is our praise and our song and that we should know nothing to sing or say but Jesus Christ our Savior, as Paul says in 1 Corinthians [1:31]."[9]

Proclamatory Hymns

Luther frequently employed the phrase "say and sing" or "sing and say" to describe the proper work of a believer. The content of the proclamation is always the gospel—the work of Christ. He wrote in his commentary on Psalm 118, "They [the righteous] praise only God's grace, works, words, and power as they are revealed to them in Christ. This is their *sermon and song*, their hymn of praise."[10] One of his best-loved Christmas chorales, *Vom Himmel hoch*, states it this way:

> From heav'n above to earth I come
> To bear good news to ev'ry home;
> Glad tidings of great joy I bring,
> Whereof I now will *say and sing*.
> [Davon ich *sing'n und sagen* will.]

Musical proclamation can be broadly defined to include any text that teaches or sets a passage of Scripture, recounts God's work, issues a call to repentance, or reminds us of God's promises. Many proclamatory hymns focus on the basic tenets of the gospel—the birth, life, death, resurrection, and ascension of Christ—and the life available to us because of Christ's sacrifice. Some examples of such hymns are these: "Arise, My Soul, Arise" (Charles Wesley); "My Hope Is Built on Nothing Less" (Edward Mote); and "Alas! and Did My Savior Bleed" (Isaac Watts).

Since the gospel can be preached through music, and since biblical teaching can be recalled through music and appropriated, then there is an obligation to ensure that this is done well. When music is like a sermon, it follows that it must have responsibilities and characteristics similar to those of a sermon. Many of the same criteria we use to define great preaching and teaching can be employed to define great church music. Church music needs to be well prepared and presented. It requires unity and coherence. It should make sense to the listener. It should evidence thought and skill. Church music should feed the people by teaching the Word of God. It is a work of the Spirit of God.

Thinking about music ministry in such terms today will change the nature of worship in the evangelical church. As Donald Hustad points out, "Though mainline evangelicals claim to be leaders in Scripture study, biblical research to determine worship practice seems to be at the bottom of their priority list."[11] It is time for that record to change.

Notes

1. Walter Buszin, *Luther on Music* (Saint Paul: North Central, 1958), 14, quoting Luther, "Treatise on the Last Words of David," in vol. 15 of *Luther's Works*, ed. Jeroslav Pelikan; and Martin Luther, "Preface to the Burial Hymns (1542)," in *Liturgy and Hymns*, ed. Ulrich S. Leupold, vol. 53 of *Luther's Works*, ed. Helmut T. Lehmann (Philadelphia: Fortress Press, 1965), 327 (italics added).

2. Paul Westermeyer, *Te Deum: The Church and Music* (Minneapolis: Augsburg Fortress, 1998), 144–46.

3. Luther's foreword to the first edition of Johann Walter's hymnal, the *Wittenberg Geistliche Gesangbüchlein* (1524), ed. Ulrich S. Leupold, vol. 53 of *Luther's Works*, ed. Helmut T. Lehmann (Philadelphia: Fortress Press, 1965), 315–16.

4. Georg Motz, *Die vertheidigte Kirchen-Music* . . . (Tilsit, East Prussia, 1703), 14–15, as quoted in Ulrich Leisinger, "Affections, Rhetoric, and Musical Expression," in *The World of the Bach Cantatas: Johann Sebastian Bach's Early Sacred Cantatas,* ed. Christoph Wolff (New York: W. W. Norton, 1997), 194–95nn10–12.

5. Ibid., 195.

6. Horton Davies, *The Worship of the English Puritans* (Morgan, PA: Soli Deo Gloria Publications, 1997), 179.

7. Psalms 78, 105, and 136 come to mind. This was a form of instruction as well as worship, particularly tied in with the wisdom literature of the Old Testament. The Jewish feast of Passover and other high holy days also featured the use of songs in the celebration of deliverance and as reminder of God's works. In addition, the 288 Levites set apart because of their special musical abilities were teachers of the other 3,712, who in turn taught their own sons and daughters.

8. *Selected Pauline Epistles,* ed. E. Sittler, vol. 28 of *Luther's Works,* ed. Jaroslav Pelikan (Philadelphia: Fortress Press, 1973), 213. See also Carl F. Schalk, *Luther on Music: Paradigms of Praise* (St Louis: Concordia, 1988), 39.

9. Luther, *Geistliche Gesangbüchlein* (1524).

10. *Selected Psalms III,* vol. 14 of *Luther's Works,* ed. Jaroslav Pelikan (St. Louis: Concordia, 1958), 81 (italics added).

11. Donald P. Hustad, *True Worship: Reclaiming the Wonder and Majesty* (Wheaton, IL: Harold Shaw Publishers, 1998), 101.

2
Sacred Music as Prayer

By day the LORD commands his steadfast love,
and at night his song is with me,
a prayer to the God of my life.
—Psalm 42:8

A significant aspect of worship music is its role as prayer. Perhaps there is still an understanding of this concept in Covenanter congregations where only psalms are sung, but overall we tend to view singing and praying as separate categories. Why we have come to see them so distinctly is uncertain, but the rise of music as entertainment within the evangelical church undoubtedly contributes to this view.

When music in church becomes entertainment, it is objectified as "an event." It turns into something to watch, a spectacle. Such events are necessarily detached from the immediacy of being something in which we are involved. Other worship elements can be treated this way, too. Pastoral prayer can be an aural "spectacle" if members of the congregation are not praying along with the minister. But perhaps more than with spoken prayer, music becomes something done *for* us instead of being done *by* us. This disconnection may be amplified by the music-suffused society in which we live (music in the malls, restaurants, elevators, etc.—when it is a mindless backdrop for other activity). We thus become desensitized to music in a public setting, as something in which we are not involved as "doers"—whether we are listening or singing. This musical alienation is a danger prevalent in services with soloists and even choirs—that the parishioner views music as an event he is watching or to which he is listening as a bystander instead of as a participant.[1]

Music, however, often takes the role of prayer. And prayer in the midst of the congregation is to be a group activity. Such is the case with Psalms, which served as a hymnbook and liturgy for the whole "congregation" of the children of Israel. Printing in the bulletin the text of all music presented by choirs or soloists will help. Not only will the congregation experience better textual clarity (irrespective of vocal diction, projection, or volume), but this speaks to intention—one is *meant* to understand and participate in what is being sung. We should avoid using the terms "performance" and "special music" when it comes to music used in worship.[2] A solo piece or anthem is fittingly called a "musical offering." (See chapter 8, "Service Music: What's It All About?") We must remember that what we sing is being sung to God.

Direct Address

Many passages from the psalms, as well as biblical canticles, hymns of Christ, and various other songs, address God directly. Direct address is one of the most recognizable characteristics of a prayer hymn. Here are a few examples:

- "Be Thou My Vision"
- "Holy, Holy, Holy!"
- "My Jesus, I Love Thee"
- "Come, Thou Fount of Every Blessing"
- "Create in Me a Clean Heart, O God

Thinking of such songs as anything other than prayers is simply insupportable. One can find prayer hymns addressed to each person of the Trinity:

- Father: "Dear Lord and Father of Mankind"
- Son: "O Jesus, I Have Promised"
- Spirit: "Breathe on Me, Breath of God"

It is both logical and biblical to conclude that *any communication to God*—verbal or nonverbal, spoken, sung, written, or thought—is prayer. Communication does not stop when one sings, and yet we often separate, at least subconsciously, the act of singing from the acts of thinking, speaking, or "meaning" (intending). Perhaps this is somehow tied in to the flawed idea that prayer must be spontaneous—that unless it is improvisatory in nature, it is not Spirit-directed. Such thinking does not align with the fact that canonical psalms and other biblical songs are recorded prayers. These prayers are written and have been used in worship from ancient to modern times. In fact, noncanonical written prayers are often more substantial and biblical than those we extemporize.

Support from Scripture

John Calvin understood the singing of the psalms to be prayer, which aligns with the teaching of the last verse of the second book: "The prayers of David, the son of Jesse, are ended" (Ps. 72:20). The third chapter of Habakkuk is a prayer designated "according to Shigionoth" in its first verse (possibly a tune, mode, or instrument) and "To the choirmaster: with stringed instruments" in its last—just like many of the psalms. In fact, it was used as a psalm in temple worship. Certainly this prayer was to be sung. "Spontaneous prayer only" rules out use of the inspired Psalter and other biblical songs. On the other hand, using only the canonical psalms excludes obvious New Testament passages and examples from the early church such as the Lord's Prayer, or the "Sovereign Lord" prayer of Acts 4:23ff. Both fixed and spontaneous prayers are valid and supported by the example of Scripture.

Other New Testament passages relate singing to praying:

- James 5:13: "Is anyone among you suffering? Let him pray. Is anyone cheerful? Let him sing praise."
- 1 Corinthians 14:15: ". . . I will pray with my spirit, but I will pray with my mind also; I will sing praise with my spirit, but I will sing with my mind also."[3]

Prayer and singing are closely associated in the James and 1 Corinthians passages, and we read that *both* should be done with the spirit and also with the mind.[4] In other words, we should *mean* what we pray with all our hearts, and we should *know* what we mean. We should also mean what we sing and know what we are singing. A lapse in either element (intention or understanding) has often rendered the singing of hymns and the worship of God irrelevant, even *irreverent.* Isaac Watts had this in mind when creating Christian paraphrases of the psalms: "I would neither indulge any bold metaphors, nor admit of hard words, nor tempt the ignorant worshipper to sing without his understanding."[5]

Modern Implications/Pastoral Choices

One welcome characteristic that the charismatic movement has reintroduced to modern Christianity is the importance of emotion in worship, and what it means to worship God with all our hearts. Emotion and energy have been missing from hymn and psalm singing in many churches. Unfortunately, the packaging and seeming success of these otherwise fine qualities in the Contemporary Christian Music movement have led to a consumer-oriented church-music industry—one that caters to the megachurch and promotes it as the ideal. It would be good (and right) to have both emotion and thought in our worship music, without digressing to the consumerist trappings of our culture.

Most pastors have not had musical training and received little to no church-music or worship instruction in seminary. Without training it is easy to succumb to the pragmatic answers fostered by church-growth "experts." In hopes of bringing vitality to the church, contemporary services are added, with psalms and hymns often demoted in or excluded from worship. A flaw in this thinking is the mistaken belief that growth in church attendance on the basis of musical style secures spiritual growth. Another error is the notion that we are responsible for producing new means or methods to build the church—that we have to package the gospel in modernity's clothing. While men seek to build kingdoms for themselves, it is God who builds his church through the faithful preaching of his Word and the biblical worship of his people. That is a timeless, unchanging means and method—and it is the truth.

Pastors are often the people who select congregational song, though more and more this significant role is delegated to others. Irrespective of who carries this responsibility, the charge is an important one. Hughes Oliphant Old states in *Leading in Prayer*, his book on worship for pastors:

> Choosing appropriate hymns is an important part of leading the congregation in prayer. We may not always regard hymnody as prayer, but theologically that is how it makes the best sense. In hymns the people of God pray together with one voice. As Luke puts it in his report of an early Christian prayer meeting, "they lifted their voices together to God" (Acts 4:24). Luke actually says this about psalm singing, but the same is true of hymnody as well. Uniting our voices together is just what we do when we sing.[6]

German Protestants actually refer to their hymnals as "prayer books." The great Lutheran church composer Johann Sebastian Bach evidently understood the singing of chorales to be prayer—that hymn singing was a manner of communicating with God—because the chorale responses at the conclusion of many cantatas not only summarize the sermonic thought preceding them, but often invoke God's help to accomplish change.[7] One of many possible examples is Cantata 77, *Du sollt Gott, deinen Herren, lieben* ("You shall love God with all your heart"). This cantata preaches the great commandment from Luke 10:27 and expounds on it, and our failing to keep it, in the recitatives and arias that follow. The cantata appropriately concludes with a chorale that acts as a prayer: "Lord, through faith live in me, let it [my faith] always grow stronger, that it be fruitful forever and ever and rich in good works; that it be active in love, exercise itself in joy and patience, my neighbor ever to serve."

If we truly comprehend that many of our hymns are prayers, might we approach them (and sing them) differently? When we sing psalms and great hymns of the faith together, we are corporately praying not only in the present but also in solidarity with saints of the past who have walked with God and who have uttered the same words.

One Example

One of Scotland's finest preachers, Eric J. Alexander, has written several prayer hymns, among them "O Lord God, How Great Your Mercy" (in response to Rom. 12:1–2), "Sovereign Lord of All Creation" (in response to Acts 4:23–30), "My Gracious Lord, Your Love Is Vast" (a hymn based on biblical teaching regarding God's love), and "Lord Jesus Christ, How Far You Came" (in response to Phil. 2:5–11). The last hymn mentioned (see fig. 2.1) responds to the great passage from Paul's letter to the Philippians, which describes for us the humility of Jesus and the doctrines of the hypostatic union (the union of God and man in the person of Christ) and *kenosis* (the "self-emptying" of Christ of the prerogatives of his deity in order to become man). In chapter 13 ("Song in the Bible"), this passage is identified as a Pauline poem that functions solidly as a "Hymn of Christ." It describes our Lord's nature and ascribes praise to him to the glory of God the Father. It makes perfect sense to teach, rehearse, and pray this passage through song—to respond to its truth and power by composing a hymn and by singing it.

Each song sung in worship should be examined for biblical content and musical credibility. But in the process of doing so, one should determine whether the piece is a prayer of confession, supplication, or adoration; or perhaps it is a hymn of praise or a song of thanksgiving, or it fulfills some other kind of function. Such ideas can be shared with

Fig. 2.1

Lord Jesus Christ, How Far You Came

...He humbled himself and became obedient to death... Php. 2:8

In response to Philippians 2:5-11
Eric J. Alexander, 2001

KENOSIS 8.6.8.8.6.6.
Paul S. Jones, 2001

those who will be singing or listening and will help determine where the music best fits in the worship service. This is an important step in making our musical worship intentional. Too often our congregations are unaware that they are praying in song. Let us sing and pray with both spirit and mind.

Notes

1. There are ways to guard against this danger. For one, musicians do not have to be front and center—leave that to the pulpit and preacher. In the Presbyterian church's roots in Scotland, the pulpit was elevated and the musicians sang from the back of the church, usually in a balcony (with the possible exception of a precentor, who may have used a front lectern or lower podium/pulpit). Music is meant to be heard; but it does not need to be watched.

2. The word *performance* may actually have some merited use for what occurs in worship, but not in the way in which we commonly interpret the word. For a good discussion, see the chapter entitled "Is Worship a Performance? The Concept," in Barry Liesch, *The New Worship: Straight Talk on Music and the Church* (Grand Rapids: Baker, 2001), 121ff.

3. The NIV, as well as the ESV quoted here, uses the personal pronoun "my" before "spirit" and "mind," but this is not in the Greek, as it is in 1 Corinthians 14:14. Paul distinguishes between his own spirit and the Holy Spirit in 1 Corinthians 5:4, for example.

4. Paul seems to treat singing or praying "with the spirit" as meaning in another tongue—basically, in a language or manner that the other worshipers present would not be able to participate in or understand. "If you give thanks with your spirit, how can anyone in the position of an outsider say 'Amen' to your thanksgiving when he does not know what you are saying? For you may be giving thanks well enough, but the other person is not being built up" (1 Cor. 14:16–17).

5. Isaac Watts, as quoted in Horton Davies, *The Worship of the English Puritans* (Morgan, PA: Soli Deo Gloria Publications, 1997), 177.

6. Hughes Oliphant Old, *Leading in Prayer: A Workbook for Worship* (Grand Rapids: Eerdmans, 1995), 321.

7. These cantata-concluding chorales may or may not have been sung by the congregation, but certainly they *were* sung, and the congregation was intimately acquainted with them.

3

Applause: For Whom Are You Clapping?

Clap your hands, all peoples!
Shout to God with loud songs of joy! —Psalm 47:1

As a professional musician, I am accustomed to applause. This is what a performer walking onto the concert stage expects as a greeting and anticipates again following a successful performance. But musicians and pastors alike are quick to affirm that when it comes to worship services, the musicians are not "performing."[1] Music in church, we rightly understand, is "ministry"—an act of service, an offering of prayer or praise. How, then, might clapping or applause fit into the worship service—or does it fit at all?

Psalm 47:1 urges all the nations of the world to clap their hands and exhorts them, "Shout to God with loud songs of joy!" Later, in Psalm 98:8, it is the rivers that "clap their hands" as the hills "sing for joy together," while in Isaiah 55:12, the trees of the field metaphorically partake in such joyous activity in praise of their Creator. Lamentations 2:15, however, associates the clapping of hands with hissing and shaking of the head in mockery of the daughter of Jerusalem. And in Job 27:23 the east wind "claps" in derision at the wicked, ruthless man who is judged by God.

Clapping, then, by evidence of Scripture, has more than one sociocultural meaning dependent on the circumstance in which it occurs. Thus, it is possible to intend different things when we applaud in the concert hall or in church; and further, it is possible for us to be aware of this distinction in each context. My suspicion, however, is that our understanding of such a distinction is not clear enough, nor is our consciousness of such intentions developed well enough.

On vacation one August, I visited three different churches on a Sunday morning. Since it is a rare Sunday morning that I am not on an organ or piano bench, I find it interesting to discover what is taking place in other churches. The largest of the three churches visited that day had a congregation that clapped frequently. Interestingly, they applauded at the end of each praise song led by the worship team, although there was no clapping during the singing itself. They applauded when a baby was dedicated to the Lord and also when his mother left the platform. I have also witnessed congregational applause of a preacher, particularly when a powerful demonstration of rhetorical skill was displayed. For me, this response, whether it is cognitive or intuitive, thoughtful or emotional, leads necessarily to the question, "For whom are you clapping?"

To "applaud" means, literally, "to give praise to" [*ap-* + *-laud*]. In worship, our thoughts and actions are to be directed to the subject and the object of worship—God himself. Jehovah more than merits our praise, so applauding him for his acts or attributes in the context of worship can be reasonably defended. Clapping the hands while singing and shouting to God with joy (Ps. 47:1) are biblical ideas. Actually, it seems that at every positive biblical mention of clapping the hands, this activity is always linked with singing to God in praise. Otherwise, clapping has no biblical place in worship and obviously should not be directed at musicians, preachers, or babies as applause. It is likely that few genuine "clap offerings" are exclusively offered to God, although they may exist in the case of individuals, perhaps, more so than among the masses. Yet clapping does not appear to be an activity that the Lord requested throughout Scripture. God does not require our affirmation, but he does want our joyful song—which could very well be accompanied by shouts and clapping and loud cymbals and other expressions of our delight in him.

More often in the context of worship, if we are honest, we applaud *people* with the hope of making them feel appreciated, to demonstrate our approval of the rendition or statement, or to show that we affirm the message of the music. Encouraging, approving, and affirming are not wrong actions in and of themselves. But can we find other means of accomplishing these goals? In our cultural context, applause is the stuff of the theater, the concert stage, the comic routine, and the political speech. With such strong associations for approval of a performance, clapping in worship is at best, inappropriate. At worst, it is idolatrous. Yet most worshipers sitting in the pews each Sunday are not bothered by its inclusion in worship.

As a society we applaud when we receive good news, hear a funny joke, or express appreciation. In fact, it has become so customary to clap that we instinctively applaud for almost anything we enjoy. When it comes to worship music, this response is most commonly witnessed at the end of a fast piece or one that concludes loudly and in a high tessitura. This is simply an unexamined carryover from the entertainment industry. We applaud in church because we have not thought much about why we do so. Instead, we have allowed our culture's response to entertainment to gain a place where it does not belong—worse yet, we have allowed entertainment itself a place in the church.

In fact, we demand it. We build large stages, elaborate sound and lighting systems, props and scenery for dramatic productions. We have drama teams, mime, sermon-by-skit, movies, and more. Some install theater-sized screens, put spotlights on the performers, have concession stands in the lobby, and overamplify both prerecorded and live band music in a service that is supposed to be about reverently approaching a holy God. We glamorize those with musical talent or dramatic gifts and allow the cult of celebrity to enter what should be a house of prayer. Pastors, musicians, and church leaders must address and change such things in their churches. If we do not, who can—or who will?

Musicians who recognize that their offerings in the context of worship (indeed, in all of life) are solely for the glory of God—*soli Deo gloria*—do not desire applause in worship. In fact, it probably troubles them and diminishes the joy of giving back some of what God has given them. A better response than applauding is simply to say to the musician, "I thank God for how he blessed me through you" or "I appreciate you and pray for you." Comments such as these are encouraging. The best response to music or other ministry that blesses you is to thank God for it and to share your joy with others.

Worship is a serious activity. We must consider our actions. In worship, if we applaud someone other than God, our misdirected praise is idolatrous. If we receive as ours the praise that is due him, we rob God of glory that is his alone. Will our jealous God bless such things stolen from him? No, our songs and applause will be "noise" to him—an offering of stench rather than something sweet-smelling. As Donald Gray Barnhouse put it in a brief statement in the Tenth Presbyterian Church bulletin on October 17, 1943:

> Church music can be anything from reverent worship of God to carnal exhibitionism, and in musical quality may be anything from a joyful noise to an artistic musical presentation. It goes without saying that a good voice is better than a bad one for church music, provided the hearts are equally yielded to the Lord. If the hearts are not yielded, the curse on unspiritual music is stated very definitely in the Bible. It is hateful to the Lord. Of many a cantata and many an Easter day it might well be written, "I hate, I despise your feast days . . . Take thou away from me the noise of thy songs . . ." (Amos 5:21, 23 KJV)

Surely no Christian will want this to be said of him or her. And it can be just as true of the classical musician playing Widor organ symphonies as of the "contemporary" band playing the latest Maranatha or Hillsong praise chorus. We need to think about our position on applause in worship so that the glory due our God is solely directed to him. If this includes clapping as an act of worship vis-à-vis Psalm 47:1, then it must be understood as such and offered that way.

Pastors and other worship leaders can lead the congregation in responses appropriate to worship. "Amen" (which means "so be it") is an affirming, biblical response, as is "Praise God!" or some other God-centered exclamation such as "Hallelujah" (which means "Praise the Lord"). A biblical example appears in 1 Chronicles 16:36. After David's "Song of Thanks," we read, "Then all the people said, 'Amen!' and praised the LORD."

Such ideas may warrant the occasional pastoral remark from the pulpit or a sentence or two in the church bulletin. When believers are taught and given spiritual rationale for a new action or the alteration of an existing action, they are generally responsive to it. Verbal responses may be distracting to others at times, so one should examine the value of this activity in situations in which that might be true. And even biblical responses can become rote after a time, so the occasional reminder or explanation for why something is done or not done in worship is an excellent idea.

Note

1. As noted in the previous chapter, although the word *performance* should probably be avoided for the sake of association, it may actually have some merited use for what occurs in worship, but not in the way in which we commonly use the word. Cf., chap. 2, note 2.

4

A Biblical Case for Instruments in Worship

Praise him with trumpet sound;
praise him with lute and harp!
Praise him with tambourine and dance;
praise him with strings and pipe!
Praise him with sounding cymbals;
praise him with loud clashing cymbals! —Psalm 150:3–5

Some churches believe that the use of instruments is not appropriate in worship. John Calvin had a lot to do with this, since for worship services he advocated psalms-only, unaccompanied singing. Ulrich Zwingli took an even more stringent position and excluded music from worship altogether (in spite of the fact that Zwingli was actually a very fine musician himself). Both of these men were seeking to promote and maintain integrity in worship. They did not despise music or instruments; rather, they were making a strong distinction, as Reformers, between what was practiced in the Roman church and what they wanted for their own congregations. Martin Luther, of course, took quite a different position when it came to music, believing as he did that as a gift and creation of God, music should be used at its highest and best to glorify him. But we should ask the question based on the Bible rather than on any man's reasoning: Are instruments permissible in the worship of God? Is there biblical support for this idea? I believe that there is.

On the basis of Scripture, it appears that instruments can be employed in worship so long as they contribute appropriately and do not detract from the service and its purposes. Certainly acoustic instruments are preferable to electronic ones for aesthetic and other reasons (see chapter 7, "Authenticity in Corporate Worship Music"). Instruments that have a historical connection with the church are perhaps more fitting than those that do not; and instruments that have overly negative modern associations with secularism are probably best avoided.[1] Players should be skilled and should contribute to worship in meaningful, positive ways. One should not engage instrumentalists simply because they are at hand or because they are willing to play. Neither will the use of instruments or songs ensure that what is offered is pleasing to God. The prophet Amos reminds us of the trouble for those "at ease in Zion" (6:1) who are not following the Lord's commands: "Woe to those . . . who sing idle songs to the sound of the harp and like David invent for themselves instruments of music . . . but are not grieved over the ruin of Joseph!" (Amos 6:4–6).

Old Testament Support

In 1 Chronicles 23 we find the biblical record of David's gathering the leaders of Israel and the Levites together to divide them for temple service. Of the 38,000 Levite males over the age of thirty, 4,000 were assigned to be musicians. David said that they were to "offer praises to the LORD with the instruments that I have made for praise" (v. 5). Chapter 25 explains that 288 of these 4,000 were especially trained and skilled "in singing to the LORD." Some were assigned to play specific instruments—harp, lyre, cymbals, and trumpets. The trumpets and cymbals were used to announce things or to call the assembly together, and other instruments were also used "for sacred song" (1 Chron. 16:42).

Perhaps we cannot make a direct leap from temple service to the New Testament church and declare that worship practices in David's time should be the same now. Other aspects of Old Testament worship (the sacrificial system, for example) are no more. The psalms sung in David's time, however, were still sung in the New Testament period and should be yet today. A disconnect between the Old and New to the degree that the praise of God is somehow stifled is dangerous. Further, is it not right that we have even *more* reason to praise God in even grander ways, by virtue of what he has revealed to us since the days of David (e.g., the glorious, completed work of Christ; the view of heaven's worship in the book of the Revelation)? The Old Testament teaches us so much about the worship of God—should this be abandoned? There is no reason to think that the worship instruments mentioned in the psalms and later used in the temple would suddenly vanish from use. We do not uncover any Scripture calling on Christians to silence them. The psalms, moreover, are replete with calls to worship with instruments. These are visible both in their main text and in their ascriptions (which are part of the text of the psalm in the Hebrew Scriptures [see chapter 11, "What Psalm Ascriptions Tell Us"]). Here are a few examples to refresh the memory:

Text

- Psalm 33:2: "Give thanks to the LORD with the lyre; make melody to him with the harp of ten strings!"
- Psalm 98:5–6: "Sing praises to the LORD with the lyre, with the lyre and the sound of melody!"
- Psalm 150:3–5: "Praise him with trumpet sound; praise him with lute and harp! Praise him with tambourine and dance; praise him with strings and pipe! Praise him with sounding cymbals; praise him with loud clashing cymbals!"

Ascriptions

- Psalm 5: "To the choirmaster: for the flutes. A Psalm of David."

- Psalm 55: "To the choirmaster: with stringed instruments. A Maskil of David."
- Psalm 76: "To the choirmaster: with stringed instruments. A Psalm of Asaph. A Song."

Strong rationale for the use of instruments in worship is found in Psalm 92, where the psalm ascription reads: "A Psalm. A Song for the Sabbath." The first three verses of the psalm state that this Sabbath-day music includes instruments: "It is good to give thanks to the LORD, to sing praises to your name, O Most High; to declare your steadfast love in the morning, and your faithfulness by night, to the music of the lute and the harp, to the melody of the lyre." These verses also reveal that this song and other music are fittingly sung and played to the glory of God both in the morning and at night. (Perhaps this helps to make the case for morning and evening worship services on the Lord's Day.)

Of course, it was not only the psalms that were sung; there are many other songs in the Old Testament as well. But even more significantly, it is possible that the *entire* Old Testament was sung in the context of Hebrew worship. At least this was true in Jewish medieval tradition (prior to that, we cannot be certain). In medieval times, the Old Testament was chanted and can be thought of as an immense vocal score. Suzanne Haïk-Vantoura's work on this subject—the science of such cantillation on the basis of Masoretic accents (the *te'amim*)—is published in her *La Musique de la Bible Révélée* ("The Music of the Bible Revealed").[2] She did believe that this chanting tradition extended back to the temple and wrote, "We know as well it was always a real 'music' that was performed by the Levites, and furthermore, this music was both *choral* and *instrumental*. In fact, no service of worship was celebrated in the Great Temple without a minimum of 12 singers and 12 instrumentalists."[3]

It is possible that the psalms were retained in New Testament worship while excluding the instruments prescribed in their ascriptions, but this is not certain, necessary, or even likely. We are able, of course, to spiritually appropriate the psalms even when they mention practices that are foreign to us (e.g., the altar, the sanctuary, the climb to

Jerusalem, or sacrifices). But when it comes to something as common and vibrant as instruments, which are not tied exclusively to worship in the tabernacle or temple, it is less likely that we fully benefit from the psalm without the reality of their presence. And it is, at the least, strange to sing the words "Praise the LORD with trumpets and cymbals" without any instruments to demonstrate or authenticate that which is being sung.[4]

Are only the individual words of the psalms valid and not their actual meaning? Surely this is not so. Are some imperative statements to be ignored? If this is the case, who will decide which commands in the psalms should be followed and which should be ignored? Since there are many calls in the psalms to use instruments in praising the Lord, one can rightly believe that these calls are right and heed them. The question comes down to whether instruments were so tied to the sacrificial system that they should be silenced at its abandonment. Lest we think instruments were only for the temple period, we should recall that instruments were used to praise the Lord well before the temple, too (e.g., Miriam's tambourine, David's harp, and the trumpets used for feast days and at the time of burnt offerings and fellowship offerings). A number of musical instruments are mentioned in the New Testament, but these are not necessarily related to worship. Mentioned in Matthew 9:23, 11:17, and 1 Corinthians 13 and 14, for example, are the flute, the gong, the harp, the cymbal, and the trumpet (as well as the flute player, the harpist, and the trumpeter).

New Testament Support

It is often assumed that because there are no direct references to instruments in New Testament *worship,* none were used. This is not necessarily so. It is possible that instruments were excluded or used minimally because of their association with the pagan and idolatrous worship of the Romans and Greeks. This would qualify as a cultural or associative exclusion and not one prescribed by Scripture for all people, places, and times. It is also possible that instruments fell out of use during the time of the Roman persecution of Christians. Trumpets and cymbals tend to draw attention, something that Christians in hiding would undoubtedly strive to avoid.

In 1 Corinthians 14, Paul addresses the issue of order in worship, specifically spiritual gifts and the clear use of prophecy and tongues, "so that the church may be built up" (v. 5). It is within this context that he says:

> Now, brothers, if I come to you speaking in tongues, how will I benefit you unless I bring you some revelation or knowledge or prophecy or teaching? If even lifeless instruments, such as the flute or the harp, do not give distinct notes, how will anyone know what is played? And if the bugle gives an indistinct sound, who will get ready for battle? (1 Cor. 14:6–8)

Paul may simply be making an allusion within the realm of sound, but it is interesting at least that his discussion of order in worship refers to musical instruments. Whether or not this had anything to do with the first-century church's use of instruments in worship, it could certainly by application point to the need for clarity and order when instruments are used. It is precisely at this point that Calvin believed instruments (and chanting) produced both "unknown" and "uncertain" sounds. That was his opinion, based on the idea that singing in worship is prayer, and that nothing should complicate prayer.

As noted earlier, James 5:13 says: "Is anyone among you suffering? Let him pray. Is anyone cheerful? Let him sing praise." 1 Corinthians 14:15 reads, "I will pray with my spirit, but I will pray with my mind also; I will sing praise with my spirit, but I will sing with my mind also."[5] In these verses, the verb used for "sing" is *psallō*. This particular verb is used only five times in the New Testament (Rom. 15:9; Eph. 5:19; 1 Cor. 14:15 (twice); James 5:13).[6] According to Friberg's *Lexicon*, *psallō* strictly meant "to strike the strings of an instrument," hence "sing to the accompaniment of a harp."[7] This is in the context of James's discussion of prayer and faith.

The two famous New Testament passages dealing with music in worship are Ephesians 5:19 and Colossians 3:16.

- Ephesians 5:19: "Addressing one another in psalms and hymns and spiritual songs, singing and making melody to the Lord with all your heart."
- Colossians 3:16: "Let the word of Christ dwell in you richly, teaching and admonishing one another in all wisdom, singing psalms and hymns and spiritual songs, with thankfulness in your hearts to God."

Psallō is not used in Colossians 3:16; *adō* is. *Adō* means "to produce music with the voice." One could claim that the words are interchangeable, and that here Paul simply chose *adō*. Yet both *psallō* and *adō* are used in Ephesians 5:19, as is the noun *psalmos*. So in Ephesians, Paul is essentially saying, "Address one another with psalms (*psalmos*) and hymns (*hymnos*) and spiritual songs (*ōdē pneumatikos*). Sing (*adō*) and make melody (*psallō*) to the Lord." Since the root of *psallō* is associated with the playing of an instrument, and Paul chooses to use both words (*adō* and *psallō*), one could interpret this as referring to both voice and instruments (potentially, *a cappella* singing and accompanied singing). On the other hand, Dan McCartney of Westminster Theological Seminary notes that *psallō* came to mean "sing a psalm" and that the original instrumental connotation may have faded.[8] Paul may have been using both words for emphasis, but by the same token, he may have been making a distinction between two kinds of singing (accompanied and unaccompanied).

In summary, there are at least three potential explanations for why Paul would write "*adō* and *psallō*" ("sing and sing") in the same phrase:

1. One refers to unaccompanied singing and the other to accompanied singing.
2. One refers to singing and the other to playing an instrument.
3. This is an example of reinforcement by synonym, an especially common technique in Jewish liturgical material (and yet this is a Greek letter to a Gentile church).

The preposition in the phrase "sing in your heart" can be *in* or *with*, as it appears in various translations. So the phrase does not necessarily refer to a quiet, exclusively internal activity, as one might conclude in English (as in "thinking" or even "humming to oneself"). This is what Zwingli believed, and thus he excluded music from worship altogether. Paul employs metaphoric language by using "in the heart," so it is possible that he is not literally referring to voices or instruments either. But that interpretation seems dubious. The phrase more likely means "with one's whole being," since biblical use of the word *heart* refers to the religious center of the person, which is why the ESV translates it as "with all your heart" in the Ephesians passage. This understanding draws a much closer parallel to Psalm 150's "Let everything that has breath praise the LORD!" If the use of *psallō* here means "strike the strings of an instrument," then "make melody in your heart" could also be a way of referring to instrumental music. All this is mentioned simply as food for thought when it comes to instruments in worship.

When instruments are utilized for gathered worship, logic informs us as to the suitability of particular instruments, and some of these deductions are contextual. The harp and lute are chamber instruments typically associated throughout history with a solo player and solo singer (often one and the same). The acoustic guitar would be a modern equivalent, an instrument appropriate to an intimate setting, characteristic of many of the early church's meetings. The pipe organ was not used in the church until about the ninth century A.D. It is an instrument suited to leading a larger body in the praise of God. The guitar was not designed to have its strings strummed off or to be amplified—it was made for the small, quiet gathering. Pipe organs and brass are not well suited to the home meeting or the intimate Bible study—they were designed for larger spaces and have a natural capacity for volume, although they can provide a quiet cushion of sound as well. The loud acoustic instruments of the Levites (trumpets, cymbals) were used to call huge masses to worship, which was often outdoors where sound quickly dissipates.

Instruments can make valuable contributions to congregational singing—leadership, melodic support, color, strength, energy, interpretative meaning. While all instruments may be "lawful" for use in worship, all may not be "expedient." If the early Christians avoided certain instruments because of their association with pagan ritual and false worship, we may make comparable decisions about instruments or styles of music. On the other hand, some good things can be redeemed from misuse and be appropriated for the work of the Lord. This line between liberty and legalism requires spiritual wisdom—wisdom that God promises to give liberally when we ask in faith (James 1:5).

The Lord will save me, and we will play my music on stringed instruments all the days of our lives, at the house of the Lord. —Isaiah 38:20

Notes

1. I do not wish to suggest a "ruling" on which instruments are permissible and which are not. Drums, of course, are the single greatest instrument of controversy in churches. Acoustic drums, such as timpani, bass drum, snare, and congas, are preferred over electronic drums or drum "sets," which are much more commonly associated with clubs and rock concerts. These are choices that involve aesthetic and associative inferences. They fall under the "lawful versus expedient" discussion.

2. Suzanne Haïk-Vantoura, *The Music of the Bible Revealed*, trans. Dennis Weber, ed. John Wheeler, based on the 2nd French ed. (Paris: Dessain et Tolra, 1978) (Berkeley, CA: Bibal Press/San Francisco: King David's Harp, Inc., 1991).

3. Ibid., 126.

4. While I believe this is a decent argument, one could similarly argue that it is strange to sing "I will offer bulls on your altar" from Psalm 51 without incorporating that particular physical act.

5. The NIV, as well as the ESV, uses the personal pronoun "my" before "spirit" and "mind," but this is not in the Greek, as it is in 1 Corinthians 14:14. Paul distinguishes between his own spirit and the Holy Spirit in 1 Corinthians 5:4, for example. Cf. chap. 2, note 3.

6. Romans 15:9 is Paul quoting David's song of deliverance, Psalm 18:49: "For this I will praise you, O Lord, among the nations, and sing to your name." It is likely that David accompanied himself on harp, although the psalm ascription does not indicate one way or the other.

7. Timothy Friberg, *Analytical Lexicon of the Greek New Testament* (Grand Rapids: Baker, 2000).

8. Dan McCartney, professor of New Testament, Westminster Theological Seminary, Philadelphia, e-mail correspondence to author, July 10, 2003.

5

King David's Praise Team

And 4,000 shall offer praises to the LORD with the instruments that I have made for praise. —1 Chronicles 23:5b

It is fascinating to study the books of 1 Chronicles and Psalms and to look closely at the team of musicians that David assembled. These musicians functioned in the service of God by order of the king even before the temple was constructed, as we see from the festivities at the return of the ark of the covenant. When the ark was moved to Jerusalem,

> David also commanded the chiefs of the Levites to appoint their brothers as the singers who should play loudly on musical instruments, on harps and lyres and cymbals, to raise sounds of joy . . . The singers, Heman, Asaph, and Ethan, were to sound bronze cymbals; [others] were to play harps according to Alamoth; [and still others] were to lead with lyres according to the Sheminith. Chenaniah, leader of the Levites in music, should direct the music, for he understood it . . . David was clothed with a robe of fine linen, as also were all the Levites who were carrying the ark, and the singers and Chenaniah the

> leader of the music of the singers. And David wore a linen ephod. So all Israel brought up the ark of the covenant of the LORD with shouting, to the sound of the horn, trumpets, and cymbals, and made loud music on harps and lyres.[1]

The untranslated Hebrew terms *alamoth* and *sheminith* were possibly the names of tunes or another musical indication such as a mode or performer designation (a mode is a type of musical scale or key on which a piece is based). The former term is found in the ascription of Psalm 46 and the latter in those of Psalms 6 and 12. It is also possible that these terms refer to specific instruments or their tuning. (See chapter 11, "What Psalm Ascriptions Tell Us.")

Of the 4,000 Levitical musicians set apart for temple service, David's main music men included 288 relatives of Asaph, Jeduthun, and Heman. The sons of these men were set apart by David with the commanders of the army, "who *prophesied* with lyres, with harps, and with cymbals" (1 Chron. 25:1). Verse 6 tells us, "They were all under the direction of their father in the music in the house of the LORD with cymbals, harps, and lyres for the service of the house of God." Later on, when the ark was carried into Solomon's temple, it is again these men of whom we read in 2 Chronicles 5:12–14:

> (. . . and all the Levitical singers, Asaph, Heman, and Jeduthun, their sons and kinsmen, arrayed in fine linen, with cymbals, harps, and lyres, stood east of the altar with 120 priests who were trumpeters; and it was the duty of the trumpeters and singers to make themselves heard in unison in praise and thanksgiving to the LORD), and when the song was raised, with trumpets and cymbals and other musical instruments, in praise to the LORD, "For he is good, for his steadfast love endures forever," the house, the house of the LORD, was filled with a cloud, so that the priests could not stand to minister because of the cloud, for the glory of the LORD filled the house of God.

Psalm 136 in its entirety may have been sung on this occasion. This musical fanfare occurred again following Solomon's prayer and the sacrifice of many animals as part of the dedication of the temple. Let us briefly consider the members of David's musical team (those whom he appointed to lead music in worship) and draw what applications we can from the biblical information about them and their service.

Chenaniah (*Kenanyah*)

We learn from the 1 Chronicles 15 passage cited above that Chenaniah was the head Levite. He was a wonderful singer who was charged with the responsibility of leading the other singers and the choirs, "for he understood it" (v. 22). This implies that those leading our singing should be skilled and understand the voice and music as well. Chenaniah was the *head* Levite—he had a lot of responsibility and authority. It follows, then, that leading the people in song was no common, trivial task. It was exceedingly important. Moreover, he personally saw to the leading of the people of God in musical worship. This responsibility was neither abdicated nor delegated to someone of lesser ability or stature. And why would it be? What privilege or calling could be greater than leading the people of God in the worship of God—the One who had created them for that very purpose?

Asaph

Asaph, son of Berekiah, penned at least a dozen canonical psalms (Pss. 50, 73–83). The psalm ascriptions, in these cases, identify him as the author. Asaph was the chief musician appointed by David to minister "before the ark of the LORD, to invoke, to thank, and to praise the LORD, the God of Israel. Asaph was the chief, and second to him were Zechariah [and others] . . . , who were to play harps and lyres; Asaph was to sound the cymbals . . ." (1 Chron. 16:4–5). So he was not only an author of songs but also a musician and percussionist—perhaps he was a composer as well.

We should notice that Asaph's ministry of music included prayers of petition as well as songs of thanks and praise. It was to Asaph and his associates that David first committed the psalm of thanks to the LORD that occupies the largest part of the rest of the chapter (1 Chron. 16:8–36). So Asaph, as chief musician, was entrusted with the dissemination and preservation of worship music. David left Asaph and his associates with the ark to minister there regularly "as each day required" (v. 37), which strongly suggests that a system of musical liturgy was in place. Later, in chapter 25, we read that Asaph "prophesied under the direction of the king" (v. 2). So he was also a prophet and a teacher, accountable to David.

Jeduthun and Heman

Jeduthun and Heman were among "those chosen and expressly named to give thanks to the LORD, for his steadfast love endures forever" (1 Chron. 16:41) (a possible reference to Ps. 136). They were responsible for the sounding of the trumpets and cymbals and for the playing of other instruments for sacred song. The sons of Jeduthun were stationed at the gate (1 Chron. 16:42–43).

Chapter 25 tells us that Jeduthun prophesied "with the lyre in thanksgiving and praise to the LORD" (v. 3). Three of the canonical psalms are specifically addressed or "dedicated" to Jeduthun—Psalms 39, 62, and 77. They read: "To the choirmaster: to Jeduthun." It is plausible, then, that he was a music director at the time those psalms were written. It is also possible that, in addition to referring to the celebrated singer/musician himself, "Jeduthun" was also the title of a musical term, tune, or mode named after the famed musical leader. Psalms 39 and 62 are psalms of David, while Psalm 77 is a psalm of Asaph.

Heman, son of Joel, may also have been the author of Psalm 88, a *maskil* written for the Sons of Korah, according to *mahalath leannoth.* (This Heman, however, is identified as Heman the Ezrahite, and is linked with Ethan and Calcol in 1 Chronicles 2:6 and thus may be another Heman. On the other hand, they may be one and the same person. Heman, son of Joel, was a descendant of Korah.) *Maskil* is an unknown musical or literary term that has three suggested meanings: a cultic song, a passage for learning, and a wisdom song put to music. *Mahalath leannoth* can be translated "after a sad manner" or "to make humble" and may have been the name of a tune or may have just indicated the mood of the writing or performance. It is equally possible that it referred to a mode that might have sounded "sad" to the Hebrew ear.

Heman was "the king's seer," and a man who had fourteen sons and three daughters "according to the promise of God to exalt him" (1 Chron. 25:5). As a seer, Heman would have given the king advice and counsel, so he served as a sort of musical wise man or adviser and prophet. Verse 6 notes that all fourteen sons and three daughters were "under the direction of their father in the music in the house of the LORD with cymbals, harps, and lyres for the service of the house of God." Here, then, is a clear reference to women who served as musicians in worship. (Another is Ezra 2:65, where we read of two hundred male and female singers.)

Ethan

A few men associated with David may have had the name Ethan. According to the psalm title, Ethan the Ezrahite wrote Psalm 89, another *maskil.* Frederick Putnam believes that this appears to be the same Ethan mentioned in 1 Kings 4:31, given the combination of names (son + father) and the relationship of wisdom (skill) to music.[2] There is also Ethan, son of Kushaiah (or Kishi), a descendant of Merari, whom David made a choir director and singer (cf. 1 Chron. 6:44; 15:17, 19). There was also an Ethan who was a distant Levitical ancestor of Asaph (1 Chron. 6:42), who would have lived long before David. There is possibly one other Ethan, who was a descendant of Judah (through Zerah), but since this man is linked with Heman and Calcol (1 Chron. 2:6), and since "Ezrah" and "Zerah" are phonologically related (and much more closely in Hebrew than their English forms suggest), some identify him with Ethan the Ezrahite of Psalm 89 and 1 Kings 4:31. But the biblical information is insufficient to be completely sure of this supposition.

Psalm 89 is a lengthy song of 52 verses that begins "I will sing of the steadfast love of the LORD, forever; with my mouth I will make known your faithfulness to all generations" and ends "Blessed be the LORD forever! Amen and Amen." It concludes the third book of the Psalter. Perhaps it was positioned here because of its length and strong literary format besides its obvious themes of praise. The psalm has a spirit of timelessness in its evocation of God's glory and rehearsing of his mighty acts. Ethan is listed with Heman and Asaph as one of those lead musicians designated to play the bronze cymbals in 1 Chronicles 15 (obviously a responsibility of some significance, since it is noted), but we do not hear too much more about him after that. He must have been a wise man because in 1 Kings 4:31 we find that Solomon's wisdom surpassed that of other men, but Ethan is the first to whom Solomon's greater gift is compared. (Incidentally, the Bible records in the following verse that Solomon wrote 1,005 songs.)

David

King David himself must be credited with setting up the massive organization of music for worship that lasted through the end of the second temple period. We have noted here and in other essays that it was David who set apart the 4,000 Levites for temple music and appointed the 288 skilled leaders. Yet he did not choose them arbitrarily or on his own. First Chronicles 15:16 indicates that he "commanded the chiefs of the Levites to appoint their brothers as the singers who should play loudly on musical instruments, on harps and lyres and cymbals, to raise sounds of joy." In other words, a committee of elders whom David entrusted with that task chose the leaders. These leaders taught the other selected Levitical musicians the songs of God, and they, in turn, taught them to the people of Israel. Much of this teaching would have been by oral tradition.

It is also possible, according to Suzanne Häik-Vantoura, that the Levitical scribes took great care to indicate the musical performance code with diacritical marks (the *te'amim*). She notes that the original biblical chant of the temple in Jerusalem was "preserved by the meticulous tradition of its consecrated singers (the Levites) during the times of the First Temple, then of the Second."[3] This system is known as cantillation. Haïk-Vantoura's deciphering key, if correct, could grant insight into exegesis. Although scholars debate the validity of these claims, she says of her code:

> Not only does it penetrate the very soul of highly diverse texts throughout the Old Testament, it reflects with disarming faithfulness the historical and literary circumstances behind the creation of the biblical narratives and doctrinal texts as related by the Bible itself. In the Psalms it also reflects the use of choruses, soloists, latent harmony, even instrumentation as practiced in the liturgy.[4]

We should recall that David (the "sweet psalmist of Israel" [2 Sam. 23:1]) was a musician from his youth—he probably wrote and sang songs and prayers to God as he tended his father's herds. At least many of the psalms recount the pastoral imagery with which David was familiar, and King Saul called him to court because David's musical skills were renowned while he was yet a shepherd (1 Sam. 16:18–23). Though he was Israel's second king, a great warrior, and, as the Bible points out, also a great sinner, God called David "a man after his own heart" (1 Sam. 13:14). Does God's characterization of David, together with the fact that God created man to glorify him and the corollary truth that biblical worship had music associated with it, not make it obvious that God approves of, desires, and delights in our musical worship of him?

But David's personal involvement in the organization of worship music did not cease at the appointment of musical directors. David composed many of the psalms and other recorded biblical songs (including those of 2 Sam. 1; 2 Sam. 22; and 1 Chron. 16). He personally instructed the three chief cantors of Israel named above (Heman, Jeduthun, and Asaph). These men played and led others *al yede David*—"according to the hand (or direction or chironomy) of David."[5] Chironomy refers to a system of hand gestures that symbolize degrees of a musical scale or other musical parameters (such as tempo and rhythm) for performance.

Chironomy must have existed by at least 3000 B.C. because it appears in ancient Egyptian pictures and hieroglyphs. *Al yede David* implies a system of musical performance or methodology that David must have created, adapted, or endorsed personally (or, at the least, a system developed during his reign).

To a significant degree, the Davidic system of cantillation and chironomy must have been set apart for the worship of Yahweh, distinguishing worship of the one true God from that of the false gods of Israel's neighbors. In discussing biblical cantillation based on the Tiberian neumatic notation system, Haïk-Vantoura writes, "Although it reveals itself to be archaic, it is perfectly suited to its purpose: the worship service of pure, filial love, so particular to the Hebrew people, and so far removed from the pagan rites of certain other ancient peoples."[6] The fact that the sons were taught by their musical fathers, generation after generation, could be seen as passing on a trade; but since this was temple service, it could properly be considered a family calling.

Cantillation and chironomy were musical traditions carefully guarded and attentively taught from one generation to the next. Thus, under the politically stable and culturally rich environment of the kingships of David and Solomon (a "golden age"), such musical traditions must have flourished to the level of art within the holy city of Jerusalem. It makes sense, on this basis, that the exiled Jews of the Babylonian captivity would have lamented being asked to sing the songs of Zion in a strange land (Ps. 137). The Hebrew people were known for their musical ability, but their singing and songs were thoroughly intertwined with their faith and its expression in worship. Here in the foreign land of their captors, they had hung their harps among the river's trees while vowing not to forget Jerusalem. These songs were so intricately linked to worship in the temple that it would have been excruciating for the exiles to sing them. Doing so could only remind them of their great loss as a people as well as their former joy in the glory of Solomon's temple that was now but a memory.

Truly, David sets the example for all of us. The man after God's own heart sang and played music to God throughout his life. He concerned himself with the proper worship of God. He employed his musical skills and his position of authority to organize suitable worship practices for the people of God. He entrusted this work to faithful, trained men; and he remained involved in their training and management. David evidently recognized that any organization is influenced from the top down—from its leadership—and thus he personally set an example, as a participant. He wrote music for the instruction of his people and ensured that they learned it. David was a real, thinking, emotional person who recognized that musical lament, praise, thanksgiving, confession, and petition, through voices and instruments, were appropriate aspects of the worship of God. He can still teach us much.

Notes

1. Excerpts from 1 Chronicles 15:16–28.

2. Frederick Putnam, professor of Old Testament, Biblical Seminary, Hatboro, Pennsylvania, e-mail correspondence to author, December 7, 2004. I am indebted to Professor Putnam for the information regarding the distinction between the various possible "Ethans" mentioned here. He also notes: "Psalm 89 ends with a lamentation over divine judgments on the Davidites (vv. 38–51), which suggests that Ethan must have been a relatively young man when installed by David, or else he lived a very long time, since the only disasters that this could refer to are (1) the division of the kingdom under Jeroboam and Rehoboam (1 Kings 12; 2 Chron. 10) ca. 930 BC, forty years after David's death; or (2) Shishak's invasion of Judah five years later, ca. 925 BC (1 Kings 14:25–26; 2 Chron. 12:9). Of course, there may have been some other war or temporary invasion that is unrecorded in Scripture. Since scholarship today generally rejects the validity of the psalm titles, dates for the composition of this poem range from the time right after the division of the kingdom (late 10th century) to after the exile (i.e., 5th century); the latter would certainly explain the complaint portion of the psalm."

3. Suzanne Haïk-Vantoura, *The Music of the Bible Revealed,* trans. Dennis Weber, ed. John Wheeler, based on the 2nd French ed. (Paris: Dessain et Tolra, 1978) (Berkeley, CA: Bibal Press/San Francisco: King David's Harp, Inc., 1991), 5. Scholars question her assertion that this practice existed in pre-exilic Israel, and many believe it was limited to medieval tradition.

4. Ibid.

5. Ibid., 9.

6. Ibid., 44.

6
Leading in Worship as Accompanist

Make a joyful noise to the Lord, all the earth!
Serve the Lord with gladness!
Come into his presence with singing! —Psalm 100:1–2

In contrast to postmodern thought and to Deconstructionism in particular, Christianity is based on absolutes. We have a moral compass, a standard, a center: the Word of God. Therefore, Christ is our center. Because our faith is Christocentric, it is also *Logos*-centric (John 1:1). The Deconstructionists accuse the Western world of being logocentric. In other words, we focus on an idea on the basis of words, and we are literary-bound or linguistically enslaved thereby. Christianity, to the Deconstructionist, is falsely presupposed; for as soon as one thinks or acts on the basis of a particular "truth" or point of view, one has negated or marginalized everything else and has assumed a corner on truth. According to Deconstructionism, John 14:6 (which says that Jesus is the only Way, the only Truth, and the only Life) is necessarily inaccurate because it propounds only one momentary, subjective truth among many. Of course, the Deconstructionists are wrong, since God's Word asserts the truth.

Why begin a discussion of musical accompanying by referring to language? We start here because church music is *logogenic* (or word-born). It grows out of language—out of our own national tongues, but more significantly, out of the language of the Bible and Christianity. Thus, language interprets and propagates our faith; and ultimately, it proceeds from Christ, the Word—the *Logos.* Music clothes the Word of God with sound and also reinforces its message with meaning beyond the realm of words. It communicates with our souls as a metaphysical force.

How do these thoughts relate to being a good accompanist and leader of God's people in worship? They relate in critical, meaningful ways. Language and communication are at the heart of worship, and musicians provide a mode or vehicle in which much of this conversation occurs. You may be a pianist, keyboard player, or organist who follows the direction of a song leader in your church, you may be part of a worship team, or you may lead everything from the console. In all of these cases, the way in which one plays affects the way the people sing. We probably realize this, but do we grasp the full extent and responsibility of this role?

The Accompanist's Role

The accompanist directly influences singing. This is true not only of congregations, but of choirs and soloists. An accompanist can influence the singer as much as the choir director can (and often more). Why? Because we respond naturally in music to what we hear more than to what we see, read, or are told. For example, in a band or orchestra, the percussion section must be especially attentive to the conductor. If the snare drum moves a little faster or slower than the baton, the entire ensemble will move with the drummer. The percussive nature of the piano has a similar rhythmic effect. The choir or congregation will typically move along with what it hears. The organ, if it is a good one, has sufficient sound capacity to lead with force; but even here it is articulation that provides much of the rhythmic clarity.

So, then, if the accompanist influences the way in which a congregation sings, in what ways is this true? In addition to tempo and rhythm, which have already been mentioned, the accompanist influences volume and dynamic. Pacing (time between verses and how long chords are held), style, and articulation can also be included in the list, as can breathing and ensemble (togetherness/unity). Most significantly, through these various parameters one can affect people's thinking as well as their connection to the truths being sung.

This last sphere of influence—thought—is the most important, and all the others are connected to it. Thought is missing more and more in worship today. Apparently we are more concerned about our emotional connection and what we are "getting" out of the worship experience than in being cognitively engaged or spiritually awakened. This mindset is one of the primary reasons that hymns have fallen out of popularity and use in many churches. It is because they require thought; and as a people, we do not want to think. Not many years ago I read a short article by a seminary professor in a prominent Christian periodical. He wrote something along the lines of, "Let's stop being enslaved to the present rationalistic, intellect-centered approach to church that characterizes much of evangelicalism." Well, he got his wish. Today most evangelicals come to church to be refreshed, not to work or to think.

Yet proper worship does take work. It also takes thought, preparation, and action. If we understood that our singing is not for ourselves or directed principally to each other, but to and for God, that understanding would make a difference in how we engage in it. If we were more conscious of the fact that when we sing we are praising God and praying to him, that we are in the presence of the King of Glory, we would realize how important it is to know *what* we are singing.

Congregational music should deliver Christian doctrine, quote Scripture, or offer a message of challenge or encouragement to fellow believers while pointing all to Christ. Often, congregational song is prayer. How we think about these songs and how we sing them matters.

The accompanist has a lot to do with that. In fact, I would venture that it is the single most important thing that one does as an accompanist. Such responsibility demands preparation on our parts. It requires practice. Let us look at some specific ways that the accompanist leads in worship, and consider how to prepare oneself to do so effectively.

The Introduction

What is the purpose of an accompanist's introduction to a hymn? The introduction has multiple tasks. It sets key, meter, tempo, mood, character, and style; and it acquaints the ear with the tune. So those parameters must be determined, be obvious to the congregation, and be consistent. This requires the accompanist's focused thought ahead of time. Choosing the right tempo (the right pace and character) is very important. We tend to slip into the rut of singing everything the same way, with the same sound, even with the same general tempo and volume. That is like painting everything in a grand mural one color. It is dull, does not encourage thoughtful participation, and results in disinterest.

As part of our preparation to accompany congregational song, we need to study the piece of music (text and tune) to ascertain whether it is a prayer, a praise-oriented piece, a narrative, a doctrinal statement, or a piece of some other nature. We need to sing it ourselves in rehearsal to determine what a reasonable tempo might be. Can the lines be sung without multiple breaths? Is there time to breathe? Does this feel rushed, or does it drag? Also, be sure to keep a consistent tempo in the introduction, without much or any *ritard*, so that it is clear to the congregation just when and how fast to sing.

Inhalation

Life is in the breath. Such is life; such is music. The way we breathe affects our communication. If someone speaks in a long, run-on sentence without ever stopping to breathe or reflect on what is being said and never changes inflection at all, the listener will lose interest or have trouble following the train of thought. On the other hand, if stress or *weight* is placed on significant words, if there is a sense of pace, and if there is evidence of thought and meaning, communication will occur. Music is very similar.

What is it in speech or writing that makes the difference between run-on sentences that lack form, and clear, concise, thoughtful phrases? The answer is simple but profound: *punctuation.* Those little marks (periods, commas, colons, semicolons, etc.) help us to understand the structure of the English language and the pacing of its delivery. So why do we ignore them when we sing?

My standard rule for choirs is to breathe or rearticulate with the written punctuation unless I tell them differently. If a congregation breathes together where the punctuation calls for it, and resists breathing corporately when a thought should be connected to the next, it will have good ensemble. And the people will have a greater chance of understanding the thought behind the words. The same is true of responsive reading, and here the unison breath is much more commonly and properly executed. But the track record, when it comes to congregational singing, is poor. People breathe in the middle of words and rush through phrases that should be separated. Unless the singers have had vocal training, such concepts may not have ever occurred to them. I have found that nonmusicians readily respond to the suggestion to breathe with punctuation, however, and that they benefit from it. Simply introducing the idea focuses a heightened level of attention on the text.

The way to encourage a group to breathe when you are playing a keyboard instrument is to "breathe" with your hands (and pedals). Lift them off the keys, and rearticulate the new word or phrase. This may mean all fingers, or the right hand only, or just the melody note, determined according to instance. This concept applies to organ, keyboard, and piano; and it can be applied to other instruments as well. Some phrases need to be sung through, or else their meanings will be changed or lost. Other phrases require multiple lifts or breaks in order to distinguish ideas or lists in the text. Some hymns present challenges because the musical logic fights the text somewhat, or the hymn's verbal phrasing differs from stanza to stanza (e.g., "Jesus, Thy Blood and Righteousness" [GERMANY]). The only way to play accurately in this regard is to "sing" along in each stanza by following the text carefully. In other words, one will breathe and musically phrase the successive stanzas differently.

Articulation

Articulation is a category related to inhalation. The attack, the amount of space between notes, the use of damper pedal, the length of notes, emphasis, and stress—all of these things affect the sound and character of the music. Listeners, particularly nonmusicians, frequently mistake the various parameters of articulation for speed. In other words, they think something should be (or is) faster or slower when actually it should simply be (or is) more or less articulate. Certain conventions exist in hymn playing in this regard. For example, the cathedral organist may not regularly employ or even approve of the articulative model of playing described here. Certainly various spaces, acoustics, and instruments will inform the way we play and lead. Traditions notwithstanding, our hymn playing should grow out of textual consideration and should compel the congregation to sing thoughtfully. If this means that change is necessary, so be it—make it so.

Registration

Another important means of drawing attention to the text is through choice of registration. This applies to organ, keyboard, and piano in ways germane to each instrument. Most church musicians agree that a different sound should accompany each successive stanza and that, at times, the registration may even change mid-stanza. The player, irrespective of instrument, is like an orchestra. Much sound color is at his or her disposal, and this color should be used to the advantage of the text. For example, if a stanza is prayerful, one could play more quietly and legato, without much bass, making use of strings/celestes or flutes. If a stanza is bold and praise-oriented, one could play louder and less legato, with reeds added to principals and mixtures on the organ or octaves added on the piano.

A stanza can be varied or set apart from the others by dropping the pedal/bass or by playing solely in the written octave. This provides aural relief for the congregation as well, and this change in sound can heighten awareness of the text. Pedal (or octaves) can be added again at a significant moment in the hymn—on the refrain, on the last stanza, or at a change of text or mood. Registration has a lot to do with portraying the character of the particular stanza, and it requires thought ahead of time. In the right context, certain stanzas may be best sung *a cappella*, without any accompaniment at all.

Improvisation

Improvisation affects the overall character of the musical rendering as well. One does not have to be a great improviser to be a good congregational accompanist; but if the skill exists or is developed, even modestly, it can add to effectiveness. Improvisation can be employed in an introduction or as an elaboration between stanzas, but more often befits other service music quite apart from hymn singing. Improvisation is by nature spontaneous. But "spontaneity" can also be planned or rehearsed. In hymn playing, this refers to the addition of passing tones, octaves, descants, arpeggios, or additional chords to fill out the rhythm or to alter harmony.

A common malady exists among congregations, pastors, accompanists, and song leaders that one might call "lack of rhythm." This rhythmic deficiency variously manifests itself as a tendency to "cheat" longer notes, fade away at the ends of phrases or stanzas, skip beats altogether, or lose energy mid-measure. The pianist can counter this and sustain the collective rhythm of the congregation by adding chords or notes that propel the hymn and give it rhythmic direction and energy. This technique is particularly helpful when the hymn has a slow harmonic rhythm with long notes at the ends of phrases (e.g., "Fairest Lord Jesus" [CRUSADERS' HYMN]). This type of addition is unnecessary in a hymn with a faster harmonic rhythm (e.g., "O God, Our Help in Ages Past" [St. Anne]), which tends to propel itself with continually changing harmony.

The key to improvising during hymn singing is to ensure that what is done is relevant to the text or music without drawing unnecessary attention to oneself. Lead the congregational singers into their next note. Help them gather energy to sing with more vigor. But remember, it is a congregational hymn, not a solo concerto.

Reharmonization/Key Change

Reharmonization is simply changing the standard harmony of a hymn to something else. Why do this? To enliven or enrich congregational singing. First of all, it should not be done all the time. Being an organist who *can* do it is not a good reason *to* do it. If the text of the last stanza of a hymn is summarizing, has a look to the future, or is strongly praise-oriented, this might be a good occasion to reharmonize, and thereby compel the people to sing even more forcefully than before (and in unison). Taking a broader tempo in such a circumstance may also be appropriate. It is helpful if the organist or pianist can give the congregation some kind of aural sign that this is going to happen, so that people do not begin singing in parts only to realize that they are harmonically opposed to the instrument. (Stalwart part singers tend to be distressed when this occurs.) Such a sign can be given by spoken instruction before the hymn begins (if there is a song leader) or by playing the first few notes or first phrase of the soon-to-be altered stanza in unison. An interlude or key change may suffice.

Key changes, likewise, should be used for purposeful effect rather than out of habit. Many contemporary Christian solos or choral octavos modulate three or four times, each new verse or refrain up half a step. It grows wearisome. Changing keys is appropriate if it will put greater emphasis on the text, but it is not a substitute for good writing or arranging. If you are not comfortable transposing at sight, there are solutions for you as well. One should bear in mind that there is a simple means of converting keys in proportions of seven (where flat keys can be played as sharp keys by reading the "same" notes—2:5, 3:4, 1:6, etc.). The tune may exist in a different key elsewhere in the hymnal or a different hymnal, or one could always write it out ahead of time. It is effective if one extends the modulation to four or eight measures, incorporating melodic or rhythmic elements of the tune itself into the transition. For those who are not highly skilled, this should be thought through ahead of time and even written out. There is no shame in writing modulations or reharmonizations. When it comes to worship music and creativity, planned accuracy is preferable to errant spontaneity. Any endeavor that will enhance the congregation's singing and not detract from it is a noble effort.

Preparation

Several references have been made to the need to prepare, think, and rehearse. If there are multiple accompanists, each needs to know what is happening (including the song leader, if there is one). This presupposes that the hymns or songs are chosen in advance as an important part of worship planning. One may be able to play any piece placed in front of him or her, but leading the congregation in the worship of God is important enough to merit reacquainting the hands and feet with the notes ahead of time. Texts should be reviewed to determine how the congregation can be encouraged to sing them with understanding and conviction.

Preparation is so very important to being effective. Being prepared does not mean that one must work within some sort of preplanned formula or sterile environment. There is room for spontaneity and inspiration. But as Bruce Leafblad, professor of church music at Southwestern Baptist Theological Seminary, has said, we are often less familiar with the "stewardship of preparation" and much better acquainted with the "theology of perpetual rescue." We sometimes hope that God will make up for our lack of preparation and somehow miraculously make it all work out. Sometimes we even pray this way. But while the Lord works out his glory through us—and regularly in spite of us—if we expect our congregations to approach him with thought and care, we are responsible to do the same as musicians.

7

Authenticity in Corporate Worship Music

God is spirit, and those who worship him must worship in spirit and truth. —John 4:24

We live in a world of high-tech gadgets, fiber optics, microchips, space shuttles, satellite television, video games, sound bites, and instant-everything-on-demand. While in many ways such advancements contribute to our lives and aid the global spread of Christianity, they have detriments as well. One such issue reveals itself in various forms within the church. The issue at hand is *authenticity*—or, more specifically, a lack of it: *inauthenticity*.

We all have pseudonyms these days for e-mail addresses and the various numbers by which we are known to the government, credit-card agencies, and merchants. "Pseudo" (false) things are everyday parts of our lives. In addition, vapid television programs and movies dominate our culture and are full of illusion; even the "reality" shows that are a current TV fascination are not true to life, but very much contrived.

Other things that we do or accept as real are also fake, including things in the context of gathered worship. Take music, for example. Church music can be inauthentic. Fifty years ago, Frank Gaebelein noted that "there is a great deal of music in favor among evangelicals that justly falls under condemnation; cheap, vulgar, and aesthetically false, its use for good ends does not alter its character. The fact is that American evangelicalism urgently needs to progress to a higher level of music."[1] In church music, at times one encounters false performances, fake instruments, and even phony worship. What do I mean by such audacious charges?

Inauthentic Performance:
Prerecorded Music, Accompaniment Tracks

These are less than real, and their use in worship should be eliminated. No one present in the church (save possibly the sound engineer) is playing the instruments, which is akin to worship by proxy. There is no direct control over tempo, relative volume, expression, timing, phrasing, or pitch. If the soloist or choral director wants to alter any of these parameters in the moment, he or she is unable to do so. Using prerecorded music can make things sound "professional" and can mask technical deficiencies in one's vocal ability or an undesirable choral tone. It can take the place of missing instrumentalists. But should it?

Music is organic, and it must have flexibility, subtlety, and choice. Recordings remove these dynamic parameters. A recording is a single performance trapped in time. It becomes "still life" rather than a real-time, real-life occurrence. Music in these circumstances is not creative or even re-creative; it is fixed and therefore is not really music, but a kind of pseudo-music—a reproduction. Additionally, playing a recording does not truthfully represent the *real* people in the church who should be offering the music. It imports commercial players from a static moment in time, from a recording studio that is likely many miles away. It is like hiring an agency to worship in our stead.

Inauthentic Instruments: Synthesizers, Electronic Organs, Electric Guitars, and the Like

These are not authentic instruments either. Before you shut the book in disbelief, allow me to explain. Any instrument that must be amplified to be played or that relies on "sampled" sounds from real instruments is not a natural, acoustic instrument. It is a recording apparatus of sorts. The computer situated within the instrument digitally records the sounds, and then the recording is played back instantaneously through speakers, very much as is done with a tape or CD, even if a person is moving the keys or strings. Does this negate the usefulness of such an apparatus? No, not necessarily; finances, space, or other limiting factors may make the use of less-than-real instruments necessary, at least for a time. And I am not suggesting that the players are doing anything amiss. The goal here is simply to cause us to think about the authenticity of our worship instruments. For example, for years the organ at Tenth Presbyterian Church has been a digital, electronic instrument. Such machines are not authentic instruments—they are replicas of the real. The acoustic instruments on which they are based are the real thing. By the grace of God, even what is less than desirable and less than we *should* offer can be useful in his service. But we cannot be complacent in this. We must strive to give, do, and be all that we can.

Acoustic instruments share one overarching characteristic: they are all modeled after the human voice—the first and greatest instrument, created by God. They also function similarly. All acoustic instruments require an *energizing source* (usually movement of air or activation by part of the body, a bow, a mallet), a *vibrating element* (strings, lips, membranes, reeds), and a *resonating space.* (The human voice requires air from the lungs being forced over the vocal folds that, in turn, vibrate and sound into the resonating chambers/cavities of the head and torso. A violin requires movement of the bow, which causes the strings to vibrate and then resonates through its own hollow wooden body, and so forth.)

A synthesizer playing string sounds is replacing real violin, viola, cello, and bass with a recorded version with unnatural vibrato. We should not expect more from them; after all, they are called "synthesizers" because they make synthetic sound. Unless the player is using a "solo" voice, most "string" sounds or "organ" buttons deliver more octaves than are being played without relief or variation. The versatility and color of the actual instruments are lost, as is the interplay of the artists. A digital organ trumpet stop replaces a live player with a sampled sound from a pipe organ. The difference with the pipe organ (even though it acts orchestrally and replaces many players) is that it has all the elements of an acoustic instrument—air, pipes, and resonating space—and thus is an acoustic instrument although it imitates others (in the same way all instruments, to some degree, imitate the voice). Imitation can be real or natural; synthetic cannot be either.

One redeeming factor, even for all of these pseudo-instruments, is that they require a real human being to play them. Or do they? Actually, today discs can be purchased, programs downloaded, and music sequenced ahead of time so that no live performer is required. Usually, however, someone is playing, so there is still a human agent at work. But is it not more wonderful to have real instrumentalists participating in worship on authentic instruments? This kind of participation is biblical—we only have to read through the psalms to see that. (For more discussion, see chapter 4, "A Biblical Case for Instruments in Worship.")

Inauthentic Worshipers: Organists, Worship Teams, Song Leaders, Soloists, Pastors, Congregation Members

"Hang on just a minute—these are real people!" Granted. There is no lack of authenticity in their humanity. Yet these people *can* be inauthentic worshipers (as can we all) because of that very fallen humanity. Inauthentic worship is a danger from which no worshiper is immune. While this danger is not new to our time, it is exacerbated by pop culture and shortcut technology. For example, the organist who is more concerned with virtuosity and remuneration than with congregational singing and calling is not an authentic worship leader. The worship team that is concerned more with stage presence, congregational affirmation, stardom, and solo spots than with pointing people to Christ is not authentically worshiping. The song leader who sings loudly into the microphone while ignoring the congregation's singing, talks too much, leaves hymn stanzas out, and does not adequately prepare also gets in the way of real worship.

Soloists who draw attention to themselves, attempt music they cannot perform well, and accept praise that is due to God are not authentically worshiping. The pastor who leafs through sermon notes during prayer, shares a joke with a colleague during the choral anthem, and does not participate in congregational singing is not authentically worshiping or leading people to God at those times. (Much worse, he is setting a poor example for the congregation and communicates the idea that elements of worship other than the sermon are not important.) And the church member who "tunes out" during the sermon, who allows the song leader or worship team to sing in his place, or whose chief activity on Sunday morning is being critical of what is taking place is not authentically worshiping. Of course, none of these inauthenticities need occur.

Arguments and Applications for Authenticity in Corporate Worship

Each of these potential areas for inauthentic worship can be answered by something authentic.

Authentic worshipers. God must be worshiped "in spirit and truth" (John 4:24). We need the help of the Spirit of God to be true worshipers. We need the right focus as well—God himself—because worship is not primarily about us. It involves us and we benefit from it, but Christ is rightly the center of attention. Keeping Christ at the center may mean less time in front of the microphone for musicians. It may mean more time in rehearsal. It may mean moving the musicians to the side or back of the church. It may mean singing more psalms and hymns. It may mean *not* singing certain hymns or choruses. It may be that Gertrude needs to retire from her thirty-year post as organist (or Elmer from his). It may be that Pastor Smith needs to prepare his call to worship in advance of the prelude. It may be that music director Jones needs to be more involved in Bible study, or that Kathy needs to pray upon arrival in the sanctuary instead of getting her weekly digest from a friend. Are we open to change in our churches and in our lives so that we can fully receive and fully give in the context of worship?

Authentic instruments. The argument can be made that something real is better than something unreal. Since we are to worship God with the best we can bring, can we not do better than pseudo-music? Perhaps we need to invest in a real piano or a pipe organ. Perhaps we should have a music budget that permits us to engage and compensate excellent wind, string, or brass musicians once a month or more. Perhaps that young person who plays electric guitar needs to have an acoustic instrument purchased for him, be willing to take some much needed lessons, and wait until he is more proficient to be part of leading in worship. The point is this: if we *can* do better, we should. Are we saving our best for someone more important than God?

Authentic performance/presentation. The use of live musicians is always preferable to recorded tracks, even though the sound of Nashville or Hollywood strings, the impeccable and omnipresent drum machine, and the wind chimes may be missing. Use your musicians and provide training and encouragement to those who need it. Do not mask the lack of tone or diction in your choir with backup vocals on an accompaniment CD. Build up the choir instead. If you do not know how, consult with someone who does. Any choir can improve.

Encourage solo singers and young people to take voice lessons; help them discover their real voices. Too many church soloists attempt to imitate recording artists and harm their voices in the process. Be careful that the opportunity to present solo music does not turn into an occasion for celebrity. Plan ahead so that the information needed to adequately prepare music (sermon information, hymn selection, etc.) does not arrive later than it should. And could it be that we need to stay in on Saturday night to be better rested for gathered worship the next morning?

Inauthenticity can be a kind of hypocrisy of which we all are guilty at times. No doubt we all can be better worshipers. Some practical suggestions have been articulated here. The Bible gives both instruction and examples of how to worship God aright. If we follow its commands and claim its promises, it will be a lamp to our feet and a light to our path (Ps. 119:105). We can thank God that his grace is sufficient for us even in our many weaknesses and that the Spirit makes intercession for us (2 Cor. 12:9; Rom. 8:26–27).

Note

1. Frank E. Gaebelein, *The Pattern of God's Truth* (New York: Oxford, 1954), 76.

8

Service Music: What's It All About?

Oh, magnify the LORD with me,
and let us exalt his name together!—Psalm 34:3

Our church services are filled with music. Do you ever wonder what purpose certain music serves or what its various names mean? In many evangelical churches, one will find events called "prelude," "praise and worship," "special music," and "offertory," as well as transition music and perhaps a postlude. In more liturgical evangelical churches, one might also discover an Introit, a *Gloria Patri*, a Doxology, Scripture sentences, responses, canticles, parts of the Mass (such as Gradual, Tract, Kyrie, and Sanctus), and anthems (also known in various congregations as "choir numbers" or "specials").

What does it all mean, and why do these various categories of worship music exist? Some reading this may not have heard of an "introit" and may have never sung a *Gloria Patri*. Demystifying such musical terminology may help to uncover *why* this music exists and give it greater meaning for us.

Prelude

"Prelude" is a generic name for music that comes before something else, as its prefix indicates. In the world of Western classical music, preludes (like overtures) came before operas, ballets, suites, plays, and various instrumental forms. They would often introduce the themes of the major work to follow. "Prelude" also served as a nonspecific title for short pieces that might be paired with others (e.g., "Prelude and Fugue") or stand-alone works performed to open a program (e.g., Debussy's *Prélude à l'après-midi d'un faune*).

When it comes to church services, what exactly is the prelude about? It is a prelude *to* something—to worship, of course. That is both its name and its function. If its purpose were to provide background music for conversation or to announce the entrance of guests as they arrived, or some other purpose, it would be named differently. The prelude provides musical clothing for the sanctuary, so that the arriving worshiper can more easily comprehend a sense of place and purpose as being different from that of the world. Prelude music should either turn the mind toward God directly or provide a setting in which one can focus on the important and serious work ahead—the worship of God. It may introduce a specific theme or it may contextualize, in broader terms, the primary elements to follow. It is a time to pray, to listen, and to think.

Praise and Worship

This title is rather misleading unless it is the title of the entire service, and even then it is errant. Praise is, after all, not exclusive of worship, and vice versa. In fact, praise is part of our worship of God, but only one part. So there is a semantic problem inherent in this oft-used and misused phrase. Another problem, which is theological and philosophical in nature, arises when one views "praise and worship" as a set time in the service when music is performed or participated in—as though the praise of God does not happen at other times, and worship occurs only when one is singing or listening to others sing.

Hardly anyone actually believes this to be the case, and yet we go on talking about "the praise" or "the praise and worship" as though we were properly using such terminology, and this leads to confusion. One of the problems is that members and church leaders come to think of these musical elements of worship as "pre-sermon activities"—making them peripheral. As a result, parishioners may show up late for morning worship, having passively come to believe that the pre-sermon activities do not matter. Anecdotal evidence suggests that if people do not really enjoy singing or dislike the songs that are sung, they may purposely come late. Another problem with the phrase "praise and worship" is the implication that all church music must be grouped into either the "praise" column (usually interpreted as loud and fast) or the "worship" column (usually implying slower and quieter). This distinction is absurd. Much church music defies this sort of categorical classification, and the terms are far from precise. For example, praise can be weighty or reflective and adoration can be energetic or serene. Such terminology is not useful for describing parts of the worship service.

Introit

Historically in the Protestant church, the "Introit" (entrance) has been a brief choral or congregational song that fulfills two functions. It serves as a processional for the ministerial staff and serves as a choral call to worship for the congregation. In the former case, it provides music for the grand entrance of the service leaders in a solemn ceremony that announces the start of worship. In the latter, it calls the people of God to lay aside their worldly cares and actively begin to participate in worship. Often, the introit is a psalm or a hymn. In the Roman service, the introit was more complex than the Protestant form described here.

Doxology

A doxology is a hymn of praise, although in a broader sense, all worship is doxological.[1] Typically, a doxology calls the people to praise the Trinity (often each person by name) and invokes God's blessing on his people. There are many forms and musical renderings of doxology. The title is not limited to the common setting of the OLD HUNDREDTH tune to which many refer as "The Doxology," although that is a fine example. The *Gloria Patri* is another example of a doxology, as is Psalm 150. (For more information, see chapter 13, "Song in the Bible.")

Gloria Patri

The *Gloria Patri* is a Latin hymn that originated as early as the second century A.D. and was fully formed by the fourth century. It takes as its primary subject matter praise to the triune God. It is named "*Gloria Patri*" from its first words, which mean "Glory be to the Father." For centuries it has been used as a response to psalm and canticle singing to the extent that many composers wrote settings of the *Gloria Patri* directly into their musical compositions as a conclusion. Previously, it was a standard component of the Mass, used several times in each service.

Hymns/Chorales

Hymns (or "chorales," if they are of Germanic or Lutheran origin) have come to be known as the primary music of the church and specifically of the congregation. In its earliest Greek usage, *hymn* referred to a poem or ode of praise to a divine being, hero, or mythological figure. One can therefore find in literature hymns that are not expressly sacred or linked with music. In the church, however, Martin Luther and subsequent theologians were convinced of music's power to transmit theological substance. They believed that hymns, as music of the people, would serve to bolster faith and carry the gospel. Luther held that one realization of the "priesthood of all believers" was that the common people should sing in worship. So he wrote 37 chorales for his congregations to sing and subsequently became known as "the father of evangelical hymnody."

Communion

Originally, Communion music consisted of the singing of a psalm and the *Gloria Patri* as the clergy distributed the sacramental elements, and the organist would improvise and the choir sing as the elements were received. Still today, in most churches, music is played or sung during the distribution of the bread and wine. This music should be appropriate to thinking about the Lord's Supper, Christ's sacrifice for us, confession of sin, or other aspects of the sacrament. Instrumental music, choral or congregational song, or even silence are all suitable in this context.

Anthem

An anthem is a piece of music with sacred text, normally intended for performance by a choir. It is distinguished from choral introits or responses in that it is a stand-alone part of the service and from the motet in that it is more homophonic than polyphonic. It makes a contribution outside of other verbal elements. This text would not usually be classified as a hymn, though hymn-anthems are an exception (hymns arranged in anthem form and designated for choral singing). The typical nineteenth-century English "verse" anthem for soloists, chorus, and instrumental accompaniment begins in unison, includes a stanza for a soloist, features at least one stanza in parts (often *a cappella*), and concludes with the choir in unison amid boy-soprano descant. "Full" anthems were for chorus without soloists. Until recent decades, church choirs were almost always composed of men and boys, and this remains the practice in many European assemblies.

Solo Music

Solo music in worship, as we know it, is primarily a phenomenon of the twentieth century, although it certainly existed previously in other forms (e.g., the solo cantatas of Bach). The twentieth-century "crusades" and tent meetings of Dwight Moody, Billy Sunday, and Billy Graham, among others, often featured the song leader or a designated soloist in a well-loved hymn or a gospel song (e.g., George Beverly Shea and "I'd Rather Have Jesus"). The rise of the pop-music industry, particularly in the 1930s to 1970s, exalted the soloist (as well as bands) to previously unheard-of popularity. Before that, the closest corollary to this kind of "singer celebrity" may have been the reception of great opera singers in Italy, but opera had little effect on modern solo music of the church. Christian radio broadcasts often featured soloists as well. It was principally the influence of the superstar singer in American culture that brought soloists (as we think of them) into the church. For generations, cantors (chief singers) or priests have led services in Jewish, Lutheran, Roman Catholic, and Episcopal worship by chanting (as soloists of a sort, but unlike those we are discussing).

The manner in which modern solo song came into the church does not negate the possibility of its proper use, but it does make it more difficult to overcome the baggage associated with it. By this I refer to the cult of celebrity, the focus on the individual, the pressure to "perform," the importance that we arbitrarily attach to this activity over choral or congregational singing, and so forth. Yet it is entirely possible for a soloist to have an effective ministry in the context of corporate worship and for the solo, as a category, to fill a niche.

In order for these postulations to be true, however, the focus of both text and delivery (including placement of the piece in the service and the singer in the room) must be on God and his Word, the song sung must be capable of being universally applied to the congregation, and the event should actually be more of a nonevent that does not interrupt or estrange one from the momentum of the service. There should be no applause, no excessive talking or testimonial from the singer, no accompaniment tracks, no use of singers who are unprepared (musically, spiritually, or emotionally), and no expectation on the singer's part of being publicly lauded for this ministry. Unless one has trained soloists in the church who are mature believers and who understand the function of a soloist in worship, this is a service component that should probably be avoided. Some would argue that all music in corporate worship should be congregational.

"Special Music"

"Special music" is the inaccurate, nonspecific title given to solo pieces, choral anthems, ensemble selections, and various other musical events that should either be properly titled or fall under the general heading of "musical offering." To call something "special" is to set it apart as unique, unusual, or extraordinary. Not only is it inappropriate for some service music to be exalted in this fashion over other (e.g., the soloist over the congregational hymn), it is rarely a true description of what is actually heard. Further, if it occurs in the service every week, not much about it could be considered unique, unusual, or extraordinary (unless those concepts apply in a pejorative sense). We would do well to eliminate "special music" as a regular title for service music of any kind. Using a term such as "musical offering" instead not only properly categorizes the musical event, but is instructive in that it describes the music's function and points people toward the Object of the offering—the Lord.

Offertory

The "Offertorium" was originally part of the Mass in the Roman rite. It was a psalm or chant sung while the "offering" of bread and wine was brought in procession to the altar. In this context, it carried a strong sense of sacrifice that the sixteenth-century Reformers attempted to alter as much as possible if they included it in their orders of service at all. It was so abhorrent to Luther that he said it "reeked" of oblation.

In our time, the "offerings" are our tithes and gifts of money. Music utilized during the collection of offerings should be purposeful if this practice is part of the service proper. Some churches customarily have retiring offerings on the way out the door, or at the end of the service during announcements and following the sermon (which is an appropriate place for this element in the Reformed tradition, since it is another fitting response to receiving the Word of God). Offertory music need not be relegated to the mere function of transition music or background noise to avoid silence.[2]

Vocal music is more captivating in the midst of other activity than is instrumental music, and song texts printed in the order of service will help one focus on the musical message, rather than on what the usher is wearing or some other distraction. Instrumental music is easier to ignore than its vocal counterpart. But if the church's ministers make it a practice to pray, meditate, or otherwise focus on the musical message during the offertory, and if on occasion this idea is verbally or textually relayed to the congregation, undue noise and chatter should not be an issue.

Canticles

Canticles are biblical songs found outside the book of Psalms. Certain canticles, such as the *Magnificat* (the Song of Mary) and the *Nunc dimittis* (the Song of Simeon), are regularly sung in Vespers and Evensong services in several denominations. The latter is used at Matins and Communion in the Lutheran tradition as well. These two biblical songs are from the gospel of Luke and are generally followed in service performance by renditions of the *Gloria Patri.* There are other major (*cantica majora,* New Testament) and minor (*cantica minora,* Old Testament) canticles recorded in Scripture. (See chapter 13, "Song in the Bible.")

Responses

Choral or congregational responses to other service elements can be meaningful if intention and thought propel and receive them. Otherwise, responses that are part of blind tradition or ceremony retain minimal value. Responses can take the form of "Amens," "Alleluias," or musical sentences such as "Thanks be to God" or "God be with you." They may follow Scripture readings, confessional prayer, assurance of pardon, the sermon, or other elements of the service. The regular use of meaningful responses provides opportunity for members of the congregation to be personally involved in the service, and it likewise offers signposts or liturgical markers that provide order, rhetorical cadence, and a sense of pacing—important aspects of corporate worship. A "responsorial" in chant has to do with a choral response to the sung statement of a soloist or group.

Mass

The name "Mass" came from the Latin service's dismissal formula "*Ite, missa est*" ("Go, the gathering is dismissed"). So the "Mass" is simply the gathering of the people for worship, centered on the Eucharist. When most evangelicals hear the word "Mass," they associate it with Roman Catholicism. This is not incorrect. But the Mass is not limited to the Roman liturgy. For what, then, of the English Catholics (the Anglicans/Episcopalians) and the Lutherans, and other Protestant denominations that have made use of the Mass and adapted it over the years? Indeed, most of our Protestant services are, at some level, indebted to the formulation of the Mass, and many still employ it or sections of it in daily or weekly worship. Reformers who used the Mass include Luther, Ulrich Zwingli, Martin Bucer, and even John Calvin (who abhorred it in its Roman manifestation, but based his own order of service on Bucer's Strasbourg liturgy—which Bucer had adapted from the Mass itself).

When it comes to the Mass "Ordinary" (Kyrie, Gloria, Credo, Sanctus, Agnus Dei), other than one line or two of the Credo that can be mishandled theologically, the text is tremendously rich in biblical language and true doctrine. In its essence, the Mass is a memorial to the passion of Christ, a celebration of the Lord's Supper, and a sacrifice of the church.[3] It was in this last "sacrificial" sense that error most profoundly asserted itself. When the Mass came to be said or sung for the dead, for travelers, for wealth, or for whatever else people could think up (and pay for), the Mass took on a sacrificial, works-centered sense of oblation. This was blasphemous and was decried by the Reformers.

But this does not mean, in any sense, that the text of the Mass itself was suddenly unbiblical or not useful. It was simply misused. Many aspects of evangelical worship evidence their origins in the liturgy of the Roman and Sarum rites of which the Mass was central (e.g., the Introit, the Offertory, the *Gloria Patri*, and Communion). So as to defuse undue concern about the Mass as a text (itself not laden with the trappings of Roman works-righteousness)—and at least briefly to expose ourselves to its value—let us survey the basic elements of the Ordinary.

- The *Kyrie* is a simple prayer for mercy that is positioned at the beginning of the service and acknowledges our dependence on the mercy of God ("Lord, have mercy; Christ have mercy; Lord, have mercy.").
- The *Gloria* is the angelic hymn of praise capturing language from the angels' declaration to the shepherds at the advent of Christ (Luke 2:14) and from the *Te Deum.*
- The *Credo* is a statement of the cardinal beliefs of the Christian church, based on the Nicene Creed, approved by the Council of Nicaea in 325 A.D. Many times it is spoken rather than sung, chiefly on account of its length.
- The *Sanctus* and the *Benedictus* that accompanies it are based, respectively, on the thrice-holy lauds of the heavenly angels in Isaiah 6 and the New Testament statement "Blessed is he who comes in the name of the Lord" (Ps. 118:26; Matt. 23:39; Mark 11:9; Luke 13:35).
- The *Agnus Dei* restates John 1:29—"Behold, the Lamb of God who takes away the sin of the world." It also recalls the Kyrie in asking God for mercy at the end of worship.

The Mass is a marvelous structure for organized worship—it is liturgy at its finest, imbued with Scripture, carefully honed and internationally utilized for centuries. It begins with acknowledgment of our need for God's mercy, moves into praise and thanksgiving, declares our faith, reminds us of God's holiness and the significance of the one who speaks in his Name, and finally confirms the finished work of Christ while recalling our daily need of him. We should not fear the Mass as liturgy but feel the liberty to employ it or elements of it to aid our gathered worship.

Postlude

Postlude music is perhaps even less understood than prelude music. Its name indicates its function—music to come "after" the service. As such, it rightly serves as a commentary, reflection, response, or summary of what preceded it. A spirit of joy, thankfulness, and energy is usually the appropriate character for this music, although that will be determined by the nature of the service. In some sense, the postlude serves as "exit music," but it does not follow that one must rush out of the church. Listening to the postlude with a thankful heart for having been in the presence of God with one's brothers and sisters and having received his Word is appropriate. One is exiting the service of worship with this music, not necessarily the building. (The clamor of chatter that inevitably ensues the moment the postlude begins is not an essential service element.) There are always the few organ enthusiasts who linger to hear what is probably the most technically challenging music of the morning for the organist, but it would be fitting if the majority of worshipers took these last few minutes to stand and listen, or to remain seated and reflect on the service, or on the nature and attributes of God.

Notes

1. See Hughes Oliphant Old, *Themes and Variations for a Christian Doxology* (Grand Rapids: Eerdmans, 1992).

2. Silence is something that many Americans are nervous to experience, particularly in corporate settings. We often do not consider the reflective, spiritual, and restorative values of silence. We would do well to experience it more often in the context of worship.

3. Bard Thompson, *Liturgies of the Western Church* (Philadelphia: Fortress Press, 1961), 48–51.

PART TWO

Hymnody and Psalmody

Current patterns of worship in evangelicalism may suggest otherwise, but hymnody and psalmody are still integral to the Christian faith. Herein lies the rich repository of centuries of Christian worship—a heritage that should be embraced and built upon, not shunned or artificially made palatable. Hymns and psalms are not simply an optional part of worship; they are central to it. They are not a "style" of worship; they are a spiritual and physical element of it. They represent the corporate voice of God's people, over the span of many generations, responding to his Word, to creation, to teaching, to creeds, and to truth. Good Christian hymns help protect us from a theology-of-the-moment, and they bolster our knowledge of God. This is no dead form or antiquated art. It is a living, organic, energizing force that often calls us to service and reminds us of why we should serve. Hymns and psalms communicate cardinal Christian doctrines and biblical teaching. These are our devotional responses and considered thoughts, our prayers and battle songs. They are part of our spiritual DNA, if you will—our history, our present, our future.

And the tunes are important, too. While not judged on the basis of doctrinal content as texts are, the music of hymnody and psalmody must be judged on the basis of musical merit (melody, harmony, rhythm, form) on aesthetic grounds, and on its capacity to match and deliver the meaning of the texts it accompanies. The legacy of long-lasting hymn and psalm tunes is another link to our living spiritual history. This music is part of our collective Christian repertory, irrespective of one's familiarity with them or regard for them. There is no need to reinvent such enduring mediums of our song. To do so is to diminish their strength. New tunes should be written, but excellent tunes of previous eras do not require the musical clothing of postmodernity. Each age makes its contribution to the ongoing, growing hymn repertoire, as it rightly and necessarily should. Style and sound may change somewhat, but solidity, quality, beauty, and universality are among the characteristics of any substantial music that will endure. These characteristics transcend time and speak authentically to any age.

The essays in this section attempt to make a case for the strong presence of hymnody and psalmody in our day. They explore biblical categories and examples of song. They make practical suggestions for ways to further or to revive the use of hymns by individuals and congregations. They look inside the process of writing new hymns and give evidence of the importance of singing in the Christian life.

9
Trinitarian Hymnody

Holy, holy, holy, is the Lord God Almighty,
who was and is and is to come! —*Revelation 4:8b*

Hymns regularly teach fundamental Christian doctrine. This teaching is one of the great benefits derived from singing them. Martin Luther recognized that writing hymns and teaching them to his people was an efficient and effective way to disseminate the gospel to the Germanic lands. Little did he realize how important this would be for all of Europe in what became the Protestant Reformation. But Luther was not the first to appreciate the pedagogical power of hymnody. The second-century hymn writers had worked to counter the heretical teachings of the Gnostics by writing hymns of Christ to affirm his deity, which was in dispute. Later, the Council of Nicaea met in 325 A.D. to formulate a doctrinal statement concerning the Trinity because the nature of our triune God was under attack. This event, in turn, led to the development of hymnody that championed the Trinity. Ever since, the doctrine of the Trinity has held an important place in the hymnody of the Christian church all over the world.

Ancient Trinitarian Hymns

The Greek form of the *Gloria Patri* ("Glory be to the Father, and to the Son, and to the Holy Ghost . . .") had three early variations that were already old in St. Basil's days (370 A.D.).[1] The oldest known Christian hymn, the *Gloria* found in the Liturgy of St. James (which is not the *Gloria Patri* as we know it, but has an extended form in the *Codex Alexandrinus*, end of the fifth century), is patterned after the Angels' Song of Luke 2, and has a Trinitarian reference: "Thou only, O Christ, with the Holy Ghost: art most high in the glory of God the Father."

Ambrose of Milan (340–397 A.D.) in the fourth century is generally credited with the serious introduction of hymnody to the Western church. He reintroduced the concept of congregational song in psalms and hymns that had previously been recited by individuals or priests. His Advent hymn "Savior of the Nations, Come" emphasizes the life and work of Christ and, as we will see in many other hymns, concludes with a Trinitarian doxology reminiscent of the *Gloria Patri.*

Stanza 1:
Savior of the nations, come;
Virgin's Son, make here your home!
Marvel now, O heav'n and earth,
That the Lord chose such a birth.

Stanza 6:
Praise to God the Father sing,
Praise to God the Son, our King,
Praise to God the Spirit be
Ever and eternally.

Another early hymn invoking the Trinity and usually attributed to the emperor Justinian (527–565 A.D.) has been suggested by scholars to have been written no later than the Council of Ephesus in 431 A.D.: "*Only-begotten Son and Word of God, Immortal . . . being One of the Holy Trinity, and glorified together with the Father and the Holy Ghost, Save us.*"

Modern Trinitarian Hymns

"Holy, Holy, Holy!" is a strong hymn of the Trinity by Reginald Heber. Patterned after the *Trisagion* (the early Greek hymn of the thrice-holy God), this famous hymn explicitly heralds the praise of "God in three Persons, blessed Trinity!" The tune associated with the hymn (NICAEA, by John B. Dykes) was named after the aforementioned doctrinal council, which considered the Trinity. The hymn tune's first melodic intervals outline the three tones of the triad, each stated twice (or, one could say, "reinforced")—a thoughtful and interpretative choice on the part of the composer, since the text reinforces Trinitarian doctrine.

On occasion, I have witnessed a pastor or song leader in the context of worship say something like this: "Let's all stand and sing 'Come, Thou Almighty King,' and we'll do verses 1 and 3." In so doing, he has failed to notice that the hymn is a hymn to the Trinity (in spite of the fact that this text is usually sung to the tune TRINITY [a.k.a. ITALIAN HYMN] and that it clearly outlines praise to the triune God in its stanzas):

Stanza 1: "Come, thou Almighty King"—*God the Father*
Stanza 2: "Come, thou Incarnate Word"—*God the Son*
Stanza 3: "Come, Holy Comforter"—*God the Spirit*
Stanza 4: "To the great One in Three"—*the Trinity*

It might make some sense to sing the fourth stanza alone, since the doctrine remains intact, but hymns should normally be sung in their entirety. By omitting the second stanza, one leaves God the Son out of the picture, misses the point of the Trinitarian hymn, and unwittingly perpetuates incomplete, heretical doctrine. A bit of planning with forethought and a read-through of the hymn's text would prevent such an error. Moreover, it might occasion an appropriate comment to alert the congregation to what it was about to sing.

Hymn writers frequently use the concluding stanza of a hymn to summarize its preceding verses or to make application of its overall message. Quite often as well, the final stanza will be a form of doxology to the Trinity even if the hymn had a different subject previously. This seems to be particularly true when the hymn focuses on one person of the Trinity as its chief theme. Also regularly linked to this adoration of the Trinity is the concept of eternal praise or timeless worship, such as one finds in the *Gloria Patri* (. . . world without end . . . *et omnia saecula saeculorum*). Here are seven examples of such hymn conclusions:

"Now Thank We All Our God" (Martin Rinkart; trans. Catherine Winkworth)

> All praise and thanks to God the Father now be given, the Son, and him who reigns with them in highest heaven—the one eternal God, whom earth and heav'n adore; for thus it was, is now, and shall be evermore.

"Christ Is Made the Sure Foundation" (Latin, seventh century; trans. John Mason Neale)

> Laud and honor to the Father, laud and honor to the Son, laud and honor to the Spirit, ever Three and ever One, consubstantial, co-eternal, while unending ages run.

"Holy God, We Praise Your Name" (from the *Te Deum*; trans. Clarence A. Walworth)

> Holy Father, Holy Son, Holy Spirit, Three we name you; while in essence only One, undivided God we claim you, and adoring bend the knee, while we sing this mystery.

"For Your Gift of God the Spirit" (Margaret Clarkson)

> Father, grant your Holy Spirit in our hearts may rule today, grieved not, quenched not, but unhindered, work in us his sovereign way. Fill us with your holy fullness, God the Father, Spirit,

Son; in us, through us, then, forever, shall your perfect will be done.

"O Perfect Love" (John Ellerton, fourth stanza)

Hear us, O Father, gracious and forgiving, through Jesus Christ thy coeternal Word, who, with the Holy Ghost, by all things living now and to endless ages art adored.

"Angels, from the Realms of Glory" (James Montgomery)

All creation, join in praising God the Father, Spirit, Son; evermore your voices raising to th'eternal Three in One: Come and worship Christ, the newborn King.

"The God of Abraham Praise" (Thomas Olivers)

The whole triumphant host gives thanks to God on high; "Hail, Father, Son, and Holy Ghost!" they ever cry. Hail, Abraham's God and mine! I join the heav'nly lays; all might and majesty are thine, and endless praise.

The Importance of Trinitarian References

There are many other hymns that conclude in similar fashion and still more that refer to the Father, Son, and Holy Spirit somewhere within their stanzas irrespective of the manner in which they conclude. Settings of the Doxology and the *Gloria Patri* offer praise to the three persons of the Trinity, as do numerous invocations and benedictions. The *Gloria Patri*, historically, is sung after the reading or singing of a psalm or canticle, and it is not uncommon in Anglican and other liturgical services to hear it more than once within the same hour of worship. Far from being redundant, this practice reminds us, as worshipers, of the triune nature of our God. In so doing, it accentuates one of the great distinctions of the Christian faith from the theology of other religions.

When we are aware of a hymn's substance before we sing, we are more apt to sing the text with energy and conviction than if this were simply a standard, rote activity. If you are the song leader in a worship service or the Bible study leader in a small group or Sunday-school class, be sure to look ahead of time at the texts of hymns or other songs that will be sung. When there are Trinitarian references in the hymns to be sung (such as the ones described here) or other great biblical doctrines, it would be helpful to those singing to highlight those references with a comment or two. It is a solemn responsibility of those who lead corporate worship to make each service element as biblical, thoughtful, and meaningful an experience as possible.

Note

1. H. Leigh Bennett, "Greek Hymnody," in John Julian, *A Dictionary of Hymnology*, vol. 1 (New York: Dover, 1957), 460.

10
Hymns in Your Church

Praise the Lord*!*
I will give thanks to the Lord *with my whole heart,*
in the company of the upright, in the congregation. —Psalm 111:1

In some congregations there has been a resurgence of the psalmody and hymnody that is our heritage as evangelicals. As the value of this heritage is grasped, a desire to expand the repertoire of psalms and hymns sung in worship may accompany it. (From this point forward, "hymns" will denote both psalms and hymns.) Obstacles and prejudices may need to be overcome in the effort to recover or to introduce new hymns. Clearly, education is the optimal means of introducing songs of a more challenging musical language to one's congregation. Explanation of the meaning of a particular text, its scriptural origin, and its composition, musical form, or author/composer will heighten the appreciation and reception of new music. The discussion that follows is intended to give practical ideas to help achieve what is needed—a modern reformation of hymnody and psalmody in the worship of the evangelical church.

Personal Worship

Since we can rightly consider the hymnal to be a collection of prayers and praise, it would be fitting for every Christian to own and utilize one or several. Hymnals can be used privately, with family members, or in small groups. Consider including the hymnal as an aid in your devotional life. One might employ an index of scriptural allusions to search for a hymn corresponding to a passage of Scripture being studied. A hymn can be chosen to guide prayer and then be memorized and sung as a prayer each day for a week or throughout a month. Many people discover that the tune will spontaneously arise in their "ear" or thoughts throughout the day, bringing the text to mind. Music helps us recall teaching, and it aids in maintaining a spirit of prayer before the Lord. Take time to think through hymn texts, and explain them to children. A text understood is one that can be meaningfully sung. This kind of study is important because worship must be intentional and thoughtful.

Corporate Worship

Congregational singing may seem like the most obvious place for hymns to be employed, but hymn selection and singing should be more than simply a routine activity. Irrespective of whether the minister or the music director chooses congregational songs, the same criteria apply. The texts should be biblically sound and meaningful. The music that accompanies a text should be excellent and should facilitate its comprehension. For ministers without musical training or musicians lacking doctrinal clarity, hymn selection is a precarious task that would be best done in partnership with an informed colleague. In the progression of the worship service, care must be taken to include elements of praise, confession, and thanksgiving. Hymns may be linked to these elements of worship, to a common theme for the service, or to Scripture readings.

Most modern hymnals provide helpful indexes that will assist in hymn selection. For example, an index of scriptural quotations or allusions can quickly direct one to hymn texts that correspond to the sermon. Subject headings can help locate hymns that deal with "Sovereignty of God" or "Stewardship" or another relevant topic. The metrical index will list other tunes with an identical meter, so that if a strong text in a particular hymnal is accompanied by an unknown or lousy tune (yes, there are some), that text can be matched with a better or more familiar one. Periodically alternating the tune used for a particular hymn text in this manner will heighten the congregation's interaction with it.

Hymn Services

One method of introducing hymns to a congregation or Bible study group is through a short, organized hymn-sing or service. This might last ten to twenty minutes and include three or more hymns. It is useful for the person leading such a service to have consulted resources for the purpose of learning about a hymn's author or composer.[1] This information can then be shared with the congregation. A theme will help to unify such a service—for example, "Hymns of Luther," "Hymns of Philip Doddridge," "Hymns of Joy," "Passion Hymns," "Hymns from 1 Corinthians 15," "Evening Hymns," "Welsh Hymns," "Hymns Written by Missionaries," or something akin to these.

More significantly, the leader should have considered the role(s) of each hymn—praise, proclamation, prayer, etc.—and should share such insights with those singing. The focus must properly be on God and his Word. A verse or passage of Scripture on which the hymn is based can be read and its teaching in the hymn noted so as to draw attention to the Word of God. Such pedagogical, preplanned hymn services will enrich and enliven the hymn-singing experience and are more significant than choosing "favorites" or having the congregation do so randomly. It is good, though, to include well-known hymns as well as those less frequently sung. There is joy and strength in sharing known repertoire. Since planning has occurred ahead of time, the choir can also assist by introducing new tunes or by singing a median stanza as a means of setting it apart. If members of the congregation do not understand what is being sung, the principle about the "uncertain sound" from 1 Corinthians 14:6–17 applies. Although Paul was addressing the interpretation of tongues, the principle for corporate worship is that while one may be giving thanks "well enough," another may not be edified. If there is a way to help others better understand, appreciate, or participate in worship, let it be done.

Hymns of the Month

Another useful means of introducing hymns to one's household or congregation is to select a hymn of the month and to sing it each day or each Sunday at the same service consistently throughout that month. Permission to print the hymn as a bulletin insert can be obtained from the publisher if required, and the hymn could then travel home with families to be learned together. Better yet, each family could purchase several copies of the church's hymnal. The same hymn might appear in the Sunday-school curriculum or at the youth-group meeting, generating a collective, church-wide effort. This would demonstrate value to the entire congregation and make hymn learning a shared experience. Singing hymns is a unifying activity, for when we sing we lift up our voices as one to God. Both the hymns themselves and our freedom to sing them as members of the congregation are aspects of our Reformation heritage. Reformers such as Martin Luther and John Calvin gave the common people biblical songs to sing.

An explanation of the hymn text or information concerning its provenance might appear in the church bulletin or be recited by a song leader. If the church has a choir, the choir could prepare the hymn and introduce it immediately before the congregation sings it for the first time, or the choir may serve as a force to help lead the singing. A choir can function as a corporate teaching ensemble and should be employed in helpful, creative ways in worship. The choir need not be limited to presenting an anthem or identical service music week after week. A trumpet or other leading instrument is valuable for reinforcing a lesser-known melody for the benefit of the congregation as it sings.

Hymn Festivals

Any time of year is a good time for a hymn festival, but certain seasons or events are especially well suited: Advent, Christmas, Lent, Easter, Pentecost, Trinity, Reformation Day, the opening of a new church, the dedication of a pipe organ, the installation of a pastor. At a hymn festival, the concepts of a hymn service expand in grander context into a fully integrated service of sixty to ninety minutes. This is a wonderful chance for pastors and music directors to work together to prepare a meaningful service of worship, particularly if this is not their regular practice. Planning is an essential aspect. Theme, timing, and texts all need careful consideration. The structure of the service should be solid. The "flow" of events, ideas, genres, keys, and mood should be thought through, and a printed order of service is of excellent help and guidance to those attending. A hymn festival can center on one doctrine, era, country, theme, or composer; or it can have considerable diversity. Employing rehearsed choirs and instrumental ensembles contributes to the effective leading and accompanying of hymns. The chart that follows is the outline of a hymn festival held on Reformation Sunday 2000 at Tenth Presbyterian Church, when *Hymns for a Modern Reformation* was first released (see fig. 10.1).

The preceding list of suggestions for hymn use is by no means exhaustive. Any activity that will set forth great hymns in an atmosphere conducive to education, good singing, and the praise of God will be worthwhile. Start with children. It is exceedingly important that we teach hymns and psalms to covenant children as part of their catechetical training. If the next generation will learn to love great hymnody and psalmody, they will love sound doctrine. We can and we must equip them to praise God well with their voices as well as with their spirits.

Fig. 10.1

Reformation Hymn Festival

Prelude
Welcome
Call to Worship/Prayer
Hymn: "A Mighty Fortress Is Our God" (EIN' FESTE BURG)

I. *Sola scriptura* (Scripture alone)
Scripture: 2 Timothy 3:10–17
Hymn: "God's Amazing Word" (SOLA SCRIPTURA)

II. *Sola fide* (Faith alone)
Scripture: Romans 3:21–28
Hymn: "Heaven's Gift" (SOLA FIDE)

III. *Sola gratia* (Grace alone)
Scripture: Ephesians 2:1–10
Hymn: "Alive in Christ" (SOLA GRATIA)

IV. *Solus Christus* (Christ alone)
Hymn: "O Sacred Head, Now Wounded" (PASSION CHORALE)
Prayer
Offering/Offertory
Scripture: 1 Corinthians 1:18–31
Hymn: "Christ Alone" (SOLUS CHRISTUS)
Sermon: "Christ Alone" (1 Corinthians 2:2)

V. *Soli Deo gloria* (Glory to God alone)
Hymn: "Now Thank We All Our God" (NUN DANKET)
Scripture: Revelation 4 and 5
Hymn: "'Round the Throne in Radiant Glory" (QADOSH)
Hymn: "Give Praise to God" (SOLI DEO)
Benediction: Romans 11:33–36
Postlude

Note

1. Many modern hymnal publishers now print a "companion" to the hymnal as a separate volume that provides information about the author or composer, text, or tune. John Julian's *A Dictionary of Hymnology* (two volumes) is essential in any church musician's library, as are books of "hymn stories." It is also helpful for ministers and music directors to own a collection of numerous hymnals spanning one's own tradition and other denominations as reference and resource material.

11
What Psalm Ascriptions Tell Us

To the choirmaster. A Song. A Psalm.
Shout for joy to God, all the earth;
sing the glory of his name;
give to him glorious praise! —*Psalm 66:1–2*

We know that the psalms were songs and that as texts they are divinely inspired. But what about the other information attached to them? I refer here to the psalm headings or "ascriptions" and to the diacritical marks above the Hebrew text itself. Let us briefly consider these extratextual elements and find out. Do they reveal important information?

The *Te'Amim*

We do not know exactly what the psalm melodies of the ancient Hebrews sounded like. There is no surviving written music or oral tradition to inform us. Or is there? The French composer, organist, and music theoretician Suzanne Haïk-Vantoura suggested that the Tiberian

Masoretic Accents (the *te'amim*) are an intricate system of notation indicating how the entire Old Testament was to be chanted. Her results were published in 1976 in the book *La Musique de la Bible Révélée* ("The Music of the Bible Revealed"), and recordings have been made of musical scores based on this system.[1]

The cantillation of these melodies was guided by a well-developed type of chironomy—musical hand gestures to indicate pitches and how the music would be chanted. The Bible itself may allude to chironomy when it refers to the antiphonal Levitical choirs' having been directed by a practice called "of David" or what is translated in the English Standard Version as "according to the order of David" (2 Chron. 23:18) or "according to the directions of David" (Ezra 3:10). In Hebrew the biblical text reads "*al yede David*,"[2] which also might be rendered "according to the chironomy of David."

Biblical scholars who have given attention to Haïk-Vantoura's landmark work on cantillation and chironomy are divided as to its value. Many believe it is too speculative, particularly because the author bases much on medieval Jewish tradition, which is difficult to demonstrably link to worship before Christ. Even if it can be traced to postexilic times, the jump to the pre-exilic period is still difficult. We are confronted with three basic problems:

1. We do not know the original relationship between the ascriptions and the psalms themselves.
2. We do not know how Hebrew was pronounced in the Iron Age (time of David, Solomon, etc.).
3. We are dealing with a medieval tradition of pronunciation (including the *te'amim*).[3]

Yet an interesting and validating aspect of Haïk-Vantoura's deciphering key is that when applied to biblical texts it always yields coherent music, well suited to the mood of the words it accompanies.[4] She writes, "The Tiberian musical notation has been deciphered in both of its systems, and it appears in fact . . . that it is perfectly designed. It allows us, without the least hypothetical suggestion, to reconstruct the biblical cantillation with great faithfulness—a cantillation which amazes us by its originality and expressive power."[5] That the psalms were sung and were part of Old Testament and New Testament worship is certain. That some psalms are acrostic poems, some were antiphonally presented, and instruments accompanied many or most—all of this is generally known and accepted, even by the average layperson. According to Haïk-Vantoura's work, the psalms employed varied vocal forms deduced from the construction of the melodies or monody itself. These forms include solo voice, solo with concluding choir, choir alone, two alternating choirs, two alternating choirs and tutti, and solo voice with choirs alternating in response.[6]

Psalm Ascriptions

As a musician, and specifically as a music director, I have always loved the psalms and felt a connection to them that I suppose might be as strong as or stronger than it might be for a nonmusician. It seems reasonable to assume that the psalm headings tell us something significant, or else they would not exist. But until recently I had not taken the time to study these superscriptions to see what they reveal about the psalms themselves or details surrounding their performance or use. I am not a Hebrew scholar, which poses significant limitations. But while knowing the Hebrew language would undoubtedly aid in understanding more in these ascriptions, the translations reveal a great deal as well.

In the Hebrew Bible the psalm ascriptions form all or part of the first verse of the psalm itself and are read along with the rest of the psalm. Often in English services or personal reading we simply skip over these headers and do not stop to ponder them, even to provide context. One reason may be that we are uncertain whether or not the ascriptions are part of the inspired text. There are at least two related issues. First, no one knows for sure how old the ascriptions are. They clearly are ancient, but it is difficult to determine whether they are second century B.C., fifth century B.C., or possibly even the work of the original authors. In other words, the question can be asked: are they inspired, or are they *anacoloutha* (scribal glosses) added at a later date, as at the conclusion of some of Paul's epistles? Second, the *meaning* of the ascriptions is debated. Yet helpful information can still be gleaned from the study of them.

Having now spent focused time with the psalm headings, which some call "incipits," I would like to share with the reader what was discovered in the process. This is data gleaned from the ascriptions only. Study of the full bodies of the psalms themselves will yield much more information. After listing each finding, inferences will be drawn and applications made concerning worship in the modern-day church.

Names/Types

There are several names for the individual types of psalms that make up the canonical book. It seems, at least in the case of the first three listed below, that these were literary/musical forms or kinds of songs:

- shiggaion—7
- miktam—16, 56–60
- maskil—32, 42, 44–45, 52–55, 74, 78, 88–89, 142
- song—7, 18, 30, 45, 48, 65–68, 75–76, 83, 87–88, 92, 108, 120–134
- psalm—57 psalms, including some that are also designated by other terms, e.g., 30, 48, 65, 68, 88
- prayer—17, 86, 90, 102, 142
- petition—38, 70 (NIV; "for a memorial," NASB)
- songs of ascent—120–134

From these designations we learn several things. The psalms are varied, not only in theme but also in type. More than one kind of song is appropriate for use in worship, and more than one type of prayer is appropriate to offer to God. At least some of the psalm authors (or preservers) thought it important enough to designate the musical or literary form and to include it within the psalm text. If Haïk-Vantoura was correct, this designation would extend to the monodic chanting of the psalms as well.

Tunes/Modes

Some of the titles may identify the "tune" to which the psalm was to be sung (this is true of at least five, but possibly as many as thirteen). Several indicate specific tunes, while others indicate that the psalm is "according to" a particular Hebrew word or phrase. These "according to" Hebrew terms may be tunes, or they may be modes or an indication of mood or style. It has also been suggested that these may refer to certain types of accompanying instruments.

"To the tune of" (NIV).

- *Muth-labben* (The Death of the Son, NIV)—9 (and 10)[7]
- The Doe of the Dawn—22
- Lilies—45, 69 (possibly the same as *Shushan Eduth,* "The lily of testimony"—60 and 80)
- The Dove on Far-off Terebinths—56
- Do Not Destroy—57, 58, 59, 75
- Lily of the Covenant/The Lilies of the Covenant (NIV; "The Lily of Testimony," NASB)—60, 80 (possibly the same as 45 and 69)

"According to" (ESV, NIV).

- *The Sheminith*—6, 12 (see also 1 Chron. 15:21)
- *The Gittith*—8, 81, 84
- *Alamoth*—46 (see also 1 Chron. 15:20)
- *Mahalath*—53
- *Mahalath Leannoth*—88

From the listing of tunes, if indeed this is what they are, we learn that at least some of the psalms were sung to the same music, or at least music with the same designation. This concept points to a mode, style, or flexible melodic outline more than to a codified melody, because the differences inherent in the psalm texts would preclude identical melodies. Of course, this is the nature of chant—the music suits the text above all and is commonly and normally modified by it. These tunes may have been widely known among the Hebrew people. The fact that

David and Asaph used the same or similar tunes may support the idea that suitable melodies or modes were limited in number. On the other hand, Asaph was appointed by David and was under his direct supervision, so Asaph may have been making a gesture of honor to his king, or David may have suggested the tune; we can only speculate.

Several of the tune titles make reference to nature (The Doe of the Dawn, The Dove on Far-off Terebinths, etc.), a factor that points toward folk music in our modern estimation. Yet Israel was an agrarian society closely connected to nature. It is possible, even likely, that David (who we know played the harp and spent much of his youth in nature as a shepherd) wrote some of these tunes. Most of the psalms that indicate specific tunes, in fact, were psalms of David. Perhaps, since he was an instrumentalist (and probably a composer) as well as a singer, it was important to him that a specific tune or instrument be used. In any case, it would not be unreasonable for melodies, modes, or instruments to be named after things in nature.

The fact that 1 Chronicles 15 refers to two of the same tunes/modes/instruments (*Sheminith* and *Alamoth*) that later appear in the psalms when the ark of the covenant was brought to Jerusalem (under David's leadership) may underscore David's control over this element. *Alamoth,* it has been suggested, has several ideas associated with it: "young girls, maidens," "instruments of music," "soprano voices," or "harps tuned to a higher register." Perhaps, then, this was music for a women's chorus or for female voices in some other configuration. Whether or not these melodies were widely used in Hebrew music other than for worship is not known. This is possible, though it seems more likely that music for worship in the temple was consecrated music with a sense of place. It is probably safe to assume that these would be original melodies of the Hebrew people, the children of God, not melodies of the neighboring pagan countries (cf. Ps. 137). So a professional Levitical musician, when it was not David himself, was likely the composer.

Purposes/Occasions

Several purposes or occasions for the psalms are listed in their headings, including prayer, thanks, and praise (although these three are purposes of many of the psalms even if their ascriptions do not so specifically state). Psalms are specifically designated for:

- Dedication of the temple—30
- Petition (NIV; "Memorial offering," ESV)—38, 70
- Wedding song (NIV; "Love song," ESV)—45
- Teaching (NIV; "Instruction," ESV)—60
- Prayer—86, 90, 102, 142 (although most psalms are prayers)
- Sabbath—92
- Giving thanks—100
- Praise—145

The psalms give many reasons to sing and show many occasions on which to do so. Music is important for celebratory events, such as the dedication of a place of worship or a wedding ceremony. It is appropriate and apparently biblical for music to be specially composed for such occasions. While it is common knowledge that music is a good teaching tool, finding a direct statement to support this idea in the Old Testament heading of Psalm 60 as well as in the New Testament in Ephesians 5 and Colossians 3 is helpful. Music is appropriate to worship, an idea reinforced by the heading of Psalm 92. Music can be a medium for prayer, whether the form of prayer is petition, praise, or thanksgiving (among others not expressly identified here).

Authors

A number of authors are listed in the canonic psalms (David was not the sole author):

- David—(one-half of the Psalter; 75 psalms)
- Solomon—72, 127
- Asaph—50, 73–83
- Moses—90
- Ethan—89
- Sons of Korah—42, 44–49, 84–85, 87–88
- Heman—88

Here we see that more than one author/composer wrote worship music for God's people. At the same time, we should note that two of the psalm authors were divinely appointed kings (David and Solomon); one was a prophet and leader of his people (Moses); and the others were the chief Levitical musicians who were appointed by David and who also "prophesied" (Asaph, Ethan, Heman, and the Sons of Korah). In other words, not just anyone should be writing the prayers and praise of the people of God, and highly skilled, consecrated, theologian-musicians should write most of them. While those in Psalms are all men, one also finds scriptural examples of women singer-composer-poets, such as Miriam (Ex. 15:21), Deborah (Judg. 5:1), Hannah (1 Sam. 2:1–10), and Mary (Luke 1:46–55).

We discover that as far as the ascriptions indicate, three psalmists (Moses, Ethan, and Heman) have only one psalm included in the canon (although other songs by Moses are included in the Pentateuch; cf. Deut. 32 and 33). While no songs written in our day are divinely inspired as the psalms were, authors and composers may be encouraged to learn that even one excellent work that survives for use in the worship of God's people is a worthy contribution.

Dedications

The psalms contain two primary dedications:

- For the Director of Music (55 psalms)
- For Jeduthun—39, 62, 77 (who may have been a "Director of Music"; cf. 1 Chron. 16:41–42; 25:1–6)

From the dedications in the psalm ascriptions, it appears that a director of music was entrusted with the inspired psalms used in worship. This fact clearly supports the concept and importance of such a position existing for every body of believers—something that churches today would be well advised to notice. It also implies that the director of music would preserve these holy songs, would determine how and when to employ them, and would be responsible for teaching them to the people. It makes the case (along with the passages in 1 Chronicles) for a trained, highly skilled professional musician to organize, teach, and lead the choirs and instrumentalists in this calling.

Accompanying instruments

Some ascriptions identify musical instruments to accompany the singing. Other instruments are mentioned within the psalm texts. Those mentioned in the ascriptions include:

- Stringed instruments—4, 6, 54–55, 61, 67
- Flutes—5

As previously stated, certain Hebrew words that seem to be related to tunes or literary styles may have denoted use of particular instruments. We cannot be sure. David wrote all but one of the psalms that specify an instrument in their headings. Obviously, the psalmists had these instruments in mind and felt that they would best accompany the psalm. This implies that there was more than one possibility for instrumental accompaniment and that some instruments might be more appropriate for a certain topic or mood than others. It also reveals that more than one kind of instrument was used in worship and that authors/composers should be concerned with such details. David must have had an opinion about instrumentation, since he specifically mentions certain instruments in the opening words of several psalms.

Place/Time of composition

A number of David's psalms were written in hiding/trouble, in the wilderness, or "in the cave." These include:

- In hiding/trouble—3, 7, 34, 51–52, 54, 56–57, 59
- In the wilderness—63
- In the cave—57, 142
- In victory—18, 60

It is not just during the "good" times that we should sing and pray to the Lord. Difficult circumstances can lead to some of our closest times of fellowship with God and are often the catalyst to artistic production. Sorrow, lament, concern, fear—all of these can be ably expressed in music, even realized *through* it, as can the care of our heavenly Father and the peace of Christ. The reality of God's presence, love, light, and protection (while never changing) often becomes more obvious when we walk through lonesome, dark, and fearful valleys.

Two of the psalm ascriptions (18 and 60) specifically state that they were written to celebrate the victory that God gave David over his enemies, although many others carry similar themes within their texts. Singing is obviously a wonderful response to God's deliverance and redemption of his people, and we find this theme time and time again in the Scriptures (see chapter 13, "Song in the Bible").

Summary

From the psalm ascriptions we can conclude several things about biblical worship:

- There are many reasons and seasons to sing to God.
- There are many reasons to pray to God.
- Prayers can be sung.
- Prayers and songs can be carefully constructed poems and can take many forms.
- Worship music can include soloists and choirs.
- Worship music can include instrumentalists to accompany songs and prayers to God.
- Our songs and prayers may be full of joy and praise or they may be sorrowful laments. They express a full range of human emotions, including yearning (Ps. 63), despair (Ps. 88), and so forth.
- When we are in trouble or afraid, it is good to sing and pray to God.
- Music often accompanies special events in the life of God's people and his church and is appropriate to them.
- A director of music should lead the people and be the guardian of the people's praise.
- Skilled theologians and musicians should write the songs of the people of God.
- Musical prayers can also be useful for teaching.

In spite of these deductions and inferences, some important unanswered questions remain. Were the psalm ascriptions added after the inspired text had been given to the author, or were they part of the inspired writ itself? And what of the music of the psalms? Was that added to the text later, or could the process have been simultaneous and as such inspired by the Spirit even if no record of it is extant? When Moses (Ex. 15) and David (2 Sam. 1) and others sang to the Lord and their words were recorded, was the music of their songs also from the Lord?

We may be forced to conclude that this is not the case, or that even if the music itself accompanied the moments of inspiration, since the tune was subservient to the text, it was less significant (which rings true). If the music was inspired, no doubt it would have been preserved for us by the Spirit as the texts have been. Still, if some of the Old Testament's "music" has actually been preserved and deciphered, are we possibly given a glimpse into the "soul" of the Bible itself? To hear what may have been the music David employed as he sang to God could give us a much deeper and more intimate insight into his person and the expression of his faith. Since David was a man "after God's own heart," it could also grant us a greater understanding of God himself. At least the prospect is worth considering.

Notes

1. Suzanne Haïk-Vantoura, *The Music of the Bible Revealed*, trans. Dennis Weber, ed. John Wheeler, based on the 2nd French ed. (Paris: Dessain et Tolra, 1978) (Berkeley, CA: Bibal Press/San Francisco: King David's Harp, Inc., 1991).

2. Ibid., "Foreword," 9.

3. Frederick Putnam, professor of Old Testament, Biblical Seminary, Hatboro, Pennsylvania, e-mail correspondence to author, October 20, 2004.

4. See "Music of the Bible Revealed," http://www.cgmusic.com/library/musicofthebible.htm.

5. Haïk-Vantoura, *The Music of the Bible Revealed*, 44.

6. Ibid. See also pp. 408–15.

7. Psalms 9 and 10 may have been a single acrostic poem. Each verse begins with successive letters of the Hebrew alphabet, and in the Septuagint, the two constitute one psalm. So even though Psalm 10 does not contain the tune name in its ascription, it is likely that the same tune as Psalm 9 was employed.

12
Writing Hymns

Sing to him, sing praises to him;
tell of all his wondrous works! —*Psalm 105:2*

Many people have asked questions about the process of writing hymns.[1] How is it done? Who writes hymns? Why should we write them? There are more possible answers to these questions than one point of view or space will permit, but progress is often made in the very act of trying to explain; so here, at least, is an attempt.

The Bible says: "Oh sing to the LORD a new song; sing to the LORD, all the earth! Sing to the LORD, bless his name; tell of his salvation from day to day. Declare his glory among the nations, his marvelous works among all the peoples!" (Ps. 96:1–3). Here we find the command to sing to the Lord a new song—a *canticum novum.* The passage also tells us what to sing about and to whom we are to sing; in fact, it gives us several direct commands about our singing and songs. We are to sing . . .

• *what?*	a new song
• *to whom?*	to the Lord
• *when?*	from day to day
• *about what?*	his salvation; his glory; his marvelous works
• *where?*	among the nations and all peoples

In other words, our new songs are to be directed to God. They should speak of his acts and attributes. And they should be sung every day anywhere and everywhere in the hearing of all people, Christian and non-Christian alike.

Those with gifts to write or compose should heed this call for new biblical songs and be writing or composing them for our worship of God and, indeed, as an act of worship itself—something done to glorify God. While those lacking the necessary skills and training sometimes write worship music today, others who have the essential abilities may not be exercising their gifts. What follows is a brief reflection on the process of hymn writing. It is included in this volume with the hope of stimulating readers who may have such gifts to exercise their minds and hands in this realm. At the same time, it may deepen the awareness or appreciation we all have for those who write the hymns we sing.

Authors/Texts

Many of the best hymn writers have been ministers who penned hymn texts to summarize the salient points of their sermons for the congregation. In this way the truths of the sermon could "live on" in the minds of the people, who would recall the poetry and tune more easily than they might the sermon itself. Seasoned pastors are especially well suited to hymn writing, as a survey of Protestant hymnody readily verifies. Biblical learning, life experience, and knowledge of great literature and other hymns provide requisite subject matter, poetic models, and ample fare for allusion.

Whether preacher or poet, the hymn writer finds inspiration in the same places that all other Christian poets do—in Scripture, in nature, in a life experience that prompts reflection on spiritual neediness, or in an overpowering awareness of God's glory. Hymn writing can be an act of Christian devotion. It both germinates and develops through study of the Bible, and it may, in fact, lead one to deeper levels of spiritual discovery.

Not every good poem makes a good hymn, and not every good hymn necessarily meets the criteria of great poetry. Hymn poetry, in general, should be limited to six strophes or fewer of consistent length.

There are many hymns of greater length, but a glance at those published in hymnals demonstrates that hymnal editors often reduce them. Four to six lines per stanza will be best managed, and each line should maintain meter, rhythm, and stress with its parallel line in other stanzas to avoid an awkward rendering when put to music. Strong and weak syllables should appropriately correspond to the musical beats, something that cannot occur if the hymn writer is inconsistent. Most hymn texts rhyme, and there are numerous rhyme scheme options. Although some good hymns and psalm paraphrases do not rhyme, rhyming is preferable. Also, one should be sure to end each stanza on a strong (accented) syllable. This ensures that the music can resolutely conclude.

Because the melody, mode, and rhythm cannot be altered strophe by strophe, a consistent mood in the poetry works best, since the hymn will be stronger if its verbal and musical sentiments agree. A refrain provides opportunity for a change of spirit or direction, or it can serve to summarize or reinforce the theme. Consistency in the mood and tone of the text will help the composer determine an appropriate key and spirit for the music. Likewise, if the text is being written to fit a currently existing tune, one will want to ensure that a strong union of character between the two is possible throughout all stanzas.

While a hymn text may contain metaphors or other figures of speech, the primary goal should be the delivery of an identifiable message. This goal is similar to the aim of a well-crafted sermon. Hymn singing is a forum in which a broad public encounters Christian doctrine; therefore, the poetry should permit the least educated to comprehend (although not necessarily at first reading), yet give the discerning mind something to ponder. Sentimentality should be avoided, but the language need not shun emotion. Any hymn text tending toward testimony or personal experience should be able to be applied in a more universal context—something that is a shared or common experience for many or all Christians. The congregation must be able to identify with the text, so concepts or experiences of a unique or overly subjective nature should be avoided.

The Hymn Society in the United States and Canada states it this way:

> A Christian hymn is a lyric poem, reverently conceived, designed to be sung, which expresses the worshiper's attitude to God or God's purposes in human life. It should be simple and metrical in form, genuinely emotional, poetic and literary in style, and its idea so direct and so immediately apparent as to unify a congregation while singing it.[2]

Composers/Tunes

A good composer chooses a worthy hymn poem, considers its meaning, and identifies its rhyme scheme, metrical pattern, and syntax. The composer will want to allow time for the text to work itself into his or her consciousness. A standard or modified hymn form will probably suggest itself on the basis of the text's pattern, and the composer will be mindful of this in outlining the piece. One seeks to discover the architecture and overall sense of the poem—metrical rhythm, mood, energy, and pacing—so that fitting music can be fashioned for it.

On these bases a key and range befitting the spirit of the poem are chosen. Keys and modes, by virtue of their physical properties within the equal system of tuning and its corresponding overtone series, have colors and qualities. Some are more powerful than others; some are brighter, while others are more melancholy. Choice of key, then, has much to do with the final product. One unfortunate aspect of hymnals whose editors have altered the original keys of hymns (usually in an effort to lower the range for our nonsinging society) is that a new key may not as well suit the spirit of the hymn. A clear example is Martin Luther's "A Mighty Fortress Is Our God," appearing in hymnals for centuries and harmonized by J. S. Bach in D major, but lowered to C major in many modern hymnals. It simply does not have the necessary brilliance or energy in the lower key. And it is perfectly singable in the original, which requires a certain energy that is inherent in the music.

In addition to choice of key, and linked to it, is the melodic range. It is important to pick a range for the melody that can be ably managed by untrained voices. The melody is what the singer will remember most vividly; thus, it should be singable, lyrical, and logical, yet fresh and not overly predictable. It should creatively strengthen the singer's attention to and understanding of the text. Melodies should normally be step-wise, with larger intervals approached intuitively and typically according to the rules of music theory.

Several options for time signature and rhythm may present themselves as possibilities after studying the text, but the composer must determine whether one draws attention toward or away from the textual meaning more than another. The rhythm can also assist the meter and rhyme of the verse so that these recurring aspects do not result in a hymn that seems trite or commonplace. The text of a particular stanza (not necessarily the first) may suggest a certain rhythm that will work well in all stanzas. On occasion one might alter the rhythm of a preexisting hymn tune for the better while retaining its harmony and melody. This kind of musical recycling is valid as long as the piece is within the public domain.

A composer will sometimes "hear" the harmony while conceiving the melody, but this basic chord structure can be refined once melodic and rhythmic elements are determined. The value of "line" within voice parts should not be underestimated. Too many hymns, for instance, leave the altos with two notes side by side over multiple measures. Typically, hymn composing that follows the rules of good counterpoint, and at the same time creates interesting lines for each of the four parts, will result in a strong piece of music.

Once written, the whole work should be examined and proofread multiple times, leading to further subtle changes in tone or nuance. This process unfolds in the same manner that one might employ to polish a poem or an essay, by selecting a more colorful word or fashioning a more economical phrase. The result may be a welcome addition to the rich repertory of hymns from which we benefit, finding resonance in the congregations who value this living heritage.

Notes

1. Some of this essay was adapted from my article in Leland Ryken, *The Christian Imagination* (Colorado Springs, CO: WaterBrook Press, 2002). Used by permission. All rights reserved.

2. Carl F. Price, "What Is a Hymn?" Hymn Society Paper VI, 1937.

13
Song in the Bible

My lips will pour forth praise,
for you teach me your statutes. —*Psalm 119:171*

Various kinds of songs appear in the pages of Scripture. In addition to the 150 canonical psalms, there are major and minor canticles, hymns of Christ, doxologies, and excerpts from various poetic benedictions, prayers, eulogies, and so forth. A look at these biblical songs should grant us insight into the various concepts and content that should characterize the songs we sing in worship. We also should not miss the fact that these biblical songs are the very Word of God. As his children, we claim them as part of our birthright, and they should be a significant part of our collective repertoire. We must begin with the psalms.

Psalms

Psalms has been called "the Hymnbook of Israel" and is divided into five books (1–41, 42–72, 73–89, 90–106, and 107–150). The psalms have been the primary source of worship music for God's people for millennia. Their function in worship changed throughout Israel's temple history, and their employment in the synagogue and the New Testament church was transformed as well. Psalms were understood as praise when first used in Israel's worship. Later, the psalms were sung in Solomon's temple at two primary times: upon entering the temple and at the immolation of the sacrifice. In the synagogue, the psalms became spiritual sacrifices (1 Peter 2:5), since the system of animal sacrifice was no longer in place.[1]

The early church kept many synagogue worship traditions, which included the singing of psalms, predominantly in the context of prayer. According to Hughes Oliphant Old, Psalm 118:27 provides a good example of the changing use of psalms: "Bind the festal sacrifice with cords, up to the horns of the altar!" In temple worship the action sung about here was literal; the animal would have been bound. In synagogue worship this was symbolic, since a sacrifice was not actually being tied down to the altar. In the early church, this psalm verse would have been understood as a celebration of Christ's death and resurrection.[2] Christ had fulfilled God's demand for blood sacrifice and thereby abolished the need for such a practice in worship.

Psalm singing is commanded as part of New Testament worship in Ephesians 5:19 and Colossians 3:16.[3] These passages direct us to sing psalms, hymns, and spiritual songs (or odes). Some have argued that the three designations are simply three interchangeable words for canonical psalms, pointing out that the Septuagint uses all three words in psalm subtitles. Thus, these three are terms with which Paul and other believers of his day would have been familiar.[4] Wesley Isenberg writes that "the very use of diverse terminology such as this suggests that the early church encouraged a creative variety of musical and poetic expression in its corporate worship. Had the church sought to discourage such expression, the variety of terms would eventually have given way to a single term, by which we would now be able to define and delimit the 'hymn form.' "[5] Robert Rayburn wrote something similar:

> When we turn to the Word of God, we find that it would be difficult to establish on any sound exegetical basis that "psalms,

> hymns and spiritual songs" in Ephesians and Colossians refers to the inspired psalms of the Old Testament only. This is the argument of our Covenanter brethren, based upon the fact that the Hebrew words for hymn and song do appear in the titles of the psalms, and further that the reference to "spiritual songs" means that they must be inspired by the Holy Spirit. We do not have space for a detailed answer to this argument. Suffice it to say that the very fact that three types of song are mentioned rather than one alone is significant. If the Holy Spirit had intended that we sing psalms exclusively, He would have made this very clear by using only the one word . . . And the argument that the word *spiritual* before songs means that they must be divinely inspired songs cannot be sustained, for the word *spiritual* is used in the New Testament in connection with men who are not divinely inspired of the Holy Spirit (e.g., 1 Cor. 14:37; Gal. 6:1) and in Ephesians 6:12 it is used to refer to spiritual wickedness.[6]

Irrespective of one's conclusion about the terminology, singing psalms is not an optional activity, and yet we find it missing from many worship services in our time. It is insufficient to sing choruses based on a few verses of a psalm; in fact, songs of this nature tend to ignore the reasons the psalms give for worshiping God. Such reasons should be recalled if our thanks, praise, and prayers to God are to be properly contextualized and purposeful.

At the same time, psalms are not the only appropriate worship songs of the people of God. The Westminster Confession's "regulative principle" from chapter 21 does not mention hymns and spiritual songs when it says "singing of psalms with grace in the heart." But Rayburn rightly notes, "This omission does not mean that we should sing the Old Testament psalms only. The Confession uses the word in a wider sense to refer to hymns sung to God."[7] From New Testament examples, worship should also include our Christian response to the finished work of Calvary. This response could be characterized as a "Christian interpretation of the psalms" through hymns and canticles as well as biblical songs and hymns of the present day. According to Old, "The doxology of the earliest Christians kept psalmody and hymnody in a dynamic balance."[8] Without Christian hymns, our praise of God through the psalms would still be rich, but it would be missing our acknowledgment of and gratitude for the manner in which Christ has redeemed us and fulfilled what the Old Testament promised.

The psalms teach us how to worship, and they provide fitting, biblical language with which to thank, praise, implore, and glorify God. They also demonstrate confession and lament. Some are messianic; others recount Israel's redemptive history. A historical study of sung psalms in worship of the church reveals a number of traditions spanning Gregorian psalmody to the metrical psalms of the *Strasbourg Psalter* (1539) and the *Genevan Psalter* (1562), to the early American *Bay Psalm Book* (1640), to Anglican chant, to the psalm-hymns of Martin Luther, Isaac Watts, and James Montgomery, among other authors. In other words, the psalms must be sung, but the manner in which they should be sung (language, medium, mode, music) is a matter of some choice.

Canticles

As one studies the Bible, it becomes apparent that singing hymns of praise was the response of many saints to God's deliverance and other blessings. Like the Old Testament psalms, these biblical songs, recorded in written form, were passed on by oral tradition from priests to people and parents to children. Although the Old Testament also includes laments, such as David's great *Elegy* for Jonathan and Saul in 2 Samuel 1:17–27 (which, incidentally, David said should be taught to the people of Judah, and so he recorded it in the Book of Jashar), canticles typically rehearse the attributes of God and his mighty acts on behalf of his people—specifically his acts of *creation* and *redemption*. They give glory to God and manifest a spirit of joy and thankfulness for his work and deliverance.

- *Moses and Miriam* and all Israel sang after the nation was delivered from the hand of Pharaoh at the Red Sea (Ex. 15).

- *Deborah and Barak* sang when God gave victory to the Israelites over the Canaanites (Judg. 5).
- *David* sang as the Lord delivered him from the hand of all his enemies and from Saul (2 Sam. 22).
- *Mary* sang upon seeing Elizabeth, who understood that God's promise of a Redeemer was going to be realized through Mary (Luke 1—*Magnificat*).[9]
- *Zechariah* sang following the return of his speech as he was filled with the Holy Spirit and verified his son's name—John, the one who would prepare the way for the Savior (Luke 1—*Benedictus Dominus Deus Israel*).
- *Simeon* had a similar response a chapter later, when he held Jesus, the Messiah, in his arms, having entered the temple "in the Spirit" (Luke 2—*Nunc dimittis*).

There are other Old Testament songs of Jacob (Gen. 49), Hannah (1 Sam. 2:1–10), Moses (Deut. 32), and Habakkuk (Hab. 3), as well as numerous other *cantica minora* in Exodus, Deuteronomy, 1 Samuel, 1 Chronicles, Isaiah, and elsewhere. The three New Testament canticles mentioned above are also known as the "Lukan Psalms," or *cantica majora.* They evidence the continued writing/singing of inspired Christian psalms, apart from apocryphal songs, after the writing of the canonical Psalms had concluded. Old notes that "these are clearly Christian psalms written in the literary genre of the Hebrew votive thanksgiving psalms . . . The Old Testament psalms had for generations cried out for the Lord's anointed; now the New Testament psalms confessed that the cry had been heard and the promise fulfilled."[10]

These biblical songs were the response of Spirit-filled people to God's salvation. The biblical model is to sing of divine deliverance—to sing the gospel. Gospel-centered churches preach Christ's work of redemption (his birth, life, death, resurrection, and ascension), which is the message of the Bible. The Scriptures sing this gospel time and time again, and so should we.

Canticles such as the *Magnificat* and *Nunc dimittis* are regularly sung in Vespers and Evensong services, and these and other canticles are prominent in the Lutheran, Anglican, Orthodox, and Roman Catholic traditions. Perhaps their prominence in liturgical Protestant and non-Protestant traditions is among the excuses for not employing them in less-liturgical and nonliturgical, modern, evangelical worship. Since they are Holy Spirit–inspired biblical songs, however, all Christians would be well advised to sing them. Not doing so deprives us of their full value and overlooks some of the rich hymnody of the Scriptures.

Hymns of Christ

The New Testament quotes extensively from the psalms and canticles of the Old Testament. And in several New Testament passages (particularly in Romans and Hebrews), one finds heightened poetic language and hymn fragments (such as John 1:1–5, 9–11; Rom. 10:9ff.; 1 Cor. 12:3; Eph. 5:14; Phil. 2:5–11; Col. 1:15–20; 1 Tim. 2:5–6; 3:16; 2 Tim. 2:11–13; Heb. 1:3; and 1 Peter 3:18c–19, 22, among others). There is no conclusive way to distinguish between poetry and hymnody in the New Testament because both contain the fundamental features of Hebrew poetry. But there is little distinction between poetry and music anyway during this period of history (cf. the Greek "chorus" or the "muse"). Usually such biblical passages are Christocentric and may appear in modern translations with indented margins, italics, or quotation marks that distinguish them from the regular prose. The passages in Philippians and Colossians are hymns of Christ, which scholars feel may be representative of Greek poetic forms familiar to the Greek-speaking congregations. Certainly the doxological hymns of Revelation 4 and 5 are hymns of Christ; these will be considered in more detail shortly.

While one can read of Christ in Old Testament messianic psalms, the book of Psalms largely focuses on the worship, attributes, and acts of God the Father rather than on the Son. One would expect this, since the psalms predate Jesus' first advent. The portions of the gospels and epistles listed above, on the other hand, poetically celebrate the lordship of Christ and provide hymns specifically to and about Christ—a new genre of biblical song. As Ralph Martin puts it:

> It was in worship that the decisive step was made of setting the exalted Christ on a level with God as the recipient of the church's praise. Hymnology and Christology thus merged in the worship of one Lord, soon to be hailed after the close of the New Testament canon as worthy of hymns "as to God" (Pliny's report of Bithynian Christians at Sunday worship, A.D. 112).
>
> It was this close drawing together of the persons of the Godhead which laid the foundation for the Trinitarian creeds, and raised a bulwark against classical gnosticism in the late second century . . . While "messianic psalms" played their role in defining and defending the church's belief in the fulfillment of Old Testament types and prefigurements, it required a new species—the "hymn to Christ"—to open fruitful avenues of Christological and soteriological inquiry that set the church from its early days on a course that led eventually to Chalcedon and the *Te Deum*:
>
> You are the King of Glory, O Christ,
> You are the everlasting Son of the Father.[11]

The *Te Deum laudamus* is one of the greatest hymns of the early church, and it may be classified as a hymn of Christ. Many church fathers wrote hymns to Christ in their letters, apologies, and homilies. Such Christological Greek and Latin hymns should not be confused with Gnostic hymns that were written with the intention of replacing the psalms. On the contrary, many of the early church's hymns were written by orthodox theologians specifically to counteract the heresies of Gnostic hymn writers.

Isaac Watts authored psalm paraphrases and hymns with a related purpose—a quest to "Christianize" the psalms. Like Luther before him, Watts wanted believers to benefit from psalm singing, so that it would not be an intellectually or culturally remote activity, but one from which they would learn and with which they could associate. We see in Isaac Watts's work what Horton Davies calls a desire to create a "Christian re-orientation of the Psalms."[12] To do so, Watts abbreviated lengthy psalms and avoided potentially confusing metaphoric language. Further, he makes direct reference to Christ or the gospel within at least one stanza in most of his psalm paraphrases. For example, in the setting of Psalm 103, "O Bless the Lord, My Soul," the final stanza reads:

> His wondrous works and ways
> He made by Moses known,
> But sent the world his truth and grace
> By his beloved Son.

Another example is his paraphrase of Psalm 19, "The Heavens Declare Your Glory, Lord," where we find the stanza:

> Nor shall your spreading gospel rest
> Till through the world your truth has run;
> Till Christ has all the nations blessed
> That see the light, or feel the sun.

While we understand that many of the psalms have their prophecies fulfilled in Christ, the psalm texts do not refer to Jesus or to the gospel by name. Some of the psalms (such as Psalm 45) were understood even in Old Testament times to be messianic. Watts wanted to make Christ's fulfillment of them evident: "In all places I have kept my grand design in view; and that is to teach my author to speak like a Christian."[13] He instructed congregants to carry psalm books with them and asked the clerk to read the psalm aloud before it was sung so that people might better understand what they were to sing. In so doing, he restored Christian praise to its rightful place in the worship of the Dissenting Church of the early eighteenth century.[14] Understanding biblical principles of worship would have a similar restorative effect on the church in our day—it would enrich our worship and help to guard against the dangers of relativism, Gnosticism, narcissism, and anthropocentrism.

Doxologies

The New Testament includes numerous excerpts from benedictions, prayers, creeds, eulogies, responses, and doxologies. Doxology encompasses the full gamut of praise to God and has been referred to as "the theology of worship."[15] Extensive doxological passages occur in Romans 11:33–36 and Revelation 1:5–7, as well as Revelation 4–5; 7:10, 12; 11:15–18; 15:3–4; and 19:1–8. The five divisions of the book of Psalms each conclude with doxological passages, and Psalm 150 in its entirety serves as a doxology to close the Psalter.

Let us look more closely at two of these New Testament doxologies.

Romans 11:33–36

Romans 11:33–36 closes the great doctrinal chapters of the book and acts as the climax of the apostle Paul's testimony to all he has written. James Montgomery Boice put it this way: "As Paul contemplated the mercies of God, he was so lost in wonder that he composed the doxology . . . as an outpouring of praise . . . the song of the redeemed."[16] This doxology, which quotes both Isaiah and Job, concludes that all things come both *from* and *through* God himself and lead rightly *to* the worship of God by his redeemed creation. This is the only acceptable Christian worldview. All things are to bring God glory and bring it to him alone.

Revelation 4 and 5

There are five doxological hymns in Revelation 4 and 5, sung by many angels, four living creatures, twenty-four elders, and all creation. These songs are continuous. The first two praise God the Father. The next two praise Christ, the Lamb; and the fifth praises both the Father and the Son. God is worshiped for his holiness, for his everlasting existence, and for his creation. Christ is praised for his worthiness to open the seals and for his saving act of redemption. A "crescendo of praise" is evident in these hymns as well. The first is offered by the four living creatures, the second and third by the four living creatures and twenty-four elders, the fourth by the four living creatures, twenty-four elders, and myriads of angels, and the fifth by every creature in heaven and on earth and under the earth and in the sea.

Our understanding of heaven's eternal worship as expressed in Revelation also informs our understanding of what worship should be following the death and resurrection of Christ; for "eternal" worship necessarily encompasses the past, present, and future. As Old has pointed out, "One is struck by the fact that in Revelation's report of the heavenly worship there are constant echoes of the Psalms and canticles of the Old Testament and yet no example of a direct and simple use of one of the canonical Psalms. In every case what we have is a Christian paraphrase."[17] Since this information is the revealed Word of God, and demonstrates at least a veiled picture of perfect, heavenly worship, it would seem appropriate to imitate this revelation in our continuous worship of the present day.

Notes

1. Hughes Oliphant Old, *Worship That Is Reformed According to Scripture* (Atlanta: John Knox Press, 1984), 39–41.

2. Ibid.

3. We will not treat these verses in terms of a distinction between "psalms, hymns, and spiritual songs," an idea that has been explored by theologians and other authors. A case can be made that these three names identify different types of canonical psalms, since they do so in the Septuagint. A case can also be made for their identifying different types of musico-poetic forms (such as psalms, hymns, and choruses; or psalms, canticles, and odes; or canonical psalms, inspired hymns, and extemporaneous songs). See also note 4.

4. Anthony Cowley and Randy W. Harris, *A Diagram Defense of Psalmody* (Elkins Park, PA: Covenanter Reformation Press, 1993). The authors also argue that "psalms, hymns, and songs" are all three modified by the adjective "spiritual" (*pneumatikais*), which suggests that these "songs" are given directly by the Holy Spirit, or in other words can refer only to inspired psalms. For a fuller discussion of possible interpretations of these verses, see appendix 1 in Barry Liesch's book *The New Worship* (Grand Rapids: Baker, 2001), which gives four views based on emphases in the Greek (imperative, attendant, resultative, and instrumental/modal).

5. Wesley W. Isenberg, "Hymnody: New Testament," in *Key Words in Church Music,* ed. Carl Schalk (St. Louis: Concordia, 1978), 181.

6. Robert G. Rayburn, *O Come, Let Us Worship: Corporate Worship in the Evangelical Church* (New York: Westminster Publishing House, n.d., ca. 1950), 95.

7. Ibid.

8. Hughes Oliphant Old, "The Psalms of Praise in the Worship of the New Testament Church," *Interpretation: A Journal of Bible and Theology* 39, no. 1 (January 1985): 32.

9. Some scholars believe the *Magnificat* may have been Elizabeth's song rather than Mary's.

10. Old, *Worship That Is Reformed,* 44.

11. Ralph P. Martin, "Hymns in the New Testament: An Evolving Pattern of Worship Responses," *Ex Auditu* 8 (1992): 34–42. (These are only two lines from the *Te Deum laudamus,* not the complete text). Pliny wrote that the Christians in the first age met before the break of day and sang hymns to Christ as God in turn, one after the other.

12. Horton Davies, *The Worship of the English Puritans* (Morgan, PA: Soli Deo Gloria Publications, 1997), 176.

13. Isaac Watts, *The Psalms of David Imitated in the Language of the New Testament and Applied to the Christian State and Worship,* as quoted in Davies, *Worship of the English Puritans,* 178.

14. Davies, *Worship of the English Puritans,* 178.

15. Hughes Oliphant Old, *Themes and Variations for a Christian Doxology* (Grand Rapids: Eerdmans, 1992), 16. Old believes that doxology is the theology of worship and that the Old Testament sounds five musical themes that are fully developed in the New Testament, specifically epiclectic, kerygmatic, wisdom, prophetic, and covenantal doxology.

16. James Montgomery Boice, *God and History,* vol. 3 of *Romans: An Expositional Commentary* (Grand Rapids: Baker, 1993), 1410, 1466.

17. Old, *Worship That Is Reformed,* 32.

14
Biblical Hymns of James Montgomery Boice

Oh sing to the Lord a new song;
sing to the Lord, all the earth! —*Psalm 96:1*

Not all hymnody is great hymnody.[1] In fact, in most modern hymnals one can find some fairly saccharine and anthropocentric texts as well as some trite and skittish tunes. Even the best hymnals include a few pieces of questionable value to appease certain members of the editorial committee or to make the book more marketable. In other words, even though one may discover a song in a reputable hymnal, it does not necessarily follow that the song itself will be great or that it will even be a hymn.

Today traditional church musicians speak out against the inundation of "praise" choruses for similar theological and musical reasons. In the mid-twentieth century, Robert Rayburn and others printed similar criticisms of "gospel songs," which, interestingly enough, are often the so-called "grand old hymns of the church" to which older folks in our churches refer. According to Rayburn, "All serious Christians should examine their own preferences and perhaps they will find a need to enrich substantially their musical praise by using more of the great hymns of exalted devotion based upon thoroughly scriptural concepts rather than the more shallow sentimental songs whose appeal is largely musical."[2] The greatest hymns, the ones that have survived the test of time, are those most closely allied to Scripture and set to well-constructed music. Texts that are trendy, overly experiential, or linked to events too provincial to be applied to the church universal do not last.

Historical Models

The finest hymn writers since the Reformation—Luther, Newton, Cowper, Watts, Wesley, Doddridge, Montgomery, and others—focused on Scripture as the source of their inspiration and the dissemination of biblical teaching as their goal. Obviously, none of the hymn writers mentioned above invented the concept that the gospel could be taught through hymnody. The basis for this idea rests clearly in Scripture. Luther and these other writers knew that music would help spread the gospel, that it would bolster the spirits of the weary and give comfort to those who were hurting. In short, great hymnody through its "preaching" would effect change in the church and would minister to its members. James Montgomery Boice (1938–2000) knew this as well. In his commentary on Psalm 9:9–10, Boice wrote:

> It is striking that in each part the psalmist combines singing with preaching. And, it is interesting to remember that great periods of church history have always been marked by both. At the time of the Reformation, Martin Luther's hymns were on the lips of the German people as much as his words were in their hearts. At the time of the Wesleyan Revival in Great Britain, the recovery of the gospel was accompanied by an equally stirring recovery of gospel singing, as the hymns of John and Charles Wesley, August Toplady, William Cowper, John Newton and others show.[3]

Perhaps history will show that a reformation in the twenty-first-century church found the hymns of Boice on its members' lips as well. That would be fitting.

Boice's Purpose

As one uncovers Luther's purposes for hymn development in his prefaces to hymnals and other writings, one can do the same with Boice. The pastor-scholar's own words help to clarify his goals for hymnody and his understanding of its significance. In a sermon on Revelation 4:9–11, Boice spoke about the importance of music and singing in worship:

> Isn't it interesting that heaven's worship is expressed in words set to music, in words that are sung? This is more than interesting, of course. It is important, for music is a gift from God that allows us to express our deepest heart responses to God and his truth in meaningful and memorable ways. It is a case of our hearts joining with our minds to say, "Yes! Yes! Yes!" to the truths we are embracing . . . It is what the four living creatures, elders, angels and the entire creation are doing today in heaven. We join that great heavenly choir rightly, wisely and joyously when we sing.

With *Hymns for a Modern Reformation*, Boice revisited Luther's goal for his own hymns—to teach the Bible in a meaningful, memorable, life-changing manner. This was, of course, his calling as a preacher as well. He e-mailed me in August 1999 with a statement that delineated the *raison d'être* of our collaborative effort: "I am thinking that if we are going to have a modern reformation, we are going to need new reformation music. Bible doctrines have always gotten a hold on people this way." His hymns originated in and emerged from contemplating and teaching biblical passages. In effect, they preach through poetry set to music.

Hymns for a Modern Reformation

For example, in reviewing Boice's *sola gratia* hymn on Ephesians 2:1–10, one finds that the poem is written in the first-person singular (see fig. 14.1). It can be understood as the author's personal testimony. The titles for the chapters Boice used when explicating the Ephesians passage in his commentary on the epistle also outline his

Fig. 14.1

Alive in Christ

But. . . God, who is rich in mercy, made us alive with Christ. Eph. 2:4-5

Based on Ephesians 2:1-10
James Montgomery Boice, 2000

SOLA GRATIA
11.8.11.8.
Paul S. Jones, 2000

thoughts for this hymn. The following section titles and paragraphs are excerpted from *Hymns for a Modern Reformation* and Boice's *Ephesians* commentary:

1. The Way We Were (2:1–3)
2. But God (2:4–5)
3. Risen with Christ (2:6–7)
4. Saved by Grace Alone (2:8–9)
5. God's Workmanship (2:10)

> The five hymn stanzas mirror these five divisions of the passage precisely as they trace the Christian's past, present, and future in a cogent manner. We were dead to God in our transgressions and enslaved by our sins. As such, by nature we were objects of God's wrath and under his just sentence for our sin. "But God" has made us alive in Christ. Boice wrote, "May I put it quite simply? If you understand those two words—'but God'—they will save your soul. If you recall them daily and live by them, they will transform your life completely." Why did God do this? Because of his love (v. 4), his mercy (v. 4), his grace (v. 5), and his kindness (v. 7). God made us alive together with Christ, raised us up together with him, and made us sit down together with him in the heavenly realms. "Before, we were dead; now we are alive. Before, we were enslaved by our sins and carnal nature; now we are emancipated. Before, we were objects of wrath; now we experience God's love."
>
> We are saved "by grace" alone, "through faith." But this is not by our own doing, it is God's work and God's gift. "Faith is not from ourselves . . . If it were a virtue, then we would be able to boast in heaven . . . No, not even faith is a work. Nothing that you or I can do, however great or small, can get us into salvation . . . Salvation is by grace alone." Paul quickly moves from rejecting any notion of good works being part of our salvation to insisting that good works are precisely what God has created us to do. In fact, God created us in Christ Jesus to do good works that were

specifically "prepared in advance for us to do." This "is the re-creation of a man or woman who before was spiritually dead, utterly incapable of doing any good thing that could satisfy God, but who now, as the result of God's working, is able to do truly good 'good works.' "[4]

Another Boice hymn could be called a "hymn of Christ." Based on the Revelation 1:5–7 doxology, it is entitled "All Praise to Christ" (see fig. 14.2). Preaching on this opening passage from the Bible's final book, Boice said:

> Earlier in this study I referred to the last words of verse 6 as a doxology, which they are. But in a broader sense everything in verses 5–7 is a doxology or, to put it differently, a hymn to be sung with joy by God's people . . . It is a communal hymn, for the repetition of "us" and "our" draws John and his readers together as a confessing community of faith. This is what hymns are meant to do. They are a means given by God by which we join in confessing our beliefs, lift up our flagging spirits, encourage our hearts, and worship God together. Can anything be more joyful and uplifting than that? Nothing at all, until we do it perfectly in the presence of our Savior and God.[5]

The fourth and final stanza of the hymn gives us a glimpse of heavenly worship in which the new creation is singing together with heavenly beings and saints of past ages. This eternal song is quoted, and then our present response of praise is given in the refrain from which the concept for the hymn's tune name (Ipsi Gloria, "to him be glory") is taken:

> With angels, saints and seraphim
> The new creation sings,
> "All glory, pow'r and praise to him
> Who made us priests and kings."

Fig. 14.2

All Praise To Christ

To him be glory and power for ever and ever! Amen. Rev. 1:6

Based on Revelation 1:5-7
James Montgomery Boice, 1999

IPSI GLORIA
8.6.8.6.8.6.
Paul S. Jones, 1999

Refrain:
All praise to Christ from grateful men
Forevermore. Amen.

"How Marvelous, How Wise, How Great," based on Romans 8:28–31, proclaims the cardinal doctrines of Calvinism as it reflects and expounds on this "golden chain" passage. Its language is both proclamatory and instructive. This is not a hymn of praise, although an appropriate response to its teaching is the praise of God. Neither is it a prayer, nor a lament, nor simply a spiritual poem. Rather, it is a short sermon, or hymn of proclamation, that outlines and explains a difficult passage of Scripture; yet it does so in poetic language and form. This accounts for the rhyme scheme that pervades and links the four stanzas. Boice fashioned it in such a way that the rhyme interlocks one stanza with the next (see fig. 14.3). In each stanza of six lines, AAB-AAB, the "B" rhyme becomes the "A" rhyme of the following stanza. (For example, "plan" and "man," the "B" rhymes of stanza 1, lead to the "A" rhymes "began," "plan," "man," and "can" of stanza 2; B becomes A). This is consistent through all four strophes, resulting in a chain-link poetic form that mirrors the interlocking doctrines of the *ordo salutis* (salvation order) found in Romans 8:28–31.

Here is what Boice wrote about it in his preface to the hymn as it appears in *Hymns for a Modern Reformation*:

> There are few passages in the entire Bible that trace the full scope of God's purposes with those he has determined to save as does Romans 8:28–31. The passage begins with God's election of a people for himself, speaks of his determination to conform them to the likeness of Jesus Christ, and then completes what some have called the great "golden chain" that ends with calling, justification and glorification. The unbrokenness of the chain is important, because each act leads to the next, and in each God is describing something he has done, even the glorification of his elect in spite of the fact that it has not yet taken place for all in time.[6]

The stanzas follow the biblical text in an important order also. The first marvels at God's purpose to regenerate a faithless, fallen man. The

Fig. 14.3

How Marvelous, How Wise, How Great

For those God foreknew he also predestined... called... justified... glorified.
Rom. 8:29-30

1. How mar - ve - lous, how wise, how great, how
2. Fore - known be - fore the world be - gan, ac -
3. He bore my sin on Cal - vary's tree and
4. What have I now but to em - brace the

in - fi - nite to con - tem - plate: Je - ho - vah's sav - ing
cord - ing to his gra - cious plan, God des - tined I must
right - eous - ness be - stowed on me that I might see his
God who saved me from dis - grace and love him ev - er -

plan. He saw me in my lost es - tate yet
be con - formed to Je - sus Christ, the man, who
face. God jus - ti - fied me, set me free, and
more; and with con - tent - ment run my race my

pur - posed to re - gen - er - ate this faith - less, fal - len man.
lived and loved as no man can: a glo - ri - ous de - cree.
glo - ri - fied I soon will be: how mar - ve - lous this grace.
eyes fixed ev - er on his face to praise him and a - dore.

Based on Romans 8:28-31
James Montgomery Boice, 1999

SPRUCE STREET
8.8.6.8.8.6.
Paul S. Jones, 1999

second reflects on the election of that individual and notes that God's predestining purpose is to conform the sinner to the likeness of Christ. After rejoicing in our justification and glorification in stanza 3, as Romans 8:30 does, the hymn concludes in stanza 4 by saying that nothing remains for us now but to embrace God and his grace, run our race well, and praise God forever—the application of the sermon to daily life. This concluding stanza begins with a question ("What have I now but to embrace . . . ?"), the very same way that Boice's spoken sermons from the pulpit often had questions for the congregation as part of their closing spiritual application of the message.

The very first Boice hymn was entitled "Give Praise to God" (see fig. 14.5), a hymn written to celebrate the fiftieth anniversary of *The Bible Study Hour* radio program on September 12, 1999. The weekend's theme was "Toward a New Reformation," and the text for the Sunday-morning sermon at Tenth Presbyterian Church was Romans 11:36. Boice's hymn is based on the Pauline doxology found in Romans 11:33–36 (see fig. 14.4). This doxology acts as the climax and testimony to the great doctrinal chapters leading up to it. It may rightly be called a "hymn of the Father" because of the emphasis placed on the first person of the Trinity. Boice's several sermons on this passage appear under the chapter heading *Soli Deo Gloria* ("Glory to God alone"), which we shortened to Soli Deo as this hymn's tune name. In particular, Boice's message on verse 36 (which he used as the key verse in defining a proper Christian worldview) was titled after the Reformation motto.

The hymn proclaims the theology of this passage, arranging the thoughts in a context of poetic praise. The refrain serves as a call to respond to the teaching of the passage—to give glory to God. Notice the manner in which each stanza of the poem mirrors a verse from the biblical doxology. This is arguably one of the finest examples of a proclamatory hymn text. It both presents the scriptural passage and interprets it, providing application that every child of God can and should appropriate.

Comparison of Scriptural Text and Hymn Poem

Fig. 14.4

ROMANS 11:33–36	"GIVE PRAISE TO GOD"
Oh, the depth of the riches and wisdom and knowledge of God! How unsearchable are his judgments and how inscrutable his ways!	Give praise to God who reigns above for perfect knowledge, wisdom, love; his judgments are divine, devout, his paths beyond all tracing out.
"For who has known the mind of the Lord, or who has been his counselor?"	No one can counsel God all-wise or truths unveil to his sharp eyes; he marks our paths behind, before; he is our steadfast Counselor.
"Or who has given a gift to him that he might be repaid?"	Nothing exists that God might need for all things good from him proceed. We praise him as our Lord, and yet we never place God in our debt.
For from him and through him and to him are all things. To him be glory forever. Amen.	Creation, life, salvation too, and all things else both good and true, come from and through our God always, and fill our hearts with grateful praise.
	Refrain: Come, lift your voice to heav'n's high throne, And glory give to God alone!

If there has ever been an age so myopically transfixed on its own importance and a people so quick to dismiss its spiritual heritage, that age is ours and the people are evangelical Protestants. One of James Montgomery Boice's chief goals in preaching to the evangelical church at large was to reawaken it from its worldliness—from self-obsessed, relativistic, pluralistic values and theology—by reclaiming the doctrines of grace expressed in the *solas* of the Reformation.[7] He believed the cure for evangelical worldliness was to view all of life through the lens of Romans 11:36, where God reigns supreme, since all comes "from him and through him and to him." In his last few years, and in the final months of his earthly life in particular, Boice stated more strongly than ever that spirited singing of biblical hymns was an excellent and necessary way to exercise the mind and soul—that this was a worthy and essential spiritual occupation of every

Fig. 14.5

Give Praise to God

For from him and through him and to him are all things.
To him be the glory forever! Amen. Rom. 11:36

Based on Romans 11:33-36
James Montgomery Boice, 1999

SOLI DEO
L.M.ref.
Paul S. Jones, 1999

Christian. After all, it will be our occupation and delight for all eternity as we sing the old songs and the new, psalms and hymns, law and grace—the songs of Moses and of the Lamb.

And they sing the song of Moses, the servant of God,
and the song of the Lamb . . . —Revelation 15:3a

Notes

1. Sections of this chapter were adapted from my chapter in *Give Praise to God: Sola Scriptura et Soli Deo Gloria, a Festschrift in Memory of James Montgomery Boice,* ed. J. Ligon Duncan, Philip G. Ryken, and Derek Thomas (Phillipsburg, NJ: P&R Publishing, 2003). Used by permission.

2. Robert G. Rayburn, *O Come, Let Us Worship: Corporate Worship in the Evangelical Church* (New York: Westminster Publishing House, n.d., ca. 1950), 230. Rayburn wrote, "One of the problems that contemporary congregations face is that many of the gospel songs are popular because the tunes to which they are sung have an appealing rhythm and a lighthearted melody." Ibid.

3. James Montgomery Boice, *Psalms: An Expositional Commentary* (Grand Rapids: Baker, 1994), 1:79.

4. James Montgomery Boice and Paul Steven Jones, *Hymns for a Modern Reformation* (Philadelphia: Tenth Presbyterian Church, 2000), 24, with quotations from James Montgomery Boice, *Ephesians: An Expositional Commentary,* rev. ed. (Grand Rapids: Baker, 1997), 54, 57, 68, 74.

5. Excerpted from James Montgomery Boice's sermon on Revelation 1:5–7, unpublished. Used by permission of Linda Boice.

6. Boice and Jones, *Hymns for a Modern Reformation,* 10.

7. The "solas" of the Reformation are: *Sola Scriptura* (Scripture alone), *Sola Fide* (faith alone), *Sola Gratia* (grace alone), *Solus Christus* (Christ alone), and *Soli Deo Gloria* (glory to God alone).

15
Why Every Christian Should Sing

Sing praises to the Lord, *O you his saints,*
and give thanks to his holy name. —Psalm 30:4

As a choir director who is constantly recruiting, and as a leader of the people's song, I frequently encounter men and women who say that they "do not sing." There are many reasons for their lack of vocal participation, but I have yet to hear one from anyone with working vocal folds that would be an adequate excuse before God. Fear is the least-cited but generally all-inclusive reason. It takes many forms: fear of error or embarrassment, fear of what others think, fear of losing control, fear of criticism, fear of offending others. Such self-conscious behavior may be appropriate to certain situations or aspects of our person, but it has little place in the corporate worship of the Almighty. God never said, "If you feel good enough about yourself, sing to me," or "As long as you have a peer-approved voice, praise me in song." According to Scripture, the praise of God is not an optional activity.

Why should every child of God with a voice lift up that voice, both privately and in corporate worship? God's Word speaks for him and supplies the answers.

The Example of Biblical Saints Who Walked with God

Moses

I will sing to the LORD, for he has triumphed gloriously; the horse and his rider he has thrown into the sea. The LORD is my strength and my song, and he has become my salvation; this is my God, and I will praise him, my father's God, and I will exalt him. (Ex. 15:1–2)

For I will proclaim the name of the LORD; ascribe greatness to our God! (Deut. 32:3)

Deborah and Barak

Hear, O kings; give ear, O princes; to the LORD I will sing; I will make melody to the LORD, the God of Israel. (Judg. 5:3)

David

For this I will praise you, O LORD, among the nations, and sing praises to your name. Great salvation he brings to his king, and shows steadfast love to his anointed, to David and his offspring forever. (2 Sam. 22:50–51)

But let all who take refuge in you rejoice; let them ever sing for joy, and spread your protection over them, that those who love your name may exult in you. (Ps. 5:11)

I will give thanks to the LORD with my whole heart; I will recount all of your wonderful deeds. I will be glad and exult in you; I will sing praise to your name, O Most High. (Ps. 9:1–2)

I will sing to the LORD, because he has dealt bountifully with me. (Ps. 13:6)

Mary

My soul magnifies the Lord, and my spirit rejoices in God my Savior . . . (Luke 1:46–47)

The Command of God to His Saints Through His Word

Sing praises to the LORD, O you his saints, and give thanks to his holy name. For his anger is but for a moment, and his favor is for a lifetime. (Ps. 30:4–5)

Shout for joy in the LORD, O you righteous! Praise befits the upright. Give thanks to the LORD with the lyre; make melody to him with the harp of ten strings! Sing to him a new song; play skillfully on the strings, with loud shouts. For the word of the LORD is upright, and all his work is done in faithfulness. (Ps. 33:1–4)

I will bless the LORD at all times; his praise shall continually be in my mouth. My soul makes its boast in the LORD; let the humble hear and be glad. Oh, magnify the LORD with me, and let us exalt his name together! (Ps. 34:1–3)

Clap your hands, all peoples! Shout to God with loud songs of joy! . . . Sing praises to God, sing praises! Sing praises to our King, sing praises! For God is the King of all the earth; sing praises with a psalm! (Ps. 47:1, 6–7)

Shout for joy to God, all the earth; sing the glory of his name; give to him glorious praise! (Ps. 66:1–2)

Sing aloud to God our strength; shout for joy to the God of Jacob! Raise a song; sound the tambourine, the sweet lyre with the harp. Blow the trumpet at the new moon, at the full moon, on our feast day. (Ps. 81:1–3)

Praise the LORD! For it is good to sing praises to our God; for it is pleasant, and a song of praise is fitting . . . Sing to the LORD with thanksgiving; make melody to our God on the lyre! (Ps. 147:1, 7)

Praise the LORD! Sing to the LORD a new song, his praise in the assembly of the godly! (Ps. 149:1)

Sing praises to the LORD, for he has done gloriously; let this be made known in all the earth. Shout, and sing for joy, O inhabitant of Zion, for great in your midst is the Holy One of Israel. (Isa. 12:5–6)

Sing to the LORD a new song, his praise from the end of the earth, you who go down to the sea, and all that fills it, the coastlands and their inhabitants. (Isa. 42:10)

"Sing, O barren one, who did not bear; break forth into singing and cry aloud, you who have not been in labor! For the children of the desolate one will be more than the children of her who is married," says the LORD. (Isa. 54:1)

Addressing one another in psalms and hymns and spiritual songs, singing and making melody to the Lord with all your heart, giving thanks always and for everything to God the Father in the name of our Lord Jesus Christ . . . (Eph. 5:19–20)

Let the word of Christ dwell in you richly, teaching and admonishing one another in all wisdom, singing psalms and hymns and spiritual songs, with thankfulness in your hearts to God. And whatever you do, in word or deed, do everything in the name of the Lord Jesus, giving thanks to God the Father through him. (Col. 3:16–17)

The Example of Heaven and Heavenly Beings

Angels

Holy, holy, holy is the LORD of hosts; the whole earth is full of his glory! (Isa. 6:3)

Glory to God in the highest, and on earth peace among those with whom he is pleased! (Luke 2:14)

Four living creatures

Holy, holy, holy, is the Lord God Almighty, who was and is and is to come! (Rev. 4:8)

Twenty-four elders

Worthy are you, our Lord and God, to receive glory and honor and power, for you created all things, and by your will they existed and were created. (Rev. 4:11)

We give thanks to you, Lord God Almighty, who is and who was, for you have taken your great power and begun to reign. (Rev. 11:17)

Every creature in heaven and on earth and under the earth and in the sea

To him who sits on the throne and to the Lamb be blessing and honor and glory and might forever and ever! (Rev. 5:13)

Those who conquered the beast and its image and the number of its name

Great and amazing are your deeds, O Lord God the Almighty! Just and true are your ways, O King of the nations! (Rev. 15:3)

A great multitude in heaven

> Hallelujah! Salvation and glory and power belong to our God, for his judgments are true and just; for he has judged the great prostitute who corrupted the earth with her immorality, and has avenged on her the blood of his servants. (Rev. 19:1–2)
>
> Hallelujah! For the Lord our God the Almighty reigns. Let us rejoice and exult and give him the glory, for the marriage of the Lamb has come, and his Bride has made herself ready; it was granted her to clothe herself with fine linen, bright and pure . . . (Rev. 19:6–8)

The Example of Jesus Christ, Who Sings

> And when they had sung a hymn, they went out to the Mount of Olives. (Matt. 26:30)
>
> For he who sanctifies and those who are sanctified all have one origin. That is why he is not ashamed to call them brothers, saying, "I will tell of your name to my brothers; in the midst of the congregation I will sing your praise." (Heb. 2:11–12)

Not all the possible references in each category have been listed above; but surely even here there is sufficient evidence from the Bible to demonstrate why every Christian should sing. The reasons to sing are given in the verses themselves. We should sing because of God's attributes and acts in creation and redemption. We should sing because this was the exemplary response of biblical saints. We should sing because God has commanded us to do so. We should sing because it is a Christian and heavenly activity of eternal duration and significance.

If we do not sing, we disobey God and miss out on the rich blessing derived from this activity. Do not hold back because you lack musical training, or because your husband says you are tone-deaf, or because it does not seem like a "manly" thing to do. If Moses, David, and even

Jesus Christ sang, it is a manly thing to do, a God-fearing thing to do, and a Christian thing to do. Living according to earthly fear, irrespective of its source, is not living biblically. Pastors should set the example for their congregations by participating in singing, and by doing so with vigor and joy. God desires your praise through song, too, not by speech alone. (A small word of advice to song leaders, though: if your voice is not particularly mellifluous, avoid singing directly into the microphone. The Lord commands us to sing to him and to lift up our voices together, not necessarily to be soloists. In fact, all song leaders should step back from the microphone so that the congregation can hear itself.) And layperson, next Sunday be sure to join in song with the host of heaven and your earthly brethren as best you can. If anyone criticizes you for singing as part of the congregation in gathered worship, you can be sure that Scripture does not support their comment.

PART THREE

Issues

Musical issues are some of the most contentious areas of controversy and divisiveness in the church today, regularly confronting the church musician, pastor, leadership, and congregation. Music has been an area of mystery for many churchgoers and church leaders over the years. Since so little has been taught to seminarians, parishioners, and even musicians concerning the biblical foundations and principles of church music, it is hardly surprising to find significant discord about its place in worship. These problems are regularly "solved" as people take sides on various matters and war against each other. Then those in the weaker position, either numerically or hierarchically, surrender or leave the local congregation. That may solve the momentary dilemma for the particular church, but it does not answer the larger questions—questions that were probably not even being asked.

Why is it that we preach, teach, and refer to the Bible on all matters spiritual, and yet when we come to consider worship music (a spiritual and biblical activity), we turn to opinion, preference, and limited experience as our allies and sources? This pattern must change. Questions we need to ask, questions that would reduce or eliminate much of the "worship wars" debate, include the following:

- What is the purpose of worship music, according to Scripture?
- Who is worship music about, according to Scripture?
- What does the Bible evidence/model about worship music?
- Who should write and lead our worship music, according to Scripture?
- What kind of musical education should we have to fulfill this model?
- To whom should musical decisions for the church be entrusted?

A few of the musical matters facing churches today are discussed in this section. This is not the only part of this book dealing with issues in church music, but it includes a number of diverse themes while striving to be informative and practical. Topics run from remuneration for musicians to the musical education of children, from debunking a popular myth about Luther's music to encounters with various stereotypical positions on music in the church. Some churches desire practical help in finding a music director or improving their primary worship instrument, so such matters are considered here. By no means is this section exhaustive. It does not deal with all the "issues" that one may face, but it is intended to be a helpful beginning.

16

Choir for Hire: Should Church Musicians Be Paid?

And all the Levitical singers, Asaph, Heman, and Jeduthun, their sons and kinsmen, arrayed in fine linen, with cymbals, harps, and lyres, stood east of the altar with 120 priests who were trumpeters; and it was the duty of the trumpeters and singers to make themselves heard in unison in praise and thanksgiving to the LORD . . . —2 Chronicles 5:12–13a

I have been a church musician since the age of nine, from the day I first accompanied the children's choir of which I was a member. We had a full-time minister of music in the church by that point, and he was a salaried member of the staff. Our suburban Atlantic Canadian church was progressive and was blessed to have a professional musical leader on staff. So many did not. His wife was the children's choir director, and she thought it was time for me to contribute at the keyboard. Thus began many years of sitting on a piano or organ bench for worship services. I was privileged to have this kind of encouragement and opportunity at a young age.

In our church, none of the pianists or organists were compensated for their service, and no one, not even those playing, ever really noticed or questioned this practice. After all, this was a fitting use of our talents for the Lord within the context of worship. It is not at all wrong for musicians to view their contribution this way. Had anyone suggested that the pianists or soloists should be paid, however, there would have been controversy. And if the notion that trained choir members or soloists might receive compensation for their singing ever arose, a localized war would have broken out, with a church split not far behind.

Why? Well, for one thing, it was not our custom to pay church musicians. In other words, *not* paying our musicians was our *tradition.* The same is true today of many evangelical churches in numerous denominations. Paying musicians was something that Roman Catholic or liberal churches did, so naturally we would avoid it. Another objection would have had to do with equity. Since the Sunday-school teachers were not paid, and the deacons were not paid, and the nursery workers were not paid, why would musicians be paid? There must be some sense of fair play. One could argue that only full-time church personnel should be compensated. This makes some sense because the pastors, the secretary, the administrator, and the custodian all depend on this payment for their livelihoods. Granted.

But what about the freelance musician who depends on honoraria or payment from musical engagements for his living? This is his profession. What about the conservatory-trained pianist who has invested thousands of dollars in lesson and tuition fees for her training? Deacons and nursery workers do not encounter expenses or training of that degree to serve in their respective areas. What about the singer whose operatic career is sporadic in engagements and who cannot afford health insurance? What about the Bible-college music majors who are close to penniless but can make a significant contribution to a church's musical health? Perhaps these are all circumstantial situations in which rationalization will lead us to one conclusion or another. But are we missing something? In the course of maintaining our traditions and solving problems with logical answers and rationalization, have we considered what the Bible evidences?

What Does the Bible Say?

Direct reference to paying church musicians will not be found by searching the Scriptures. Then again, neither will salaries, housing allowances, retirement programs, and expense accounts for ministers be evident. One does not readily find payment for secretaries, clerks, superintendents, or custodians, either. Looking to the Old Testament, however, we find examples to follow. At the time of David's order for the temple (1 Chron. 23), there were 38,000 Levite males over the age of thirty. Some 4,000 of these men were selected and trained for temple service as musicians—to "offer praises to the LORD with the instruments that I have made for praise" (v. 5). Out of those, as 25:7 explains, "The number of them along with their brothers, who were trained in singing to the LORD, all who were skillful, was 288." Some were assigned to play specific instruments, such as harp, lyre, cymbals, and trumpets. Music *for the service of the house of God* (25:6) clearly designates that these men were skilled in worship music.

We recall that the Levites were the tribe of Israel set apart by God for priestly ministry. They were given special tax-free, Levitical cities, and their needs for food, clothing, and shelter were provided by the rest of God's people (including the needs of their families, of course). These Levites led the people of Israel in worship of God. They were trained and skilled at doing so. They were set apart by God as professionals to carry on this activity. Music and other service for the Lord was their occupation, and they were compensated for it. Even at the rebuilding of the temple and then the walls after the Babylonian captivity, this practice was resumed:

> And at the dedication of the wall of Jerusalem they sought the Levites in all their places, to bring them to Jerusalem to celebrate the dedication with gladness, with thanksgivings and with singing, with cymbals, harps, and lyres. And the sons of the singers gathered together . . . , for the singers had built for themselves villages around Jerusalem. (Neh. 12:27–29)

> For long ago in the days of David and Asaph there were directors of the singers, and there were songs of praise and thanks-

> giving to God. And all Israel in the days of Zerubbabel and in the days of Nehemiah gave the daily portions for the singers and the gatekeepers . . . (Neh. 12:46–47a)

How completely stunning is this concept—thousands of professional singers, living in villages where they trained and rehearsed for their profession—music for the Lord! And the rest of the nation fed them and honored them for this work. Yet we tend to find it difficult to justify the hiring of even one full-time musician for our congregation. Can this be right? From the New Testament, both "the laborer deserves his wages" (Luke 10:7) and the "worthy of double honor" statements for teachers and preachers of 1 Timothy 5:17 could be applied here also, since church music is part of the teaching and preaching ministry. The musician's worship can also be his work without lessening its value.

Present-Day Application

In other words, if we were to follow the biblical model in principle, we would have more "professional" involvement in worship music. Instrumental and vocal leaders would have training, be dedicated to the Lord, be set apart for church ministry, and be appropriately compensated for their roles in leading the people. A modern application might be to have salaries for trained and skilled trumpeters, choristers, song leaders, organists, pianists, and others. These musicians would work full-time in church music. They would compose, train, teach, rehearse, and lead. The church would value and respect them. Why? The answer is that we would want the most skilled, accomplished professional Christian musicians leading us in our praise of God—because he is worthy of the best we can offer.

Does this mean that all musicians must be paid or that musicians cannot "give" their talents in sacrificial service? Not at all. Rather, it demonstrates biblical support for the concept that those whose livelihood and occupation is music, and specifically those set apart for church ministry, can and should be compensated, with full congregational support. It should correct the view that musicians must be volunteers. Does this mean that volunteer musicians should not participate in worship? No, this is not the case. A return to the medieval/Renaissance separation of priests/musicians from the congregation is not what is being advocated here. Laypersons should be involved, and all Christians must sing. Congregational song is a manifestation of the priesthood of all believers. We should not expect laypersons or amateurs to *lead* our musical worship, however, nor should we expect our trained, skilled leaders to work for nothing.

The Significance of Musical Ministry

This musical occupation, as I have discussed in other essays, is part of the preaching and teaching ministry in addition to being a ministry of praise and prayer. In 1 Chronicles 25:1 we read, "David and the chiefs of the service also set apart for the service the sons of Asaph, and of Heman, and of Jeduthun, *who prophesied with lyres, with harps, and with cymbals.*" Paul exhorted in Colossians 3:16, "Let the word of Christ dwell in you richly, *teaching and admonishing* one another in all wisdom, singing psalms and hymns and spiritual songs, with thankfulness in your hearts to God."

If we truly understood the ministry of music to have the level of significance that David and Paul attached to it, this understanding would change our attitudes and actions. It could result in changes to our staff composition, to our salary structures, and to our budgetary allocations. It would mean that all churches—yes, even small ones—would invest in the ministry of music. As musicians, we would gain a deepened perspective about the importance of preparation, the noble calling of church music, and the training of young people for service. Our churches would have more mature men (age thirty and above, cf. the Levites) leading in worship. Teaching people to sing and play instruments, writing new music, preserving musical heritage, carefully selecting music employed in worship—all of these are elements of a biblical music ministry.

Where We Are

But what is our modern-day reality? We "can't afford it." We train few musicians for church service. We do not properly compensate those who are dedicated and called to it. We hire commercial companies to write our worship songs by purchasing their products, which are geared to sell and to be current. We depend on secular community schools or private secular teachers to train our children in music (and there is nothing wrong with this training, other than that it should be available through the church). In many cases we have amateur, musically unskilled people leading our worship music. We bow at the shrine of popular culture. We endeavor to entertain, to please our constituency, to be relevant. Basically, as James Montgomery Boice often said, we "try to do the Lord's work in the world's way" instead of following biblical examples. Sometimes this methodology is even disguised as stewardship or good business practice—well intentioned, perhaps, but not biblical.

Should qualified church musicians be paid? Yes. There is no disputing this principle on biblical grounds. But first we need to define who a biblical church musician is (see chapter 17, "What Does a Biblical Music Director Look Like?"). Then we need to change our practices accordingly. So, should we hire the choir or our other musicians? Well, certainly not as mercenaries and not every member, necessarily; but when there are skilled, committed Christians whose livelihood comes from singing or musical occupation, then yes, we can find support in Scripture for compensating them—chief singers to lead the people's praise of God. We can even find this idea supported in the Reformed tradition. Martin Bucer appointed precentors—"specially decent singers"—to conduct the laity, who were for so many years untaught in the way to sing as a congregation.[1] Finally, in a similar way to ministers, church musicians need to know the Word, they need to seek to teach and proclaim it in musical forms, they need accountability to a larger body of their peers, and they need to be prepared to live lives of service in as high a calling as ever was given to man—musical leadership in the worship of God.

Note

1. Bard Thompson, *Liturgies of the Western Church* (Philadelphia: Fortress Press, 1961), 164.

17

What Does a Biblical Music Director Look Like?

Behold, I have seen a son of Jesse the Bethlehemite, who is skillful in playing, a man of valor, a man of war, prudent in speech, and a man of good presence, and the LORD is with him. —1 Samuel 16:18

The music director (also known in various congregations as the minister of music, director of music, cantor, worship pastor, chief musician, worship leader, choir director, choirmaster, song leader, etc.), whether he leads singing from the pulpit/lectern or from the organ bench, is involved in leading worship—in helping the congregation to praise God, to pray to him, and even to proclaim his Word. In the best-case scenario, what would the *ideal* music director look like? He would have a great love and understanding of the Bible, music, and people. Donald Hustad says that he should be a musician, administrator, educator, and pastor.[1] He would have Bible school or seminary-level theological education and hold earned graduate degrees in music. He might even be ordained. He would manifest rhetorical ability, administrative prowess, interpersonal skills, personal charisma, leadership qualities, and a servant's heart.

Perhaps a handful of people in the country meet all these criteria, some of whom may be Presbyterian or Reformed, and a few might be ordained. Evidently the "ultimate" music director is too rare a find to expect in most local churches. But many good possibilities should be at hand, even at that. Who are they, and from where do they come? College and seminary church-music programs are charged with the responsibility of developing such persons. We could be doing more in our churches as well. Music teachers and parents can begin training and creating opportunities for young people to garner the necessary skills and qualities. Some of these qualities and abilities are less essential, while others are vital. Let us examine some of the indispensable characteristics more carefully.

Musician

A music director needs to be a trained, skilled, professional musician. This may seem obvious enough to most people, but one might be surprised at some churches' choices for their musical worship leaders. These days it is not uncommon to find amateurs, self-taught guitarists, youth pastors, and other musically untrained persons beset with duties in music that are well beyond their capabilities and expertise. "Chenaniah, leader of the Levites in music, should direct the music, *for he understood it*" (1 Chron. 15:22). This is the biblical model.

There is no reason to believe that the music director must be a master of every musical instrument or idiom. He may not have the same level of expertise in singing as an opera singer. He may not be able to play a certain instrument as well as another member of the congregation. But he should be versatile, well informed, and exceptionally competent in one or more instruments (one of which could be voice). Vocal training, including basic training in diction, is especially important, since there are sure to be responsibilities related to choir, vocal ensembles, and soloists. Keyboard training is also very helpful. Many choir directors and other church musicians wish they had a greater level of piano proficiency when it comes time to choose new music, accompany a singer, or interview for a new position. Organ proficiency is important too.

The music director must gain and retain the respect of even the finest musicians in the congregation. Such a comprehensive musician will be well grounded in music history, theory, and performance. The ability to conduct is equally important; this skill will be employed often. Knowledge of hymnody, psalmody, and the history of worship and choral literature will also prove to be of great value. Ultimately, such a person will live the credo articulated for us by Samuel Hsu: "Every musician who names the Name of Christ has the obligation to develop his talent to the fullest and to confront the church and the world with music that is technically unashamed and spiritually indicative of his personal relationship with God."[2]

Theologian-Pastor

The Lutherans have understood the nature and role of the pastoral musician since the days of Luther himself. Some others of us seem to have missed this biblical concept. A minister of music who is not only musically trained but biblically grounded is a wonderful find. But such a person is increasingly rare. To properly lead the people of God in worship, knowledge of the Word of God and some conception of one's doctrinal tradition is essential. Along with the pastor, the music director is the guardian of the people's praise and prayer. He must ensure that sung texts are biblical and legitimate. He must make certain that the music utilized in worship matches its text and tone, and that it has substance and quality. Since he works directly with other pastoral staff, it is of great benefit to be familiar with their language and world. Of course, every Christian should be a student of the Word and a theologian at some level, musicians included.

It would not be unreasonable for chief musicians to have seminary training—particularly if more seminaries were offering music degrees and one did not have to sacrifice musical education to attend. But this is rarely the case. Why education of such importance to the church is not occurring in more seminaries is a mystery and a great tragedy. After training pastors to preach and teach and scholars to write and expound on Scripture, what could possibly be a higher mission for these schools? Martin Luther, who said, "Next to the Word of God, music deserves the highest praise,"[3] and "We shouldn't ordain young men to the ministry unless they be well schooled in music,"[4] would not be pleased with the present scenario. Neither musical education for pastors nor theological education for musicians is sufficient in most seminaries or music graduate schools.

The music director should also have a pastor's heart. In many ways he is a shepherd to the congregation, but especially to the choir and to the individual musicians working alongside him. Music will minister to individuals, particularly those who are sick or terminally ill, in ways in which other types of ministry simply will not. On occasion the music director will meet with these people to encourage them or to participate in planning funeral/memorial services. Although not a counselor per se (although one could receive such training), the music pastor will regularly deal with both professional and volunteer musicians and their stage egos, inferiority complexes, and performance-related maladies. He should strive to help all musicians under his care understand the nature and value of their contribution. He must be confident in his ability and yet teachable; not easily manipulated, but flexible. He is likely to be a target for criticism from all sides, and in the same day will offer music that one member of the congregation appreciates and another despises. He needs to be a man of prayer.

Administrator

Administrative skills are never lost on a music director. These skills will be needed for service and rehearsal planning (which are each worlds of their own), concerts (including all the logistics of time, facilities, instruments, programming, advertising, contracting, printed materials, and so forth), selecting and ordering repertoire, preparing budgets, communicating with the congregation and leadership, organizing volunteers, preparing musician/accompanist schedules, and any number of other sundry duties. Less essential but helpful skills include computer literacy, typing ability, the facility to speed-read, the ability to write well, and the power to recruit. Music-related skills such as transposition, orchestration, score reduction, score-reading, basic composition, arranging, knowledge of music notation/computer software, piano-tuning, and other related abilities are often put to use and serve a music director in good stead. Personnel and ensemble management, particularly in larger churches, is another duty that comes with the territory. As in any other pastoral role, there are many interpersonal relationships for the music director to nurture (too numerous to list here but encompassing the sphere of pastoral staff, administrative/secretarial staff, other musicians, board members, sound engineers, choirs, congregation, vendors, and visitors).

Teacher

The music director should enjoy teaching and should be skilled at it. Rehearsing a choir requires one to be a musician, pastor, teacher, comedian, and disciplinarian all at once (but not necessarily in that order). Music directors can and should act as mentors to younger musicians, as introducers of new songs and musical information to church members, and possibly as music teachers for children. As with any other teacher, a love of the subject matter, a desire to pass it on, and the skills to do so engagingly are essential to success. The music director may directly or indirectly tutor pastoral staff in musical matters (tactfully and appropriately, of course). Articles written for the benefit of the congregation, synopses of hymns, and even Sunday-school classes on hymnody/psalmody may very well be part of the chief musician's opportunity to raise the musical standards and awareness of a congregation. Public-speaking skills and poise are requisite, but they can be developed and are not always present in a potentially fine musical leader. Energy, joy, the gift of encouragement, high standards, a quest for excellence—all these are necessary, too.

Basing a list of requirements for God's musician on the qualifications of David in 1 Samuel 16:18, Hsu writes: "He is skilled; . . . he has a good character; . . . he has a commanding presence; . . . and most importantly, he is spiritual."[5] Does this set of biblical qualifications coupled with the criteria listed above sound easy to find in one person? Of course not, and every candidate is human, totally depraved, saved by grace alone, and in need of help. So whether you are looking for a music director, you yourself are a music director, or you aspire to be a music director, do not despair. The Spirit of God will provide, sanctify, and lead in the path God has for us. We have to lean on him rather than laboring in our own strength; but, of course, we must labor.

"Where Do You Find Such a Person?"

This is a difficult question to answer. Reformed seminaries are not producing music directors, though some are training "worship pastors." There are musicians who choose to attend seminary, but many of them have a call to pastoral ministry outside of music. This is wonderful, but means, with few exceptions, that they are probably not going to be active as musicians. We cannot have too many ministers with musical training, however, so there is no room for complaint on this particular front. On the other hand, many musicians have insufficient theological education to fulfill their responsibilities thoroughly. In these cases it is especially helpful to have pastors willing to work closely with them.

The Baptist seminaries and independent Bible colleges are training church musicians, and have been for years, predominantly for service in churches of a congregational nature. They must be given credit for actually doing something, and the required coursework in theology/Bible is an excellent beginning. In this author's estimation, the focus on "worship techniques" in such schools (with credit-level coursework in clowning, puppetry, mime, dance, play- and scene-writing, drama teams, contemporary worship ensembles, and such graduate-level required courses as "Leadership in Contemporary Expressions of Corporate Worship" and "Producing and Staging Church Drama") indicates an attempt to equip musical leaders with what is "currently out there" in evangelical churches. Unfortunately, it also seems to exhibit a degree of willingness to compromise musical excellence to accommodate the relativism of the postmodern church. One wonders how much stronger the graduates of these programs could be if hours spent on such courses were instead allotted to a deeper study of great music, history, and liturgy. But all institutions feel the pressing need to find prospective students (and to graduate them "employable"), and this factor wins out over a commitment to change the musical landscape for the better.

The Lutheran schools are producing church musicians, as they have been for years. Yet most of these will not desire to serve in congregations where they are not valued, and not all of these graduates have a solid, conservative theological grounding, either. Secular music schools and conservatories produce some very fine musicians, of which a few will have had undergraduate biblical training or at least a good knowledge of the Scriptures from their upbringing. Schools that were founded to produce musical leaders for the church, such as Westminster Choir College, while still being fine music schools, are now dark places indeed when it comes to matters of true Christian faith, although there are exceptions to this generalization on the faculties. Basically, there is no graduate school or seminary where a Reformed young person can study both music and theology at the highest possible level, without having to compromise. In short, we need to pray for these people, and we need to be actively involved in shaping more of them in our churches, schools, and places of higher learning.

One suggestion, if you are searching for a potential musical leader, is to contact heads of music departments in Bible colleges and Christian liberal-arts schools. Then bring a good prospect to your church and help that person continue to grow—by financing some seminary or graduate-school education and by providing both time to practice and some form of accountability. In churches where a fine musician is present, interns can be brought on (even quite economically) who can both assist the music program and apprentice their craft. In fact, every mature music director should be systematically doing this for younger people to some extent. What better training ground could there be for the next generation of church-music leaders than to work alongside an experienced person in the field? You can also support and send students to a graduate-level school of church music.

A Vision for the Future

Someday, by God's grace, we may establish a thriving music graduate school, at long last, for the Presbyterian, Reformed, and other churches that still desire biblical musicians or are awakening to such a need. A program or institution of this nature is sorely needed. Ideally, it would be born into an existing conservative seminary. Perhaps that concept is too grand, but one would hope not. In such a place, the next generation of pastors and the next generation of pastoral musicians would train side by side. They would meet and dialogue with each other. When their career work began, they could go out in teams, or at least would know whom to contact when a position was available. In such a school, all musicians would take a core set of theology/Bible courses, and M.A.R./M.Div./D.Min. students would take music-related courses, such as basic music appreciation, hymnology, history of Christian worship, and so forth. A historical, classical approach to musical curriculum would be essential both for its inherent value and for its ability to equip church musicians and pastors to navigate and influence music of the present day.

Music graduates of such programs (and other existing music graduate schools or conservatories) should be able to undertake a specialized qualifying process akin to ordination within their denominations that would help to verify musical/biblical learning, the call of God to ministry, and their readiness for it. This would be of the same nature as ordination for pastors to the ministry, except that some of the qualifications, prerequisites, and areas of knowledge would be different. Why do our evangelical and Reformed denominations not have such a process? Clearly, the reason is that the role, or what J. S. Bach and others have considered an "office," of the pastoral musician (and what surely could be termed a "calling") is not regarded either as real or as important enough to warrant such a process. How different things would be if we followed the Bible's portrayal of the roles of music and musicians instead of allowing our practices to be determined by the failings of tradition, popular whim, and modern trend. Let us join together in praying and working to this end.

Notes

1. Donald P. Hustad, *Jubilate II: Church Music in Worship and Renewal* (Carol Stream, IL: Hope, 1993), 80ff.

2. Samuel Hsu, "Sacred Music," in *Toward a Harmony of Faith and Learning: Essays on Bible College Curriculum*, ed. Kenneth O. Gangel (Farmington Hills, MI: William Tyndale College Press, 1983), 144.

3. Martin Luther, "Preface to Georg Rhau's *Symphoniae iucundae*," in *Liturgy and Hymns*, ed. Ulrich S. Leupold, vol. 53 of *Luther's Works*, ed. Helmut T. Lehmann (Philadelphia: Fortress Press, 1965), 323.

4. Martin Luther, *Table Talk*, German ed. (Irmischer) 62, no. 2848 (Erlangen: Verlag von Hender & Zimmer, 1854): 308ff. See also Ewald M. Plass, *What Luther Says* (St. Louis: Concordia, 1959), 980.

5. Hsu, "Sacred Music," 138.

18
Teaching Children Music at Church

From the lips of children and infants
you have ordained praise . . . —*Psalm 8:2a* NIV

According to Scripture, music serves as a visible expression of the Christian faith for every person. It is indispensable to worship and should be a daily part of one's spiritual life. How many people, though, feel entirely incompetent as musicians? Many think that musical training is only for the elite few, the talented. But this thinking is flawed. A lack of confidence and competence in music is usually the consequence of poor musical instruction or environment rather than a genuine lack of ability. Music education theorists tell us that "music aptitude is normally distributed among children at birth."[1] This means that God has endowed every person with at least some potential to be musical. Such thinking may seem revolutionary to us, but it is undoubtedly not so to God, since we are commanded by him to sing his praises. Singing is a *known* eternal activity and one that is clearly mandated in Scripture.

The church actually used to be the center of musical education, but this responsibility was handed over to the state decades ago. Sadly, more and more we are witnessing the removal of music from the core of American education. Where does this leave the church now that most public education has made music an extracurricular subject? If the church does not teach the children of God to sing, who will? If the children of God do not have something to sing about, then one might well ask, "Who does?" When we abdicate this responsibility, we forfeit our right and duty to teach to covenant children the songs of the people of God. What songs will be learned instead?

Research tells us that a child's musical aptitude (or potential for making music) is in flux until he or she is approximately nine years of age. Before that, a child's musical environment has a significant effect on this aptitude. This means that children's music-making potential can either be increased by solid music teaching and environment or be lowered by an instructional or environmental deficiency. Another crucial revelation of current research is that early instruction has a measurable result on a child's aptitude. In other words, we need to reach children early in life in order to effectively increase their musical potential. One reason for the music crisis in American worship is that neither our church-music heritage nor music itself has been properly learned or valued from childhood. Most of our parents could not teach us because they did not learn it either. If we are to encourage a modern reformation in worship and Christian living, we must begin by reaching and teaching the next generation of church leaders—the children.

Encouraging our young people in the use and development of their musical abilities is a task that can and should be shared by many in the church community. As one would expect, parents have the pivotal role in providing their children with opportunities both to make and to listen to music. The joy and learning that occur when families make music together should not be downplayed. Additionally, older, trained musicians should invest in these younger people by providing instruction tailored to the needs of children. The bottom line is this: our churches and Sunday schools need to be involved in teaching singing and basic musical proficiency. Through such efforts, children can and should learn melody, rhythm, music appreciation, hymnody, biblical truth, teamwork, discipline, abstract thinking, and proper singing technique.

Martin Luther had young people in mind when he wrote new church music. In fact, he claimed that this was the primary impetus for his work in hymnody:

> Therefore, I too, with the help of others, have brought together some sacred songs . . . And these songs were arranged in four parts for no other reason than that I wanted to attract the youth (who should and must be trained in music and other fine arts) away from love songs and carnal pieces and to give them something wholesome to learn instead . . . It is unfortunate that everyone else forgets to teach and train the poor young people; we must not be responsible for this too.[2]

Luther also specifically addressed the need to have the musical education of children in the schools when he wrote in "To the Councilmen of All Cities in Germany That They Establish and Maintain Christian Schools" (1524): "For my part, if I had children and could manage it, I would have them study not only languages and history, but also singing and music . . . The ancient Greeks trained their children in these disciplines; yet they grew up to be people of wondrous ability, subsequently fit for everything."[3]

With these thoughts as a context, the Music Committee, Family Life Commission, and Session of Tenth Presbyterian Church set out in 2003 to make a difference in the lives of children in our congregation. It was overdue. Other churches in the nation have invested in similar efforts for years, and it will be increasingly important for other assemblies to do the same. The Tenth *Schola Cantorum* began in September 2003 with the goal of offering our children the quality musical education they need and deserve. We hope to equip them with the musical knowledge and abilities necessary to participate in lifelong musical worship. Our hope and aim is that they will become musically literate, capable performers who will benefit from the ability to fully participate in musical aspects of the church and the world beyond.

The following excerpts from an article published in the Tenth Presbyterian Church bulletin on June 8, 2003, give more information on the background, need, and purpose of this program.

> From the Middle Ages the Church was the center of musical, religious and even general education. Churches had schools of singing called *schola cantorum* in which the music of the church was learned by young choirboys and men. In the twentieth century the Church's role in the education of children was greatly reduced, and the public or private school today that provides meaningful musical education for children is a rarity.
>
> Singing is one of the few known eternal activities (Isa. 6; Rev. 4–5). We must reclaim the right and responsibility to teach young Christians "to sing and to make music for the Lord." Parents, it is incumbent upon you to help us in this regard. A child's musical aptitude is formed fully by the age of nine years, so it is important to reach children early in life. The benefits of music in learning development, memory, abstract thought, math and so forth are well documented, but aside from such benefits, the primary advantage is musical literacy. Yet the Church in recent decades largely has ignored this important opportunity to train children.
>
> Therefore we have decided to introduce a comprehensive church music education program for the purpose of developing musical literacy in children ages 3–12, focusing on the ability to sing. Inherent in such a program will be a biblical view of music in worship, an historical perspective as it relates to church music, and a dynamic application of musical skills through choral ensembles. Learning nine hymns annually (one each month of the school year, September–May) will be a fantastic complement to the Scripture memory program in place in the Bible School.
>
> The objectives[4] of the *Tenth Schola Cantorum* are:

- To develop the children's musical literacy (defined at the highest level as the ability to vocally perform unfamiliar music from notation with tonal and rhythmic accuracy combined with appropriate musical expression) for the purpose of participating in individual and corporate worship through music.
- To develop the children's singing voices through training in correct vocal production and to increase their enjoyment of music through all aspects of the program.
- To develop the children's understanding of and appreciation for the roles of music in worship and worship itself as taught in Scripture.
- To deepen the children's comprehension and love of hymnody.
- To deepen the children's knowledge of Scripture and the Lord Jesus Christ through the texts of the songs that constitute the program curriculum.

Children will be involved in tonal and rhythm classes (with many activities) and in choir, with a snack break included. There is no fee to any child or family. Parents will complete a registration form for each child, and the child's regular attendance is necessary. The staff will be comprised of professional music educators who are members of the church, assisted by others, under the authority of the Music Director and the Family Life Commission.

This may mean a change of current Sunday schedules and considerable effort for many parents, but we sincerely hope that such an important opportunity for your children will be viewed favorably. It will take commitment, but the rewards (spiritual, musical, social and intellectual) will be great. s.D.g.

As implied earlier and stated in the quoted document above, parents shoulder a great responsibility for the musical education of their children. In addition to providing musical experiences in the home, parents can assist in other specific areas. If a child senses his or her parents' support and enthusiasm, he or she will be encouraged to respond in kind. Not only will this help to prevent sporadic attendance or lack of interest on the part of the children, but it will also advance their musical progress. This personal investment serves to create an environment that is conducive to true learning. Music is more than an academic subject, of course. It is experiential, creative, and intuitive. The process of learning music can and should be fun. Parental attitude and communication strongly influence a child's perception of music's value and his or her receptivity to it.

In the Tenth *Schola Cantorum*, the children are divided into groups by age. Although the case could be made to divide by gender or musical level, for various reasons we have chosen to begin in this way. Each group rotates in a schedule that affords them instruction focusing either on melody or on rhythm in addition to weekly choir rehearsal. While there are many dimensions to be studied in music, these are the two most important when addressing musical aptitude. The two 25-minute classes specifically address tonality and rhythm. They include various developmentally appropriate activities that serve as a means of maintaining a high level of interest and keeping students "on task." In between the classes and choir rehearsal, we include time for the children to have snacks and focus on hymnody.

Under the leadership of our senior minister and music director, we have compiled small "hymnbooks" for each year that contain the nine hymns of the month for September through May (including a Christmas hymn for December, a hymn for Lent/Easter, and a selection from *Hymns for a Modern Reformation*—our congregation's own legacy vis-à-vis James Montgomery Boice—among others). A written historical and musical introduction to each hymn precedes its appearance in the booklets. We also include a CD with piano accompaniments of the nine hymns (all stanzas) so that the children can practice and regularly sing the hymns at home or in the automobile with their families. The children are asked to memorize these hymns, and they sing them in small groups together. First- and second-graders still learning to read are asked to memorize just the first two stanzas. Year-end incentives are given to encourage this activity.

Time will tell how successful our particular approach and curriculum will be. One thing, though, is certain: few activities in which a church musician can be involved have greater value than educating children so that they can better worship God. *Schola Cantorum* provides training that will help these young people throughout their lives, and the initial investment by parents and teachers will reap an exponentially greater return. It is our hope and intention that both children and their parents will begin to thoroughly enjoy and understand the process of making music, to the ultimate glory of God. This has repercussions that will echo throughout their earthly sojourn, and even into eternity, as we worship the Lord with song. For when we sing to the Lord, we join an activity already in progress—and one that does not end. Let me encourage you as a reader to consider what might be done in your church to develop musical learning in a spiritual environment for the covenant children with whom you have been entrusted.

I will sing of the steadfast love of the LORD, forever; with my mouth I will make known your faithfulness to all generations. —*Psalm 89:1*

Notes

1. See Edwin E. Gordon, *Learning Sequences in Music: Skill, Content and Patterns* (Chicago: GIA Publications, Inc., 1997), 9. Such norms assume that 68 percent of the population will have "average" musical potential and that 16 percent will be above and below that average, respectively.

2. Martin Luther, from the foreword to the first edition of Johann Walter's hymnal, the *Wittenberg Geistliche Gesangbüchlein* (1524), in *Liturgy and Hymns*, ed. Ulrich S. Leupold, vol. 53 of *Luther's Works*, ed. Helmut T. Lehmann (Philadelphia: Fortress Press, 1965), 315–16.

3. Martin Luther, "To the Councilmen of All Cities in Germany That They Establish and Maintain Christian Schools" (1524), in *Luther's Works* 45:369–70, as quoted in Carl Schalk, *Luther on Music: Paradigms of Praise* (St. Louis: Concordia, 1988), 16.

4. *Schola Cantorum* goals were developed in consultation with Kristyn Kuhlman, Ph.D., a professional music educator. The curriculum is based on Edwin Gordon's Music Learning Theory.

19

Music in the Small Church: Where Do We Go from Here?

It is good to give thanks to the LORD,
to sing praises to your name, O Most High . . . —*Psalm 92:1*

Some reading this book may believe that the ideas expressed in it apply only to large churches, or at least primarily so. This is not the case. Biblical principles apply to all churches irrespective of cultural, social, or economic context. But while the extrabiblical concepts suggested herein may vary in application, they are the product of multiple church experiences and personal reflection, and they apply to the small church with equal strength.

Small churches share common problems with larger churches, but they have issues specific to them as well. Small churches typically have fewer human and fiscal resources on which to draw. While the congregation may have the advantage of being small enough to enjoy close fellowship, it may also face the risk that everyone knows and has an opinion about everyone else's personal life. Sometimes because the giving base is smaller, undue weight or power is given to a wealthy member's wishes or opinion. Grudges are held and politics occur, unfortunately, in every size of assembly, but they tend to be amplified in the small church because of the proximity of parishioners. Personality conflicts and trouble stemming from issues of personal taste are more readily apparent. Likewise, change is difficult for any congregation, but perhaps it is more noticeable in small churches. For example, when an adequate (or somewhat less-than-adequate) musician has played or sung in a church over many years (and is likely to have been very faithful in doing so), but the desire exists for more than this person can provide, change can prove to be a real challenge.

Change is regularly accompanied by difficulty. But if a church body is following Scripture and acting in love, much good can be accomplished with little trauma or none at all. And when it comes to the quality of the music in a church, no one should expect instant change or growth. Patience, education, persistence, and commitment are all requisite. In an effort to help those who find themselves in small churches and who desire to better their music ministry, what follows are several scenarios that represent common challenges. In each case, we consider some basic steps to help move forward.

Scenario 1: "Seeking a Part-Time Organist/Choir Director"

Ethel, who had dutifully taken her volunteer place at the organ bench for more than twenty years, has just retired or expired. The church has a decent organ but no one to play it. There may be a pianist, but for this pianist (like many others) the organ pedal board and stop list are frightening mysteries. The pastor or church board wants to get help right away but has no idea where to search, whom to call, what to pay, or how to determine whether or not a person is qualified. What does one do?

1. *Form a committee.* You need more than one person making this kind of decision for a church. Pastors should not single-handedly choose musical leaders for the church. It would be best to have *at least* one

elder/church leader, a couple of educated musicians, one businessperson, and one choir member on this committee. These should be people committed to the task and to prayer. Each member should have specific areas of responsibility to the group. Begin and end each meeting with prayer with everyone participating. It is difficult to sustain grudges or criticism against others when you are genuinely praying with them. Often in small churches, one man or woman in the congregation has taken a special interest in the music program (or has had control of it) for years. While this person may have a lot to offer, he or she should not single-handedly determine the music personnel or style for the church on the basis of his or her own tastes or moneys. Knowledge, of course, should be valued.

2. *Take stock of what you have.* You need to gather information to have at your disposal when talking to potential candidates, or to give to those who may be able to provide you with names, and also to accomplish appropriate advertising:

- Organ, piano, keyboard: What make of organ do you have? How many manuals? How old is it? Does it have a full pedal board? Does it work? If it is a pipe instrument, how many ranks? What size, model, and make of piano? Is it in good condition?
- Potential salary, music budget (for music purchase, tunings/repair, honoraria, etc.) : How much can you afford to pay? Be generous—church musicians are seldom, if ever, overpaid. What room for growth is there? Is the music budget sufficient to purchase new music and other essential tools for the church musician? How many weeks' vacation are included? (Provide at least three or four.) Is there financial provision for a substitute organist as needed?
- Number of choir members, length of current choir rehearsal, current rehearsal time: Is there room for flexibility in this schedule? (For example, if the rehearsal has been only an hour long, can it be longer? Can the choir meet at another time if that is

better for the new leader?) Will the new musician be responsible for other groups or duties?

- Philosophy/theology of music: Do you have one? If not, do some reading and study to write or adopt one. Be sure that the leaders of the church understand and subscribe to it, and make it available to the congregation. Do not assume that you have musical understanding if you have little or no training. Leave room for the knowledgeable musician you are seeking to hire to move around and work. Also, ask the candidate to describe his or her philosophy/theology of music.
- Job description: Do you have one? If not, write one. A pastor and an educated musician working together should write the primary draft, and then have the document reviewed by the committee. What should it include? A good music job description will include the church name and address, a brief theological statement or position (include a statement that personal faith in Christ is necessary, etc.), a brief statement of purpose for the music ministry, the title of the position, a list of responsibilities, a potential salary range (approximate), vacation information, special services other than regular weekly events, whom to contact, whether or not you want résumés and/or references sent in and to whom, and the date by which you hope to have someone in place. Include audition and interview information as available.

3. *Advertise the position.* Advertising can be done by word of mouth, e-mail, church bulletin announcement, community announcement, newspapers, Christian magazines, Christian music service groups, music departments in colleges and universities, and calls to resource people, such as other music directors/organists in the area, chairs of academic music departments, or local performing organizations, guilds, or societies.

4. *Interview and audition candidates.* Do both. It is always a good idea to hear a church musician "do what they do" before making a decision.

Paper and personal presentations are not enough. Provide undisturbed time for candidates to familiarize themselves with your instruments before auditioning them, especially organists. The audition could consist of a couple of contrasting prepared pieces of music (perhaps a prelude and a postlude), a prepared congregational hymn, and then the spontaneous playing of a hymn or two from the church's hymnal, requested on the spot with the committee singing along. Remember that the capacity to lead the congregation in song is the most important part of the musician's job. That combination of items should take about thirty minutes and should give the committee a good idea of the candidate's musical ability. It is just as important to hear candidates speak about their faith, their philosophy of music ministry, their goals/desires for the position in your church, and any variances, requests, or needs they have.

Be open to the possibility that the job as you describe it in ideal terms may be capably handled by someone who may be deficient in one area but who has a strength you had not anticipated. For example, you may want a music director who is a fine pianist but you interview someone who is a great singer/conductor. Perhaps his wife or her husband is a fine pianist or you could engage someone else from the community as a pianist—do not be closed to the possibility that the Lord may have something better for you than you had planned.

5. *Have a written contract and a review period.* It is important for both the individual and the church to have a written understanding with each other. Such a document should include details of responsibilities, remuneration, benefits, vacation, conflict resolution, resignation/termination notice, review period, to whom the employee reports, and any other pertinent details. Both parties should sign and date the document. Too often, problems arise when one or both parties have a varying perception about expectations that could have been solved by having detail in print. A written contract will not cover every possible problem, but it should at least provide a framework that can aid in conflict resolution. A three-month or six-month review is a good opportunity for either party to voice concern about or to affirm the decision. Three months is not a

long enough time for a musician to truly build anything new, but a short review period can provide a graceful "way out" for either party. Rarely should this be necessary, though, because the process by which the musician was brought to the church should have ensured competence and the true calling of God.

Scenario 2: "In Need of a Full-Time Musician"

Small churches often do not have the budget to hire a full-time church musician right away. Others should do so but have their priorities elsewhere. But at least by the time a church has grown to between two hundred and three hundred people, it should have a full-time music director. While the trend in churches may be to hire a youth pastor, an administrator, or some other position first, the biblical emphasis on worship of God as a primary activity of the church should cause us to invest in musical leadership as a priority.

The steps to take in finding the appropriate person are similar to those taken to find the part-time musician. A greater emphasis, however, should be placed on wider searches (and being prepared to relocate the right person). Candidates can be found by talking to music department heads in Bible colleges and Christian universities and by contacting music directors of well-known churches of like mind and doctrine. Ideally, seminaries should be places in which to find these musical leaders, but unfortunately very few are making an effort in the field of church-music education. (For a fuller discussion of what to look for in a full-time music director, see chapter 17, "What Does a Biblical Music Director Look Like?")

Scenario 3: "We Don't Have Any Hymnals"

While this is a shame, it is the unfortunate truth in many churches, large and small. The church may have begun as a very small group, in a gymnasium or local school, with little money. At that time, an overhead or bulletin insert with a CCLI license was more expedient and cost-effective than moving books around or purchasing them. Now the congregation has grown or even built its own building and has been used to functioning without hymnbooks. Or perhaps the church had hymnals and, rather than replacing outdated or worn books, decided to buy the latest technology and flash words up as each stanza goes by. One problem with this is that worshipers do not have music in their hands to read—and yes, some people can still read music. Moreover, one cannot *learn* to read music without having occasion to do so. The church used to be a center of musical training and experience, and it should be once again. Please use printed music.

If you want to have a credible music program and a church where people are learning doctrine and apprehending the truth of their faith as they sing, purchase and use hymnals. Arguments that written music gets in the way of worship and hymns require too much thought are easily answered. Holding a hymnal in your hand and singing its words in your own language is one of the great gifts of the Reformation to the evangelical church. It is our heritage and privilege. The leadership of the church must first understand this value and then communicate it. Hymns are among the greatest devotional literature we have. Would it not be helpful for every Christian to own at least one hymnal and make regular use of it? Since hymns require more thought than simple choruses, they should be read, sung, and contemplated at home, in Sunday-school classes, and in Bible studies.

If the church budget has no money for hymnals, ask individuals and families to sponsor the purchase of one or more. For the price of a couple of fast-food meals or trips to the movie theater, a young person could contribute one hymnal for his or her congregation. Families could take it on as a "project" and have a yard sale or give up some regular nonessential indulgence for a time in order to do this. Such activities provide a sense of ownership and communal effort. Sacrificing for something worthwhile is an experience in which many of us (and particularly young people) have participated less and less. Those of an older generation in your congregation would probably so love to sing great hymns again that they would gladly help supply the funding.

Scenario 4: "We Have Only a Lousy Piano and a Trombone Player"

Some churches find themselves with instruments in disrepair or without any at all. Sometimes there are individuals willing to share their musical gifts, but they are imposed on too frequently (or impose themselves on the congregation too frequently). Some churches start with a simple electronic keyboard as an affordable way to supply music for the church initially. It probably has an organ sound on it, piano, and even jazz marimba. That is fine as a start if it is all a group can afford, but it is no place to remain for a long time.

The Lord never asks us for more than we have unless he will supply the need. We are called to offer our best. For most churches willing to work at it, "best" can constantly get better. It does not do for the Lord to be offered praise accompanied by an inferior instrument while members of the congregation drive around in luxury cars, eat at expensive restaurants, and take lavish vacations (though there is nothing inherently wrong with those activities). Even if the congregation is quite poor, it can seek to better its worship conditions. If you have only an "old clunker" of a piano, use it. But have it tuned and repaired, and start a fund to get a better one. Make the need known in the church and community. Often an older couple scaling down to a smaller house, or someone with a piano that was used by now-grown children, is willing to donate that instrument to a church in need. Donors and donations, however, should never dictate conditions to the church (such as placement, color, use, etc.). Not all would-be donations are helpful.

If you have a good trombone player or a fine flutist or an excellent guitarist, use them. But there is no requirement for them to play on every stanza of every song at every service every week. As humans, we require some variety and change in our diets—physical and musical—to say nothing of the interpretation of text. Furthermore, if the instrumentalist is not well trained, he or she should seek better training and practice, and "sit out" for a while. There is no call for poor playing to be part of worship just because a person *likes* to play. Poor playing will draw attention to itself and away from the text (ultimately, away from God) and will distract others. Surely no one would want such a charge laid on him or her. Occasionally someone's mother or grandfather or friend will simply have to be told by a pastor or musician that little Johnny or Great Aunt Lola has gifts that can and should be used in a ministry other than music. Such difficult tasks need to be handled with grace, love, and prayer, and with service-opportunity alternatives, but they must be accomplished.

Conclusion

Small churches will find themselves in any number of possible situations other than those mentioned above. The important thing is for churches (and their leaders) to be looking to Scripture for real insight into how they should function rather than operating on the basis of perceived norms. For too long we have neglected biblical principles of music and worship and have taken our cues from "the way it's done" elsewhere. Will this change be easy? Will it be received everywhere with open arms? Will it be cheap and quick? Obviously, the answer to all those questions is no. Is a switch to biblical music-making necessary and right? Will it be received by thinking Christians who are educated along in the process? Will God provide for our needs as we trust him and help us accomplish things in his time and strength? The answer to those questions is, without doubt, in the affirmative.

20

So You Want a Better Organ

The house that I am to build will be great, for our God is greater than all gods. But who is able to build him a house, since heaven, even highest heaven, cannot contain him? —2 Chronicles 2:5–6

I have been music director in several churches where those involved with the music ministry, and eventually the church at large, felt it was time to replace their organ with a better one for the worship of our great God. Not every church will find itself in this situation, but enough do that a practical discussion about how to approach the task seems warranted. This will not be a definitive discourse on every detail in the process, but it outlines at least the basic steps and general concepts involved.

The Organ and the Church

The pipe organ has been the primary instrument of the church since the Middle Ages. It has the capacity to lead with great volume and in the next moment to play so quietly that a holy hush fills the room. The organist, a solitary player, has at his or her disposal the sounds of many orchestral instruments—flutes, strings, reeds (e.g., oboe, bassoon, horn, trumpet)—and mutation stops (mixtures) that add color. Various pipe lengths determine range, and couplers move sounds from one keyboard to another and add octaves above or below. Called "the king of instruments," the pipe organ had been associated with the evangelical church in positive and powerful ways right up until the last three decades of the twentieth century.

It was mid–twentieth century when the little home pump organs were traded in for living-room-model electronic organs such as the Hammond and the Wurlitzer. Then, as church sanctuaries became more and more like modern carpeted American living rooms and less like the stone-and-steeple churches and cathedrals of Europe, the living-room organ entered the church, replacing the pipe instrument. This switch demonstrated a seemingly good stewardship of fiscal resources (that is to say, the newer instruments were inexpensive and required low maintenance). Electronic specialists designed solid-state analogue and eventually digital organs to mimic pipe instruments. Nowadays these are "sampled" from actual pipe instruments so that the sound of the pipes exists without the maintenance and fluctuation that accompany a pipe instrument. Because of the money to be saved, church after church has purchased these instruments instead of pipes. In the last couple of decades, the ongoing "innovations" of our time have replaced the digital organs (as well as pianos) in many churches with synthesizers and other MIDI-compatible keyboards. None of this speaks ultimately to quality, of course, but it does fit the American pocketbook and mind-set of economy and immediacy.

Today those churches still desirous of "traditional" services and great hymnody find that their twenty- to thirty-year-old electronic instruments are inferior to modern technology. As with toasters and computers, electronic organs wear down and better products are constantly being developed. Interestingly, the pipe organ has never gone "out of date," nor will it, though it does require maintenance. Unfortunately, however, the vast majority of the public, evangelicals included, associates pipe organs only with weddings or funerals—and Catholic ones at that (this being the only occasion wherein many experience a solemn service or a traditional sanctuary). There are few forums in which the general populace can hear daily pipe-organ performances in a public setting as they still do in Philadelphia's downtown Lord & Taylor department store on the famous "Wanamaker" organ.

As Christians come into contact with a great instrument played by a master musician, however, the case for "real" organ music is quickly made. Singing a majestic hymn such as "A Mighty Fortress Is Our God" or "Holy, Holy, Holy!" to the accompaniment of a pipe organ can be a tremendously moving experience. These do not have to be sung with organ, of course, nor will any argument make the organ essential. But anyone who has experienced a great instrument well played or who has compared real to fake will not need much more convincing. Education will bolster appreciation of the organ's grandeur, color, and purpose in the same way that a fine painting "speaks" for itself, but the instrument is enjoyed even more when the viewer knows something of its origin, style, or artist. The pipe organ and its music reach out to the one who listens with an "open" or educated ear. More and more we are seeing a musical renaissance within segments of the church. This occurs when Christians get in touch with their roots and want to experience their rich Reformation heritage. Artistic church music and great hymnody are part of this reawakening, and the organ has a symbiotic relationship with these as well.

What to Do?

So you want a better organ. Maybe this will be a pipe instrument; maybe it will be digital; maybe it will be a hybrid. Where does one begin? Let it be said, and not glibly, that prayer is both a good start and a constant companion throughout this process.

Committee

First, you need an intelligent, committed committee. This is going to be a lengthy process (at least months, if not years), and members must be prepared for that. The music director, the organist, a choir member, a supportive layperson, someone with business sense, a "detail person," and someone from the ruling body of the church (elder, deacon, etc.) would constitute a good committee. One or more of these positions or roles may overlap. The support of the minister(s) is also crucial. Perhaps a minister could serve on the committee, but at the least ministers should be given reading information and meeting minutes to keep them informed and involved.

All committee members should read basic information about organs so that they are versed in the differences between a rank, a manual, and a note, as well as those between tracker, electro-pneumatic, and slider actions (if a pipe instrument is being considered). The organist or another member could compile this information and distribute it at an initial meeting. Committee members should be versed in the differences between digital, hybrid, and pipe instruments, both for decision-making and so that they can intelligently answer the sure-to-be-coming questions of the congregation. At the first meeting, whoever is serving as chair should present a timeline outlining when members will be expected to have digested the material and to have accomplished certain tasks. A printed agenda for meetings of this nature is a must, as is a chair who will keep things on track.

Consultant

Next, particularly if you want a pipe organ, you will benefit from engaging an organ consultant. This person's role is that of an independent representative on the church's behalf. He or she will deal as an intermediary with the organ company that is eventually chosen, and will help sort out details, errors, and adjustments as needed. The consultant will make recommendations and take your decisions to the builder. If the church has an organist who is knowledgeable about organ construction and design, he or she can serve in this capacity, but there is also merit to having outside assistance. Inquire of organists at churches with major pipe instruments who acted as a consultant for them. If you are installing a digital instrument, it is still helpful to have a consultant, particularly if you do not have an organist experienced in organ design.

Companies

Write to several prospective companies that the committee/consultant feels might be candidates for building your instrument.

Consider the longevity of the company, its location, its service reputation and representatives, its style (some organs are better solo instruments than accompanying instruments—a German Baroque instrument will be considerably different from a French Romantic one, etc.), the company's voicing staff, and so forth. Timing may be an issue as well. Some companies may be backlogged and require three years or more to build your pipe instrument. Others might turn it around in 18 or 24 months. A digital builder may have an instrument in stock perfectly suited to your needs, or may be building one on a schedule that would enable you to acquire it when you are ready. Request information and set up meetings with organ-company representatives. They will want to see your church, take pictures, and ask questions about your hopes and plans for the instrument, in order to acquire the information necessary for them to make a formal proposal. Do not feel any need to rush. Determining the best organ for a church is not something that one does often, but it must be done well—like finding a spouse.

Congregation

After you have learned much as a committee (through reading, through your consultant, and through various representatives) and have made some preliminary decisions, you should communicate with the congregation. The congregation needs a vision for what would best benefit the church, a basic plan of attack, and a ballpark figure of the costs and timeline involved. If you need congregational approval (and this is normally the case), education, information, and communication are key. This requires that the committee and consultant have worked through these various aspects. Be prepared to justify the expense and the need with thoughtful and thorough rationale that can be disseminated in advance of a congregational meeting. Arguments about whether the money would be better spent on missions, paint, a new gym, an elevator, or better office furniture are likely to arise. Do not be surprised or alarmed, but be prepared and be reasonable.

Selection

The organ companies will present proposals, and then the process of selection, bargaining, and determining what is essential and nonessential will begin. Be sure to have the input of master organists in your city, particularly if your organist is not a design/construction expert. Your consultant will be of great help, but he or she should be open to a second and third opinion at least to raise questions, share experience, or catch something that might have been missed. Fine organists are usually excited about a prospective installation in their area and will be happy to review the stop list and offer their opinions and suggestions. Choose a company and inform the other organ vendors that your choice has been made, thanking them for their proposals and time.

Funding

Prepare a brochure, letter, or other reader-friendly fund-raising information and distribute it where appropriate. If the committee believes that a full-fledged brochure is necessary, such a brochure might include a brief history/mission of the church and music in the church, a description of the builder and project, a stop list and rendering of the proposed instrument, and details about how donors can participate. If a campaign is needed (i.e., no single donor is underwriting the entire project), this is the time to launch it. It is wise to have a good portion of the funding in place or pledged before signing a contract with the organ company. Most contracts are formulated with a payment schedule that will request a percentage up front (maybe 20 percent) and a similar percentage after various events in the building process have taken place. Final payment does not occur until installation and voicing are finished and the committee, consultant, and organist are satisfied with the result.

People like to contribute to projects such as organs, and there are ways to encourage them to do so. Most organ builders will have literature and fund-raising programs or ideas in place from which you can benefit. It is wonderful to have the entire congregation participate—breadth in congregational support will help create a sense of ownership and excitement in the project, and will make it the work of God through the people. Donors can give predetermined amounts toward a "note" or a "pipe" or a "manual," or specific items such as the festival trumpet, chimes, or bench. Children's classes could pool their dimes and quarters over a period and participate. There could be fund-raising concerts, choir bake sales, appeals in the bulletin, and updates given via e-mail. Other potential sources of funds may include companies or vendors associated with the church, memorial donations, and bequests.

Your Case

The strongest argument for a great organ—one that will speak to members of the church—is that this new instrument will aid the congregation in its worship of God. Above all, that is the purpose of church music. I sometimes use the allusion that if one were going to the airport to pick up the king of a foreign country, one would find the best motor vehicle possible to do so. Yet Sunday morning when we approach the King of kings, our praise is often carried through an instrumental vehicle that is less than our best. The premise is simple but profound: *if we can do better, we should.* Aesthetic authenticity is a strong argument for a pipe instrument (see chapter 7, "Authenticity in Corporate Worship Music"). Whenever possible, an acoustic (pipe) instrument should be used—but this will not be possible for every congregation. What then? Get the finest instrument that you can. This statement implies sacrifice and work, not the simplest and quickest solution. Strive for excellence, and lay your desires before the Lord.

A church's organ is neither strictly for the organist nor for the musical elite of the church. It is for the good of all of the church's worshipers to help them in corporate worship. Yet it will not ensure that one is worshiping well, nor will it create an influx of new members. So why should all this time and money be spent on it? Here's the answer: *because it is for God.* One needs only to look at God's specifications in Exodus for the tabernacle, or the elaborate work on Solomon's temple, or the woman at Bethany's lavish washing of Jesus' feet with precious ointment, to know that sacrifice, beauty, and extravagance are never wasted on the worship of God. When played well, a great organ will bolster the praises of his people and aid them in prayer—what price can one put on that? Moreover, the Lord is worthy of the best that one can offer.

21
Luther and Bar Song: The Truth, Please!

Praise the Lord, for the Lord is good;
sing to his name, for it is pleasant! —*Psalm 135:3*

If I had a dollar for every time I have heard that Martin Luther used tavern music for his hymns and that "A Mighty Fortress Is Our God" was a drinking song, I would be a wealthy man. Yet such assertions are simply not true. These are falsehoods perpetrated on the evangelical world. Does that seem overstated? Well it would be an overstatement if this misinformation did not have such overarching ramifications and effects on current church-music philosophy and practice.

On numerous occasions such ideas about Luther and his hymns have been verbalized and put into print to support the CCM (Contemporary Christian Music) industry. Luther's hymn was supposedly a "bar song," in turn validating the use of popular secular music in church. This assumption purportedly corresponds with a question attributed to Luther: "Why should the Devil have all the good music?" On these bases the use of popular music in the church has been championed, provided that it is "sanctified" by the addition of sacred text. The conclusion: *as long as the words are Christian words, the music is of little consequence*—worse yet, *the world's music is the best way to win worldly people to Christ.* The careless acceptance of these errant ideas has done great damage to the integrity of church music and worship in our time. There are at least four errors to counter.

First, Luther's battle hymn, *A Mighty Fortress Is Our God,* is not a tavern song, nor is it based on one. Luther composed both the text (based on Psalm 46) and the original tune for this chorale in 1529. Luther was a good composer, who worked closely with eminent musicians Johann Walter and Conrad Rupff. While some of his pieces were derived from Gregorian chant or other preexisting compositions, only one was even based on a secular tune—an extant folk song used for his Christmas hymn, "From Heaven above to Earth I Come" (VOM HIMMEL HOCH). This tune was replaced after a time because "Luther was embarrassed to hear the tune of his Christmas hymn sung in inns and dance halls."[1] Walter agreed and ejected it from the hymnbook in 1551. Perhaps this matter is the source of some of the present confusion, since it would be natural to hear folk music in such settings. None of Luther's tunes can be traced back to drinking songs.

Luther was careful in his choice of music for the church. And his purposes for composition are entirely other than secular, as is confirmed by his own words:

> Therefore, I too, with the help of others, have brought together some sacred songs, in order to make a good beginning and to give an incentive to those who can better carry on the Gospel and bring it to the people . . . And these songs were arranged in four parts for no other reason than that I wanted to attract the youth (who should and must be trained in music and other fine arts) away from love songs and carnal pieces and to give them something wholesome to learn instead . . .[2]

Luther did use preexisting musical material for some of his chorales, though. He borrowed and adapted from Gregorian chant, as well as from folk music. This was a regular practice from before Luther's time right up through the Baroque period. Such borrowings were called *contrafacta* (singular *contrafactum*) or *parody*.[3] However, borrowing from secular folk music was much more common in medieval times than in Luther's day and thereafter. Albert Schweitzer said that EIN' FESTE BURG itself was "woven out of Gregorian reminiscences. The recognition of this fact deprives the melody of none of its beauty and Luther of none of the credit for it; it really takes considerable talent to create an organic unity out of fragments."[4] In the cases where the rhythm or other aspects of a tune did not appropriately suit Luther's texts, he would alter the rhythm, smoothing it out, making it more stately or noble (the opposite, incidentally of what many are championing today). Luther was primarily after good melodies or melodic ideas. Many "folk" melodies of Luther's time originated in music of the church, not the other way around.

The primary mistake that people have made is in confusing drinking songs or tavern music with "bar form." Bar form is a standard German music and literature form of the Middle Ages. It normally consists of three or more stanzas, each stanza being divided into two *Stollen* (the "A" lines) and one *Abgesang* (the "B" section). This resulted in an AAB structure common to most Lutheran chorales.[5] A variation on bar form known as "quatrain" form or the "quatrain-stanza" concept was identified by musicologist Dénes Bartha. Quatrain form can be identified by the letters AABA^1, which the English music theorists label "rounded binary songform" and German folklorists call *Reprisenbar*.[6] This form is employed for many strophic hymns, perhaps most commonly in hymns from Germany and the British Isles. Luther's use of bar form has nothing to do with drinking.[7]

The second error is in believing that the statement "Why should the Devil have all the good music?" (as applied to Luther) has anything to do with pop music, or for that matter has anything to do with Luther. Pop music did not even exist in Luther's time; it is a phenomenon of the twentieth century. Did secular music exist? Of course it did. There was music of the courts, music of the bards and troubadours, and folk/dance music of the common people. But this music was not mass-produced with the intention of making vast amounts of money. The only association that the statement has with Christian pop music is that Larry Norman wrote a song by that very title as part of the "Jesus movement" that gave birth to CCM.[8] Norman and others used this song as a means of championing their music within the Christian church and quite successfully managed to build a commercial Christian rock empire. Music and worship in evangelicalism have not been the same since.

Norman's song typifies the attitude and philosophy that gave birth to CCM. Perhaps you are familiar with these lines from it:

> I ain't knocking the hymns; just give me a song that has a BEAT.
> I ain't knocking the hymns; just give me a song that moves my feet.
> I don't like none of those funeral marches; I ain't dead yet!

Though he says he is not "knocking the hymns," he calls them "funeral marches." He advocates rock music and claims that in place of hymnody, the music (for him) should generate a physical, dance-oriented response. In short the idea is: away with our Reformation heritage, away with the music of our parents and grandparents, away with the hymns of the church. Instead give me what makes me feel good physically and what I want now! This is somewhat different from the current move back toward hymnody's texts (which is wonderful), though with contemporary musical clothing (which is less than wonderful).

The third error has to do with the statement's attribution. The confusion is understandable. Schweitzer wrote, "Believing, as he said, that 'the devil does not need all the good tunes for himself' Luther formed his Christmas hymn *Vom Himmel hoch da komm ich her* out of the melody of the riddle-song *Ich komm aus fremden Landen her.*"[9] While Schweitzer is correct about the melody, there is no evidence that Luther made the statement about tunes and the Devil. In the January 1997 issue of *Concordia Theological Journal,* James L. Brauer offered a $25 reward to any Luther scholar who could find the quote in Luther's works. No one met the challenge. Apparently, William Booth, founder of The Salvation Army, said something similar as quoted in Helen Hosier's biography: "'Why should the devil have all the best tunes?' William replied when chided for appropriating music of popular tunes for his hymns."[10] Is it possible that Booth was quoting the Rev. Rowland

Hill (1744–1833), the famous London pastor and evangelist, who said, "The Devil should not have all the best tunes"?[11] Hill was concerned over the lamentable quality of music in his church (Surrey Chapel, built for him in 1783), and he wanted do something about it. So Hill wrote hymns and compiled and published five collections of psalms and hymns, three of which were specifically for children and schools. In spite of such readily available documentation, the statement has been misattributed to Luther as well as to both Wesley brothers, Isaac Watts, and even D. L. Moody.[12]

But even if Luther had uttered such a statement, it would not have been in an effort to bring tavern or folk music into the church. It would have been directed at the Roman Catholic church and its pope, to whom Luther frequently referred as "the Devil." In other words, "Why should the pope (i.e., the Roman church) have all the good church music? Our Lutheran churches should have it, too." The music that Luther loved and reclaimed for use in his church was music written for Rome by Josquin des Prez, Louis Senfl, Heinrich Finck, Pierre de la Rue, and other master composers of the day admired for their musical skill and attention to text. In other words, if the question had been Luther's, it would support the idea that artistic music of great composers should be employed in worship—the polar opposite of what those positing it as support for rock music or hip-hop or other pop styles would like for it to mean.

The fourth error is the belief that the simple addition of sacred text or Christian words to a tune makes it worthy of use in worship. A related error is the notion that as long as the words are inoffensive, the music is of little consequence. But adding scriptural text to a heavy-metal tune or even to vapid easy-listening rock does not make it appropriate for worship. The ideological conflict of the two forces is irreconcilable. The music's destructive and purposely anti-God, anti-authoritarian nature remains undiminished even if it is played by well-meaning Christians.

Does music of rebellion fit the worship of our majestic God? No. It may be useful in expressing *angst*, or man's sinful condition, or even the lament or oppression of minorities in some forum, but this forum is not properly a worship service. Some people will be fooled and will put themselves or their congregations in the middle of such confusion, but careful consideration will uncover the false premises and devastating results of such an action. The music used in worship is of great consequence because it communicates at a level deeper than words. In fact, the musical message in a particular song may be more powerful and insidious than its verbal message can overcome. When the two conflict, the music usually emerges as the victor.

Text and music should match each other well. If the text is trite and meaningless, it has no place in worship. Yet at times profound texts are wed to music with inferior structure or harmony, so that, as Leonard Payton put it, "the aesthetic form communicates fun and good times to most people rather than the worship of Almighty God . . ."[13] This does not mean that light or popular music is "bad"; rather, it suggests that *not all music is appropriate to worship* or to particular thoughts and ideas about God.

Our heavenly Father deserves and demands the best we have to offer. Our lives are to be living sacrifices (Rom. 12:1). We are told to think on whatever is good, lovely, and virtuous (Phil. 4:8). This requires us to make choices. As literature or art can be critiqued according to certain standards, so music can be judged according to objective parameters—specifically, melody, harmony, rhythm, and form. While some judgments will be subjective, the laws of science and nature reveal the Creator's absolute principles. Along with those borne out in human experience, it is these absolute principles apprehended through education that inform our knowledge of good form, artistic content, and musical excellence. Our relativistic, pluralistic society says otherwise, of course, in direct opposition to the gospel and to biblical standards for godly living.

Everyone will have an opinion about music and will know what they *like,* but a trained church musician with theological understanding will be best equipped to make decisions about what is "good" church music. One of the primary responsibilities of the church musician is to be a steward and protector of the church's worship music. This responsibility points to our need for musically educated, theologically astute church musicians who will care for us in this regard. It also points to our need for congregations and pastors who will search for and value these kinds of musical leaders. Such is the kind of person whom Luther commended, and such is the quality of music that he sought for the church. Any myth that misrepresents Luther and others in support of commercial "pop" music in worship (Christianized or not) should be silenced.

Notes

1. Paul Nettl, *Luther and Music*, trans. F. Best and R. Wood (Philadelphia: Muhlenberg Press, 1948), 48.

2. Martin Luther, from the foreword to the first edition of Johann Walter's hymnal, the *Wittenberg Geistliche Gesangbüchlein* (1524), in *Liturgy and Hymns*, ed. Ulrich S. Leupold, vol. 53 of *Luther's Works*, ed. Helmut T. Lehmann (Philadelphia: Fortress Press, 1965), 315–16.

3. Manfred F. Bukofzer, "Popular and Secular Music in England," in *The New Oxford History of Music 3: Ars Nova and the Renaissance, 1300–1540*, ed. Anselm Hughes and Gerald Abraham (London: Oxford University Press, 1960), 108.

4. Albert Schweitzer, *J. S. Bach* (1908), trans. [English] by Ernest Newman, 2 vols., enlarged and illustrated edition (Neptune City, NJ: Paganiniana, 1980), 1:16.

5. "*AAB* form can exist in various ways. The most important possibilities are as follows: (1) *AA/B*, (2) *ABAB/CB*, (3) *AA/BA*, (4) *AA/BB/A*, (5) *AA/BB/C*, (6) *AA/BB*. These forms are taken from medieval German song, but are also more generally applicable . . . The *AAB* form—one of the most common of all musical form genres—can be documented from the time of the classical Greek ode with its *strophe*, *antistrophe* and *epode*. In the early Middle Ages it can be found in the Gregorian chant repertories and later in many hymns . . . In Germany it was moreover of paramount importance in the *Tenorlied* of the 16th century and for the Protestant *Kirchenlied*. In the more recent history of German song it receded in importance in relation to other form schemes, but saw a significant revival in the songs of Schubert, Schumann and Brahms. The importance of bar form for Wagner has been shown exhaustively by Lorenz." Horst Brunner, "Bar Form," *Grove Music Online*, ed. L. Macy (accessed 20 October 2004), http://www.grovemusic.com.

6. Dénes Bartha, "Song Form and the Concept of 'Quatrain,' " in *Haydn Studies* (New York: W. W. Norton, 1975), 353–55. See also "Binary and Ternary Form," in *The Harvard Dictionary of Music*, 4th ed., ed. Don Michael Randel (Cambridge, MA: Harvard, 2003), 100–102.

7. This does not imply, however, that Luther did not enjoy good beer.

8. "Why Should the Devil Have All the Good Music?," words and music by Larry Norman as recorded on *Only Visiting This Planet*, Verve Records, copyright 1972. One of the refrains states it this way: "I know what's right, I know what's wrong and I don't confuse it. Why should the devil have all the good music? I feel good every day 'cause Jesus is the Rock and He rolled my blues away."

9. Schweitzer, *J. S. Bach,* 17–18.

10. In Helen K. Hosier, *William and Catherine Booth: Founders of the Salvation Army* (Uhrichsville, OH: Barbour, 1999) as quoted at http://www.apologetix.com/faq/faq-detail.

11. See John Bartlett, *Bartlett's Familiar Quotations,* 10th ed. (Boston: Little, Brown & Co., 1919), 861, as well as the *Oxford Dictionary of Quotations,* 3rd ed. (New York: Oxford, 1979), and E. W. Broom's biography of Hill, *The Rev. Rowland Hill: Preacher and Wit* (London, n.p., 1881 or 1883) all of which attribute the quote to the famous preacher, as does V. J. Charlesworth in *Rowland Hill: His Life, Anecdotes and Pulpit Sayings* (London, n.p., 1879), 156.

12. Mark Nabholz, "Give Luther a Rest" in *The Journal of the Church Music National Conference* (Fall 2002), 19.

13. Leonard Payton, *Reforming Our Worship Music* (Wheaton, IL: Crossway, 1999), 14.

22 Misconceptions about Church Music

Behold, God is my salvation;
I will trust, and will not be afraid;
for the Lord God *is my strength and my song,*
and he has become my salvation. —*Isaiah 12:2*

In our day, misconceptions about music in the church abound. Some are based on assumptions or misinformation, while others are implied or are more insidious. These ideas are frequently accepted as fact without any question of their legitimacy. In this essay, we consider some prevalent misconceptions about church music with the hope of kindling thought at the least and of effecting change at best. Please note that these statements are *mis*-conceptions—in other words, fallacies. If they sound true, there is a problem. One way to test a supposition about worship music or a church musician is to consider whether the same supposition would be true of a sermon or of a pastor. (See chapter 1, "Sermon in Song: Sacred Music as Proclamation," for more information along these lines.)

Misconception 1: Worship is about us. Worship is about the lost. Worship is about music. Whom is worship really about? It is about God. He is the Subject and Object in worship. So any argument about worship, worship music, or worship-music style must start with that perspective. This overarching truth should inform our choices, our preparation, and our presentation of music in worship. Most of the problems we encounter are specifically because we are acting under the pretense that worship is somehow about us or someone other than God.

Misconception 2: Music is the best part of the worship service. It really warms me up for the sermon. Most people would agree that it is an error to think that church music is simply "for fun." And yet sometimes this is how we behave. Music is serious, particularly when it is communicating a biblical text or spiritual truth. While it obviously can delight the heart and refresh the senses, and making music should be a joyful activity, worship music is not to be treated as entertainment. This is a problem when people are focused on their own amusement. Rather than existing for our amusement, church music presents an important opportunity for us to worship God. It is not simply a mindless pre-sermon activity. Neither is music (in whatever role it takes: praise, prayer, or proclamation) the most important element of worship. All the elements of worship are important.

The misconception that music is the "fun time" is fostered when the service is front-heavy with music, with musicians "on stage." This often takes the form of a twenty- to thirty-minute "praise and worship" time during which the congregation is up and down and moving around as others straggle into the service. Using music as a sort of calisthenic warm-up for the sermon manifests the misuse of a primary worship vehicle. Music can be used to control people this way, as a kind of energy-inducing drug or catalyst, but this is not appropriate for worship. The naturally occurring joy and energy of robust, Christian singing is sufficient.

Misconception 3: Music should be spontaneous, not too carefully planned. While it is also a good thing to sing to the Lord spontaneously out of joy, church music, like sermons, should normally be the result of study, thought, and practice (rehearsal and honing of skills). Further, spontaneity does not necessitate an ever-changing service order, or the lack of an order of worship altogether. Music should be well prepared so that it can be well presented. The four thousand professional Levitical musicians whom David set aside for temple service alternated in twenty-four different groups. Obviously, it was important for them to prepare for their opportunity to serve, and such preparation for excellent service was part of their calling. They were given time to rehearse. The Holy Spirit is at work as much in our preparation for service as in the service itself. It would be wise for us to remember that excellence is an attribute of God. God *deserves* the best we can offer. He *demands* the best we can offer. It has been said that "worship is like a mirror into which God looks and should see himself reflected." The question is, "What does He see?"[1]

Worship should be from the heart, as well as from the mind. Yet the notion that whatever I think or feel at the moment is legitimate and worthy of offering to God simply because it is "mine" is a falsehood. This kind of thinking evidences the influence of our relativistic culture—a culture in which people are self-obsessed and do not embrace the idea of absolute truth. True worship is about God. One test of a good hymn or chorus text is this: How filled with God is it? Does it actually deliver truth about God's attributes and acts, or is it chiefly about man?

Misconception 4: Everyone who volunteers to do church music should be used. Skill is not important as long as people's hearts are in the right place. This is a tough issue to navigate and even more difficult to discuss with those who hold such a view. We encourage people to praise God, and all Christians should. We want to encourage people to use their abilities in his service, and they should. But music requires study, practice, and discipline to achieve skill. And not everyone who wants to lead in some public capacity has reached a sufficient level of skill to do so. We are careful whom we ask to preach, and especially whom we hire to be our pastors. Churches conduct extensive, nationwide searches to fill their pulpits. But when it comes to direction of music, they often do not. In other words, we do not place the kind of value on chief musicians and their role as we do on ministers. Yet music, while in many senses universal, is also a specialized ministry. Are there other such fields of specialty? Not everyone has the gift of teaching, or can communicate well with children—this is another specialized ministry, and it would not take anyone long to think of other ministries that require special skill or training.

Sally, who has had four years of lessons and was once in a beauty pageant, has volunteered to play the piano, and Joe's mother insists that he sing a solo when her relatives are in town, so we feel obliged to engage them in these ways. After all, they are willing to serve; do they not have the right to lead the congregation? No, not necessarily. Sometimes the best thing we can do for people who want to serve in areas in which they are not spiritually or physically gifted is to tell them so, in kindness, as hard as that might be. Perhaps a statement such as "this is probably not the best use of your gifts" or an explanation of the level of competency or experience one needs could be offered. Then, of course, we should be ready to help these people improve or explore other avenues of service and follow through as much as we are able. More often than not, however, we cave in to the pressure of others. We do not wish to hurt feelings, or perhaps we choose the path of least resistance. Maybe we feel obligated (or are made to feel this way) because the request comes from a financial supporter. Is it possible that we would rather avoid unpleasantness and, in so doing, compromise what we offer God instead?

Nonmusicians and musicians alike can be involved in music ministry for the wrong reasons. Some tend to view it as a forum to exhibit skill (or the skills of talented children). But church music is not the right place for showmanship, and worship is not the setting for it, either. From 1 Chronicles 23–25, we know that 288 highly skilled musical leaders led the organized musicians of the temple. Israel Adler noted, "The singers of the Temple were professional musicians, trained for the preservation of the tradition from generation to generation."[2] We each have our particular roles in the body, and this is the biblical example for music leadership—Christian professionals, not Christian karaoke. This in no way minimizes the importance of congregational song, however, which rightly involves all worshipers. It also implies that we need to be training people of all ages to serve musically.

Biblical, conservative, evangelical churches should be the ones that value skilled musicians. It much better suits our theology than it does that of liberal or state churches; yet they often value artistic and musical excellence more than we do. Even the strictest of our Reformed forebears understood the need for professionalism when it came to the music of the church. John Calvin was not a musician, but he viewed music as one of the most excellent gifts of the Holy Spirit and afforded it an important place under the doctrine of common grace.[3] He convinced some of the finest French composers of his time to write tunes for his French Psalter, *Aulcuns pseaulmes et cantiques mys en chant* (Strasbourg, 1539), which later culminated in the Genevan Psalter of 1562.[4] Although Calvin was personally involved in writing and adapting the texts that his people would sing, he was not a musician. So he asked for the help of proficient musicians in his effort to strengthen the church and its worship. He did not lower the level of music to that of his own skill or the skill of the first volunteer from his Genevan congregation.

Misconception 5: It is necessary to have background music in church all through the service. It helps break up the monotony of worship and keeps things moving. It shouldn't be loud or distracting, though. This misconception could also be stated along these lines: "The prelude, offertory, or any other use of instrumental music in the service is a good time to talk with my neighbor. If the service gets too long, we should stand and sing a song to wake people up. All parts of the service should be connected by transition music." There is a simple response to this kind of thinking: *all service music should contribute to worship in meaningful ways.* In other words, church music is not fundamentally utilitarian. It should not be reduced to background music for conversation or mood music for prayer, and it is not to be employed merely to change the pace of the service or to break it into convenient sections. It may, in effect, serve to set a mood or act as a signal to stand, sing, pray, or take some other action—but these are all purposeful, intentional roles that are not meant to compete with another human activity (such as talking).

Misconception 6: Musicians should be volunteers. We need to invest financially in our church's music ministry if it is to be viable and credible. Obviously, laypeople should be involved in the music ministry (volunteers constitute most choirs, for example), but there *can* be paid music directors, organists, pianists, and even singers. These professions are biblical, as is their compensation. We pay the preacher and other staff members, but many churches still depend on volunteers to organize and carry out the musical work; or else musical responsibilities are placed on staff who are not musicians. In so doing, we make musical direction (choice, leadership, and presentation) a lay activity instead of a ministerial responsibility. We do not, however, find such a pattern modeled for us in Scripture. (For a lengthier discussion, see chapter 16, "Choir for Hire: Should Church Musicians Be Paid?")

Misconception 7: If we want to reach young people and be a growing church, we need a contemporary service. This is an extremely divisive issue in the evangelical church today. In North America two or three decades ago, a typical growing, midsize church would hire a pastor, an assistant pastor, an administrator, a youth pastor, and then perhaps a part-time or full-time music director. No one thought church music was too important. Certainly it was a necessary component, but it should not cost much. After all, money was needed for the new gymnatorium, sanctuary carpet, or some other project. By contrast, today even very small churches are hiring "worship leaders" or "ministers of worship," particularly for contemporary worship services. Everyone seems to know that music is essential to a healthy church, but adequate knowledge about how this requirement should manifest itself is lacking.

The decision to move to alternative worship services on the basis of musical style commences, more often than not, because the pastor or governing board wants the church to grow. There is nothing wrong with the desire to grow; in fact, it is right and good. Method and motivation are the questions to consider. Is our motivation fiscal? Do we believe that growth will build up the size and prosperity of the congregations and provide the money to build facilities and add programs? Such growth is a sign of success, and desiring to succeed is noble, right? Perhaps. But the question is: Will we go to any length and risk the integrity of the message in order to bring people to church? For some, the motivation for size or success stems from the desire to become more like the megachurch Christian "communities" that separate themselves from the world. And sometimes, perhaps even regularly, these actions do draw people in and achieve the desired results. I am reminded, however, of a statement that James Boice used to offer: "What you win them *with*, you win them *to*."

God calls us to be faithful, not huge or wealthy. Narrow and deep is better than broad and shallow. Music is frequently misused in many churches in an effort to "market" the church by making the atmosphere comfortable and more like the world. But the church and Christians are called to be separate from the world—in it, but not of it. If a visitor walks into your church and hears the same pop-music sounds that he or she hears in the restaurant, pub, or club, what does it tell him or her about your church?

The irony is that the music in these services is often not contemporary at all. More often it is music of the "baby boomers," who want to relive their youth in their churches. Naturally, this music sounds outmoded and phony to young people because the money, equipment, and talent needed to sound like the pop stars that recorded it are not readily available. Neither does such music appeal to "the young crowd" nearly as much as is popularly believed. Young people today typically desire neither their parents' music when they go to church nor the music they hear on the radio. Many small churches with small budgets have "contemporary services" that might be contemporary for the 1970s to the 1990s but are certainly not on the cutting edge of anything today. Yet their pastors or boards are eager to get more parishioners, and First Baptist or Third Methodist down the street has such a service, and "all the young people are going there now." The pressure mounts. All the church gains in the end is a split into two congregations according to worship-music style, which is not really a gain at all.

The seeker-sensitive megachurches that have money also have the latest music from big American or Australian Contemporary Christian Music corporations that purport to sell "the most excellent worship music available today!" Really? Is it truly the most excellent worship music available? Advertisers at Christian booksellers' conventions would have us believe so. Churches that buy into this mentality have the whole show—large stage, giant movie screens, bands, electric drums, elaborate lighting systems, Plexiglas pulpit, and TV-quality video cameras. The news quickly spreads throughout a community. "Did you see their Christmas show or the Easter passion play? It was awesome. So elaborate! So cool!" So much like the world and its values. This is what is held up as the model in American evangelicalism today. We cannot do the Lord's work in the world's way and be biblical.

We want the church to grow, and this is a godly desire. Paul encourages us to use every means possible to win the lost—but not to risk the integrity of the message (1 Cor. 9:22; Gal. 1:9–10). When the Word of God is preached boldly and truthfully, and when the worship of God's people has integrity, then the church will grow because God will bless and build it. Its needs will be met. Men build kingdoms, but God builds his church. That is the power of the gospel. That is the sufficiency of Scripture. We need to trust the divine Author when he says, "My word . . . shall not return to me empty" (Isa. 55:11).

Misconception 8: Since music is moving and powerful, we should use it any way we can to influence people to believe. It would never be stated this obviously, but this fallacy lies behind many musical efforts in the church. Unless the Holy Spirit is working through the musical offering, there will be no spiritual benefit to anyone. But this is not about how exciting the music is. The goal of church musicians should not be to create an emotional frenzy. Church music should be emotional, but not shallow or sentimental or raucous. It is not supposed to induce a manipulated emotional response. Neither can any "work" of ours bring another to faith.

As a trained musician, I have some acquaintance with the types of chord progressions, combinations of sounds, volume changes, and other effects that will achieve a certain reaction in the majority of listeners. Good film-score composers are masters in this arena. But when it comes to worship services, this manipulation does not fit. Church music can be expressive, inspirational, and performed to its potential, of course. In this sense it can be truly moving, so that, as Luther said, "those who are the least bit moved know nothing more amazing in this world."[5] Certainly Baroque composers understood how to move "the affections"; but an "affection" was a *rationalized* emotion, and the use of musical rhetoric to sway these emotions was supposed to be evident and understood.

Emotional truth can be relayed, but emotional manipulation should not be a goal. The latter occurs when we "use" music to elicit a particular response by playing on the emotions, instead of letting the Spirit naturally work in the listener what is true in the music itself. God works by his Spirit to convict, to enlighten, to strengthen, and to encourage. The Spirit does not need our help to coerce souls with yet *another* repetition of the invitational hymn or a few more vamps while the preacher repeats his altar call. The Spirit calls sinners to faith directly, in his own time.

Numerous other misconceptions could be stated and discussed if space permitted, but suffice it to say that too often we are caught in a mode of thinking or operating that is not biblical. We do not intentionally choose to be antibiblical; we just sort of slip into it by doing the things that other churches are doing, or by trying the ideas that such and such a worship magazine boasts are the latest trend, or by purchasing the up-to-the-minute music peddled at this convention or that conference. We more often err by unintentional action than by intention—by *not* thinking and measuring things by the Word. We must take time to examine our ways and methods, to measure them by the principles of Scripture, and to ensure that biblical models are followed when it comes to worshiping the One who created us for that purpose.

Notes

1. These two remarks were adapted from a seminar by Bruce Leafblad given in Philadelphia in February 2001.

2. Israel Adler, "Musique Juive" in *Encyclopédie de la musique*, vol. 2, ed. Michel François (Paris: Fasquelle, 1959), 643.

3. Frank Gaebelein, *The Pattern of God's Truth* (New York: Oxford, 1954), 72, citing Abraham Kuyper, *Calvinism* (Grand Rapids: n.p., 1931), 243–44.

4. Clément Marot wrote some of the finest metrical psalm texts, and Calvin secured the assistance of some excellent composers, among them Louis Bourgeois, Claude Goudimel, and Claudin Le Jeune. These composers also imported monophonic chants from the Genevan Psalter to create polyphonic settings of the psalms that were widely published and sung in France and other Francophone countries.

5. Martin Luther, "Preface to Georg Rhau's *Symphoniae iucundae*," in *Liturgy and Hymns*, ed. Ulrich S. Leupold, vol. 53 of *Luther's Works*, ed. Helmut T. Lehmann (Philadelphia: Fortress Press, 1965), 321–24. Luther, discussing artistic music, gives a vivid description of the polyphonic motet and advocates its use in the Lutheran church even before the Council of Trent (1546–63) banned it from the Roman Church.

23
What Happened to Hymns?

Let the word of Christ dwell in you richly, teaching and admonishing one another in all wisdom, singing psalms and hymns and spiritual songs, with thankfulness in your hearts to God. —Colossians 3:16

A few decades ago, the notion that one would need to argue in support of the existence and use of hymns in the corporate worship of the church would have been laughable. With the exception of those who held to exclusive psalmody, hymns were a staple of Christian worship as customary as bread at mealtime. Today, though, we hear questions, statements, and arguments about their use: "Hymns? Why should we sing hymns? Aren't they old-fashioned? Young people don't like them. Aren't we to sing a *new* song? That just isn't *my* kind of music. It doesn't minister to me. You won't win anyone with that music. Worship should be free of encumbrances like hymnbooks. Hymns are too hard to understand" . . . and so on. Most of these perceptions emanate from a lack of information or education rather than from any real anti-hymn agenda.

At least some of those statements must sound familiar to the reader. For some others, such as strict followers of John Calvin, hymnody in the church has no place for another reason—the belief that only canonical psalms should be sung in worship. But Calvin's strictures were established for his own assembly, not for all churches. As Hughes Oliphant Old points out: "In defending his preference for psalmody Calvin appeals not to Scripture but to John Chrysostom and Augustine. This being the case one can be sure that Calvin had no objection if in other churches hymns other than psalms were sung. His use of exclusive psalmody [in the *Genevan Psalter*] was a matter of preference."[1] In fact, one of Calvin's chief models for worship was the great liturgical leader of the Strasbourg church, Martin Bucer. Bucer was a champion of hymnody who even prepared a hymnal himself (the *Gesangbuch* of 1541). He "prized the hymn as a way to exercise both young and old in the knowledge of Christ and in true godliness."[2]

The two references to singing "psalms and hymns and spiritual songs" in the New Testament (Eph. 5:19 and Col. 3:16) have been exposited by theologians on both sides of the exclusive-psalmody debate in support of their respective positions. (See chapter 13, "Song in the Bible.") Some believe these are three different names for canonical psalms; others believe they are three different categories of song. At times, it seems, the goal of singing to the glory of God and for the instruction and edification of his saints becomes obscured by polemics.

Then there are the present-day believers for whom Calvin, psalms, and hymns are all somewhat of a mystery. Their theological reading material tends to be limited to futuristic Christian fiction, and the church music with which they are familiar consists of "contemporary" praise choruses. The average college freshman today, who has attended church all his life, is acquainted with twenty hymns or fewer; some know none at all. This is more than sad; it is tragic. Robert Rayburn, founding president of Covenant Theological Seminary in St. Louis, countered the same kind of folly fifty years ago when he wrote of the then-popular gospel song:

> It is not just the poverty of the gospel song as an instrument of praise that is of serious concern. It is the woeful ignorance which Christians today demonstrate with respect to the almost inexhaustible riches of sacred song which are theirs in the great hymns

> which have come down through the centuries. A good hymnbook is the repository of the deepest devotion of the saints of the ages. Its treasures are priceless . . . Next to the Bible a good hymnbook is a Christian's greatest devotional guide. Yet many Christians will spend money readily for daily devotional readings which are far inferior to the great poetry of the hymnbook.[3]

Hymns have always been effective carriers of Christian doctrine, and without their definitive presence our collective theological understanding has become shallower. But this should not surprise us if we take a good, hard look at ourselves. In the postmodern, post-Christian age in which we live, worship and the music of corporate worship in evangelical churches have both followed the relativistic path of our culture.

Where We Are: The Postmodern Church

Upon examination one finds that in today's church, our value systems, musical and otherwise, reflect society's primary philosophy (what "works"—*pragmatism*), its object of attention (ourselves—*narcissism*), its occupation (our own amusement or pleasure—*hedonism*), and its basis of belief (our opinions—*relativism*). In such systems, psalms and doctrinal poems set to music in the traditional forms of Reformation congregational song do not appear relevant. The postmodern church, like the rest of Western culture, is self-consumed and is largely uninterested in the rich heritage of church music imparted to us from saints of previous generations. Although *worship* is a buzzword in all ecclesiastical circles, minimal attention is given to biblical teaching regarding worship. As a result, we as evangelicals have slipped away from biblical worship and now justify our practices on the basis of the spirit of the age (what Germans refer to as the *Zeitgeist*).

A "me-focused" age, though, is hardly one that should inform and define our approach to God. And yet, it does. We measure our ecclesiastical "success" by numbers and facilities, our relevance by how technologically integrated and up-to-date we are, and our worship by how good it makes us feel. Sometimes, one fears, it is the music itself that is being worshiped (something that can happen with any style in any setting). In the minds of most contemporary saints, hymns clash with the spontaneity, simplicity, and style that have come to rule in the postmodern evangelical church. But these brothers and sisters need to know and experience something more.

Great hymns serve as praise, prayer, and proclamation in the context of worship. They say something that we still *need* to hear, something that we must believe, sing, and share. They often paraphrase a psalm, distill the teaching of a specific scriptural passage, or relate a doctrine or other spiritual truth by drawing on multiple biblical texts. Hymns are not emotionless. They make demands on the whole person—on the heart, soul, and mind. And they have special power to communicate spiritual truth and encouragement, particularly through association with a fitting tune. While some hymn texts and tunes are ancient, hymns are not antiques or artifacts. They are a living genre, important, even vital to the church; in fact, hymns are still being written today. While the church has shunned psalm and hymn singing, particularly in the last two decades of the twentieth century and the opening years of the twenty-first, both forms are biblical and necessary.

What Is the Problem?

To correct a problem, it must first be diagnosed. It is not congregations or young people who created this hymnological crisis. The fault, first of all, can be squarely placed on leadership: seminaries, Christian colleges, Christian organization heads, pastors, and musicians. Rayburn articulated the culpability of seminaries: "Perhaps the real blame rests upon the theological seminaries that have neglected the matter of practical instruction in worship, including hymnology. The evangelical church has been sadly impoverished."[4] As a result, many pastors lack sufficient training in hymnology and in a general appreciation of music and the arts. But there is no excuse to remain this way by default even if seminaries have failed. Pastors can read, listen, and ask for help. Seminaries can change, and some are making progress.

Musicians must also share the blame for the decline of hymnody. Musicians have failed when they have chosen poor hymns or played good ones like dirges. They have disrupted hymn singing with unnecessary chatter from the microphone and have shortchanged it by skipping stanzas. Musicians regularly fail to substantiate hymnody's value. We blaze the path to inferior congregational song when we sell out to what is easy, politically correct, or "safe" rather than standing up for what is best for the body of Christ. We alienate ministers and members of the congregation by reacting too defensively or egocentrically when challenged instead of taking time to answer calmly out of conviction and love. Music directors and pastors must be protectors of the church's heritage; we must defend it, teach it, write about it, and preserve it. But too often we have failed out of fear, ignorance, weariness, or worldliness.

Singing Hymns Is Biblical

Even a cursory survey of the Scriptures should lead one to the inevitable conclusion that the Bible contains too many examples of hymns to set them aside or to forbid their use in present-day worship. In answer to the concern that only canonical psalms should be sung, we must acknowledge that there are commands in Psalms, Isaiah, Revelation, and elsewhere to "sing a new song" as well as numerous accounts of both Old and New Testament saints singing new worship songs of praise and deliverance that are neither classified as psalms nor contained in the canonical book of Psalms. Therefore, to cease writing, composing, and singing new hymns of praise to our great God is contrary to the example of Scripture. Further, the pictures of perfect, heavenly worship in Revelation reveal echoes of psalms and hymns in paraphrase, combining the praises of all ages in an eternal song that is both old and new. This worshipful song is never vapid, trivial, or worldly in nature. Surely such biblical evidence must inform our current worship practices.

We must also acknowledge, though, the apostle Paul's instruction to the Ephesians and Colossians to "sing psalms." Singing psalms in worship is a biblical mandate, not an optional activity. The choice to sing psalms as unison chant or four-part harmony, with instruments or *a cap-*

pella, in a metrical form or as a paraphrase, in English, French, or Hebrew, is extrabiblical. In other words, subjective aspects and choices exist that are not expressly limited or directed by scriptural command. We no more sing in the same style as the early church did than we gather together in the same physical structures, or arrive for corporate worship by the same methods of transportation, or understand things with the same sociocultural perspectives.

The particular make and model of the "vehicle" delivering the psalm is not as significant as the fact that the inspired Word of God and its truth is sung back to him, for his glory, and for our edification and instruction. The vehicle, however, should suit the text and must not contradict it, musically, aesthetically, or otherwise. Further, the quality of the mode through which we meet our King should be our finest possible offering. We would not offer an earthly king less than our best, yet for the King of kings we regularly "make do." Why? Our view of God is too low.

In church music, the quality of the music itself—melody, harmony, rhythm, and form—plays a significant role in interpretation of the text and delivery of its truth. If the musical setting communicates a message contrary to that of the text, the textual meaning can be thwarted or even miscommunicated. This is the unfortunate case with much of the "new" music of recent decades. There has been a positive return to singing Scripture in the Contemporary Christian Music movement, and this is one of its strongest virtues. But in relatively few examples of "praise songs" do the form and other musical elements suitably support the weight and meaning of a text, in cases in which the text itself is worthy of being sung.

The Old to the New

What is happening *now* to hymns? There has recently been a remarkable move in "contemporary" music circles toward hymnody. This is particularly true of Christian rock bands (many of which play under the same label or ultimate owner). It is not clear whether this trend is motivated by a renewed desire for rich theology in Christian music or by a desire to generate new audiences and make money. One thing is certain: the act of putting "old" hymns to "new" musical styles is growing at an amazing pace. Some leaders in the evangelical world have surprisingly embraced this movement, or at least have breathed a sigh of relief that better texts are being employed. Before pastors or other leaders endorse this seemingly positive pendulum shift, however, they should consider at least two prevalent errors inherent in it.

First, great hymnody does not need postmodernity's clothes. It simply needs to be encountered genuinely and sung with understanding and energy. Why would anyone think that Martin Luther's "A Mighty Fortress" or Charles Wesley's "And Can It Be" need new music? They do not. The grandeur and power of these tunes are only lessened by removing harmony, adding static rhythmic formulas, and reducing them to "contemporary" musical language. Not only is this "decomposing" unnecessary, it diminishes the greatness of these hymns. True, some excellent hymn texts would benefit from better tunes, but the desire in the movement under discussion here is not to give the great texts *better* music. Rather, the effort appears to be an attempt to "win over" a young mass audience to hymn repertoire, or at least to a particular band's rendering, with a style that appeals to their pop-infused mindset and experience. If we believe that the postmodernization of Christian doctrine or preaching is improper, why do we permit and champion it in our worship music.

Second, when and if a new tune is better than the old, we should embrace it. But a driving rock rhythm or simplification of harmonic progression does not a new, good tune make. It simply packages the hymn text with something that people supposedly want. Their embracing of the result is characterized as "success"; therefore (so the argument goes), it must be "good." Who is really thinking critically about *the value of the music* in this process? And again, as I have said elsewhere, if the text and tune do not consonantly communicate the same message, there is an inherent conflict.

A Call to Arms

We should answer the call to "sing a new song" by following the examples of theologians such as Luther, Bucer, Isaac Watts, and James

Montgomery Boice. Their hymns are biblically derived, artistically conceived, theologically sound, and exegetically purposeful. They fulfill and reinforce biblical patterns of praise, proclamation, and prayer as the rightful roles of church music. At the same time, great thoughts should be carried by great music. We would not offer the gift of a diamond in a fast-food hamburger box to even a familiar friend or family member, let alone to a king. Why would we offer the great truths of Scripture or praise to God in a musical style similarly common simply because it appeals to the masses? Does Scripture evidence God's praise by the masses or by the remnant?

We must be willing to instruct our congregations so that they sing with understanding—with the heart and the head—as whole beings. We must properly support, both philosophically and financially, the ministry of music in our local congregations, by engaging and compensating church musicians who are professionally skilled and biblically mindful. Such musicians will understand both the seriousness and the joy of their calling, will measure their offerings by Scripture, and will be unwilling to offer less than the best they can to our heavenly King. Revive use of the hymnal in your home and in your church. Let us reclaim what is ours as children of the Reformation, and let us sing to the praise of God's glory!

Notes

1. Hughes Oliphant Old, *Worship That Is Reformed According to Scripture* (Atlanta: John Knox Press, 1984), 52.

2. Bard Thompson, *Liturgies of the Western Church* (Philadelphia: Fortress Press, 1961), 164.

3. Robert G. Rayburn, *O Come, Let Us Worship: Corporate Worship in the Evangelical Church* (New York: Westminster Publishing House, n.d., ca. 1950), 225–26. The "gospel" song referred to here is a genre of early-twentieth-century evangelistic song associated with tent meetings and crusades. It should not be confused with "gospel" musical style in the African-American tradition.

4. Ibid., 230.

24
Musical Ignorance versus Musical Arrogance

I will sing of steadfast love and justice;
to you, O Lord, I will make music. —Psalm 101:1

For some time now, music has been a divisive issue in the evangelical church. Generations ago, worshipers identified themselves as "Christian" in contradistinction to those who were "pagan." Next was a split between the Eastern and Western church. Then came Protestantism and denominations by which Christians differentiated themselves from various forms of Catholicism and from each other. Nowadays, within the very same branch of a denomination—and indeed within the very same local congregation—we are defined by "worship style" (and by this we generally mean our musical preferences). We have all heard or imagined the following stereotypical viewpoints, or even voiced one of them ourselves. The examples are somewhat extreme, and none represents a clear majority of individuals, but they tend to go something like this:

From the perspective of a "contemporary" worshiper. "I'm glad we don't have that music in our church. Hymns and classical music are old-fashioned—it seems like it is about the performers in their ivory towers. They need to get real and sing the music of the people. Thankfully, we worship with songs that let us truly feel the presence of the Lord. All kinds of people come to church to hear our band. Our hands are free from books, so we can lift them to God and clap. Worship is so free and real that you might be surprised by what happens next!"

From the perspective of a "traditional" worshiper. "I'm glad we don't have that music in our church. Those contemporary choruses are so repetitious, and I don't know them at all—it seems like it is about the performers as entertainers. At least move that stuff to a different service where I don't have to deal with it. Thankfully, we still sing great hymns of the faith (like "Because He Lives" and "The Old Rugged Cross"). Besides, aren't drums and syncopation worldly? And don't give me any of those trained voices that sound like opera, either! That's just as bad."

From the perspective of a "classical" worshiper. "I'm glad we don't have that music in our church. The drivel that some other churches call music today is so trite—it seems like it is about the performers and immediate gratification. They need to rediscover greatness and excellence. Thankfully, we worship with the best, and we know that God is pleased with the best. Those poor people don't even realize how bad off they are. I do wish the organist would play softer, though, and stay away from that modern music! What does he think we pay him for, anyway?"

These three points of view all have their obvious vices and more subtle flaws. Each represents a selfish, unloving position that is veiled by a kind of pseudo-spiritual language that supposedly justifies the position. Truths are present in each viewpoint, although these have been tooled to fit (rationalized). Often the good aspects of any of these worship contexts become distorted. It is interesting how the same rhetoric can be spun to fit almost any perspective. It is telling how each view centralizes itself and marginalizes others. It is also revealing how self-centered and subjective each view's judgments of its own merits and others' needs are. By what standard or authority are such positions informed?

The Problem

Very few arguments about church music today take biblical principles or examples of worship into consideration. Is that not odd? More often these arguments are waged on the basis of cultural context or personal opinion and experience (i.e., "taste") and are full of flawed premises and faulty assumptions. Yet people remain convinced that their beliefs are not only credible but also right. Even trained musicians are frequently at a loss to give good guidance. Musicians often cave to others' points of view because there appears to be a persuasive logic to them, or because musicians cannot distinguish (or link) the music with which they are professionally associated to music that is viable for the church. "Church music must be different from that of the concert hall, so I guess *this* must be church music" goes the reasoning.

It is surprising how often fine musicians assume that only a more common or crude music than that which they regularly perform would be suitable for worship. The implication is that either: (1) a concert-going audience is more discriminating than God; or (2) music in worship is about the common person rather than about God. While both of these inferences are incorrect, so is the inference that God "listens" to music in the same way we do. While God deserves and wants our best, he also looks on the heart and our intentions—which are probably more heavily weighted in his musical criticism than are intonation, ensemble, or style. Ignorance abounds all around—not because people are stupid, but because we assume truth rather than seek it.

As mentioned in the preface to this book, in the past few decades we have witnessed the downward spiral of principle and excellence in much church music whereby musical integrity has been abandoned more often out of ignorance than by intention. Pragmatism, relativism, narcissism, and pop culture have invaded the church subtly masked as stewardship, "progressive" thinking, and cultural relevance. We are generally unaware of their presence. They have taken a toll on church music and worship in the process. Much of this has come into play through the Contemporary Christian Music movement, which, irrespective of taste, cannot be categorically separated from the secular forces and mediocre musical ideals that inform it, no matter how Christianized the texts may be.

This judgment is not based on musical form, musical style, associative issues, or instruments alone, although those would be sufficient. The primary problems in CCM stem from the pop philosophy that propels and undergirds it. This philosophy is "consumerism." In consumerism, value is attributed to music simply because it is purchased. Music that sells is thus music with value and relevance. The idea that something not created to "sell" could be valuable or that something from a different age might have significance for us (other than as a relic) is scoffed at. Of course great music is often sold as well—and composers depend on it. It is not the sale of music that I am challenging, but the assignment of value and consumerist ideology.

The relatively small protest against this movement from traditionalists has been poorly supported without the use of biblical principles or thoughtful apologetics. Instead, people become entrenched in camps on one side or another, lash out at others, and assume no common ground. On the other hand, some have tried to blend many styles together in an attempt to please everyone. In these circles, variety or diversity itself is championed as the supreme good—a goal that generally results in pleasing very few and degenerates to pluralism and the lowest common denominator.

Arrogance

Arrogance can be linked to the assumption of knowledge when actual knowledge is missing. It occurs when one believes that he or she knows better than another while there is no ground for this presumption in actual fact-based knowledge or reality. When it comes to music, everyone has an opinion. Sometimes pastors and boards believe (and I mean this in the kindest possible sense), as do people around them and under them, that positions of leadership and power give them a high level of insight into areas or professions outside their expertise. At certain times, personal opinion may even be considered on a par with mastered truth.

For example, there is considerable presumption on the part of one who lacks musical training but is quite willing to tell a professional musician what tempo or style of music should be employed. Parishioners sometimes have the same spirit when they tell the minister what he should be preaching about or what is wrong with his delivery. Perhaps the listener has a good point, and can offer feedback to the musician or pastor in a helpful, positive manner. A pastor or parishioner might have good insight about a song or about the relative volume from his or her place in the sanctuary; something can often be learned from such comments. Yet honoring those with expertise is always wise, as is keeping one's tongue in check when underinformed, because "a little knowledge is a dangerous thing." Micromanagement, particularly in areas in which one lacks proficiency or training, is best avoided, even if one has some level of supervision. Healthy dialogue can always be encouraged, however.

And as we have noted before, laypeople have opinions about what music they like and do not like and regularly share these opinions. Every church musician has some great stories to relay in this arena. In churches where leadership is top-heavy, the music employed is often according to the tastes of those with power. In democratic settings, an attempt is sometimes made to please the majority; or, alternatively, no strong stand is taken at all.

Arrogance can appear just as readily in the trained musician who has contempt for those with less information or training. Real knowledge should not breed a spirit of superiority, but one of humility because of the responsibility attached to it. And those who "know" should realize that there is so much more to know than even they do. Pompous or cynical attitudes toward Christian brethren are never appropriate. A kind of "ivory tower" mentality among musicians sometimes occurs, albeit with less frequency than those who level the stereotypical accusation believe. People who want "different" music, whatever that may be, may employ this kind of charge. And professional church musicians can exhibit a lack of love, an unwillingness to explain, a highly critical and easily wounded spirit, or an ego that needs regular stroking. Such characteristics are sinful and need to be overcome by the grace of Christ.

Ignorance

Ignorance is a basic lack of knowledge or awareness in a given area. Ignorance may be "bliss" for some, but it affects many others in negative ways. Those who find themselves in a church where worship was once rich and deep but is now impoverished may have had very little to do with it. Sometimes the new minister or music director is responsible for the decline. Sometimes those who believed that the diagnosis of a church-growth "expert" would inject life where it was waning are to blame.

Ignorance itself, however, is rarely as deadly to the truth as is the person who supposes that his or her own ignorance does not exist. Those who know that they do not know are much less harmful than those who do not know that they do not know. The exception, of course, is when we blindly assume that those who do not know, but think they do, actually do. And perhaps the ones who do not know, but think they do, are in control. This may trigger a humanly justifiable outrage on the part of those who really do know; yet angry responses are seldom helpful and do not befit a child of God who is working in a spiritual ministry with his or her brothers and sisters.

Such has been the plight of the educated church musician in Western evangelical churches for some time. The lines between ignorance/arrogance and knowledge/humility are not easy to draw or negotiate, and no fixed answers solve the problems in all situations. Graciously demonstrating Christian deference and love, of course, is always in season.

How does one earn sufficient reputation to be heard while not compromising the truth or being too bold? How does one allow for differences in taste while maintaining some level of aesthetic judgment? How does one insist on excellence without losing perspective of the need for an educational process, and how does one find an educational approach that will be welcomed by adults who are in need of it? How does one speak the truth in love? The kind of communication skills required in a musical leader who also has theological insight, love of people, and real musical prowess rarely exist—and even when all these facets align, there is still no guarantee of a welcome reception. But all of us must press on and trust the Lord for change. We must ask for wisdom from the One who does not withhold it. Churches and missions around the world need significant change in the realm of worship music. Such change begins with how we think about it. We must think biblically.

What to Do

The answer to musical ignorance or musical illiteracy is musical education. Pastors and other church leaders need to be humble and willing to listen, read, or even take classes. Parishioners need to think for themselves, ask questions, and be willing to be taught and led. Musicians need to be ever more skillful and patient, and must have the right goal—to help people worship better to the glory of God. Knowledge of God's Word and a "quiet answer" are essential, too, as is prayer. Church musicians need biblical and theological education and ongoing musical study. Churches should hire competent, trained, professional Christian musicians to lead the people in musical worship, and they must insist on finding pastors who are educated in aspects of pastoral ministry beyond business and homiletics.

Christian colleges, universities, and seminaries need to train musicians with classical musicianship as part of their core curriculum, coupled with theological perspective and an experiential awareness of their Reformation heritage. Chapel services should model this framework—what church worship *should* be, not what it is. Likewise, Christian educational institutions need to include musical and historical worship studies in the coursework of the next generation of ministers and laypersons. We can hope that some in academia are listening and thinking past the demands of accrediting agencies, donors, and constituent churches. Here is the message: *comprehensive, integrated theological and musical education for the next generation of pastors and church musicians is paramount if we want to reclaim evangelical worship and restore biblical principles to it.*

The corrective to musical arrogance is humility. This involves putting others before oneself (following the second great commandment). It means that we must be humble enough to lay aside our preconceived notions about many things and allow our decisions and actions to be guided by the Word of God. What other rule of faith and practice will do? We cannot assume truth on the basis of tradition or the "current thinking" or the ever-present pragmatic philosophy that "this works; therefore, it is right and good" (which is essentially judging means by ends). Rather, we must examine our practices on the basis of Scripture and let neither "success" nor "failure" in the eyes of the world—or even in the eyes of fellow believers or other churches—determine how we should act and live. We must walk humbly with our God and live peaceably with our brothers and sisters. We must not remain in darkness but move toward light. For "God is light, and in him is no darkness at all" (1 John 1:5b).

> *For God, who said, "Let light shine out of darkness," has shone in our hearts to give the light of the knowledge of the glory of God in the face of Jesus Christ. —2 Corinthians 4:6*

PART FOUR

Composers and Composition

We can learn much from studying great Christian composers such as Heinrich Schütz, J. S. Bach, Felix Mendelssohn, and Igor Stravinsky. All these men were master composers, and yet more motivated them than their innate ability and desire to produce great art. They were keenly aware of their Creator and of his gifts made evident in them; and for this reason, they intentionally wrote music to the glory of God. Their musical compositions often invoke biblical or Christian themes. Although sacred themes are not an essential requirement for a composition to bring God glory, such themes can help the hearer more readily link a composer's spiritual intention with the musical work of art.

Schütz and Bach were church musicians. Naturally, then, we expect to find sacred music among their compositional output. But it is equally possible to find music of depth and intention on sacred themes among the works of Mendelssohn and Stravinsky that were intended for the secular stage. An important distinction must be made here: it is not the fact that these composers wrote sacred music that makes them "Christian" composers (for there are many examples of non-Christian composers' writing sacred music throughout the history of Western music up to the present day); rather, we know from other evidence that the particular composers being considered here had a profound Christian faith, and thus their lives and sacred compositions are likely to have added significance for other Christians. This does not necessarily make them better composers or their works better compositions; nor does it suggest that the sacred music of non-Christian composers cannot bring glory to God. According to the doctrine of common grace, all men created in the image of God can bring him glory; moreover, God is glorified in beauty and truth despite a composer's intention.

The essays in this section are written to help introduce a small portion of the amazing music given to the world by these Christian composers. In doing so, we will encounter principles that apply to both sacred and secular music-making today. Such principles should inform our own musical concepts and compositions, for any greatness found in new church music today comes from standing on the shoulders of the theological and musical giants that have come before us.

The final two essays in this part of the book consider ideas of the present author-composer rather than those of celebrated historical composers. We explore together the "blueprint" and construction of a new hymn tune with the hope of making such an experience less mysterious to the reader. Then practical help is offered for making decisions about defining and selecting good church music. Here the reader will not find a list of acceptable and unacceptable repertoire; rather, principles for determining what is good are given, so that these, in turn, can be applied in one's own context.

25

J. S. Bach and Musical Hermeneutics—Part 1: Bach, the Evangelical Composer/Preacher

My heart is steadfast, O God!
I will sing and make melody with all my being! —*Psalm 108:1*

Johann Sebastian Bach (1685–1750) was a confessing evangelical. He has been called a "second Luther" and even the "fifth Evangelist" for the way in which he heralded the message of the gospel writers in his passions and cantatas. He was confessional in his adherence to the *Book of Concord,* which contains the "symbols" or doctrinal confessions of the Lutheran church, and specifically the *Augsburg Confession* (1530). And with his gospel theology in the tradition of Martin Luther, Bach was an evangelical in the true sense of the word. *Evangelical,* derived from *euangelion*[1] ("evangel, gospel, good news"), is a term that came into modern use at the time of the Reformation to identify Protestants, especially as they held to justification by grace through faith and to the supreme authority of Scripture.

In the Lutheran service of Bach's day, the cantata (the primary piece of service music) followed the gospel reading (known as the *Evangelium*) and usually functioned as a response to and interpretation of this liturgical reading.[2] To be more specific, the cantata served a hermeneutical purpose, throwing light on the text as a "vehicle for the proclamation of the Gospel."[3] (Hermeneutics is the art and science of interpreting literary, specifically biblical, texts.) In the centuries following Luther's death, the meaning of "evangelical" has narrowed somewhat, yet it is appropriate to classify Bach as an evangelical even with the focused understanding of the word as we know it today:

> Those who espouse and experience justification and scriptural authority in an intensified way: personal conversion and a rigorous moral life, on the one hand, and concentrated attention on the Bible as a guide to conviction and behavior on the other, with a special zeal for the dissemination of Christian faith so conceived.[4]

Bach's Theological Perspective

Much has been written about Bach's theology. There are those who argue for his Lutheran orthodoxy, others who claim that he was a Pietist, and still others who state that he was primarily influenced by mystic theologians. In some sense they are all correct, for Bach was a confessional Lutheran of great personal piety with mystical leanings. This is not to imply that every pious person was officially a Pietist. Some have tried to argue by inference or anecdote that Bach was intolerant of Pietists or mystics in his adherence to Lutheran orthodoxy. But there is no real proof of this, and for a time he even served in the Reformed court of Cöthen.

While their distinctive aspects appear too disparate to reconcile, the formative ideals of Lutheran orthodoxy and Lutheran Pietism were not so far apart. Both found their roots in Luther. To generalize somewhat simplistically, the Orthodox were desirous of maintaining doctrinal purity, and so they codified theological statements and tended to be polemical. The Pietists strove for a faith evident in one's life; desired to minister to the poor, orphans, and widows; and promoted personal Bible study. All of these doctrinal and practical matters of faith resided in Luther and Lutheranism.

But as still happens today after the death of a great leader, followers of Luther splintered into more extreme positions. It is impossible to reconcile the Pietist and Orthodox positions regarding artistic music in the church. Pietists were against it (as were Calvinists), and wherever their teaching took hold, both liturgy and music in the church suffered. Such ideas were offensive to Bach. To him, the person who rejected artistic church music was a natural and spiritual foe; so Bach could not have been a Pietist officially even though he empathized with the general tenor of the Pietist movement. A summary of theological discussion pertaining to Bach conclusively grants that he was a devout student of Luther who, by his own statements, believed he occupied the biblical "office" of church musician. Bach's stated life goal was to compose "well-regulated church music" for the glory of God.[5]

Bach's Heritage: Hermeneutical Church Music and Musicians

Bach was not the first German church composer to demonstrate a synthesis of Lutheran theology in the context of service music. A tradition in Lutheran church music had been passed down through Heinrich Schütz (1585–1672), Johann Hermann Schein (1586–1630), and Samuel Scheidt (1587–1654). Less than a century before Bach's time, these Lutheran musicians held positions similar to his musically, ecclesiastically, and theologically. One compositional tradition that they all share is the use of Baroque musical rhetoric, a generic class of musical devices derived from the effort to imitate linguistic/literary devices associated with oratory. Musical rhetorical gestures are compositional figures that add literary or interpretive meaning to music.[6] Musical rhetoric can serve a hermeneutical function, and has been called "the single most important aesthetic concept of all of Schütz's music."[7] (See chapter 27, "Heinrich Schütz: A Hermeneutical Composer.")

While secular Baroque composers employed musical rhetoric as well, the difference between them and the three church musicians now being considered is theological. Schütz, for example, had theological training and purposely determined to elucidate spiritual truth in the way he wrote music. Schütz was entirely committed to the interpretive musical setting of the Word of God and made this his life's work, providing the perfect paradigm for Bach. "Schütz's church music . . . not only conveys the Word, but it actively carries the Word forth. It doesn't merely make known, but it preaches, it proclaims."[8]

Schein was a predecessor of Bach as *Thomaskantor* in Leipzig. Musicologist Paul Nettl notes that Schein "delved deeply into the meaning of the biblical texts and tried to express their spiritual message in music" and that Bach became heir to this tradition.[9] Scheidt, Schütz, and Schein were also devoted to the German chorale (hymn), as was Bach. The chorale plays a prominent role in much of his church music, be it for keyboard, choral forces, or solo voice. Bach resembles these three German masters, especially Schütz, in his approach to text. For Bach and Schütz, attention to German speech rhythm and cadence made them linguistic sons of Luther and gave to him the posthumous role of being their finest librettist vis-à-vis his translation of the Bible and formulation of the *Deutsche Messe.*

Bach's immediate predecessor at the St. Thomas Church in Leipzig was Johann Kuhnau (1660–1722), appointed in 1684. Kuhnau was a pioneer of the keyboard sonata, of which his six programmatic "Biblical" sonatas are the most famous. With them he strove to demonstrate how keyboard music could capture emotional states without the benefit of a poetic text. In other words, here was a composer seeking to communicate emotional, theological, and musical truth without words, through instrumental music alone. Bach regularly accomplished this kind of instrumental communication in his organ, solo-instrument, and orchestral works in addition to his cantatas, passions, and other "texted" works.

Bach the Preacher

One of the most significant aspects of compositional technique that Bach shared with Schütz was a hermeneutical approach in setting Scripture to music.[10] This activity was in complete accordance with Luther's views that music should be employed "in the service of exegesis and of the enlivening of the Word" in order to "intensify the biblical text through melodic, rhythmic, harmonic, and contrapuntal means," allowing it to "strike the hearer in full force."[11] All evangelical church music from the time of the Reformation to Bach was intent on finding a compositional technique that could, with integrity, do justice to the language and interpret the Word successfully.[12] Bach's familiarity with Luther's theology, coupled with his own classical education, intuition, and logic, allowed him to develop a musical language of his own. Andreas Werckmeister (1645–1706), the German organist, composer, and musical theorist who developed the chromatic tuning used in all the churches in which Bach served, indicated that at the deepest level, musical meaning is theological and that it is to be uncovered by a practice analogous to hermeneutics.[13] This principle was never truer of another composer than it was for Johann Sebastian Bach.

Bach's cantatas were *Predigtmusik* (sermon music)—music that proclaimed the message of the text. In this sense the cantatas functioned as another sermon for the day, having the same goal as the sermon spoken from the pulpit: the proclamation of Scripture.[14] One might recall Luther's words: "God has His Gospel preached through music too . . ."[15] Of Bach and of other Christian composers who are mindful of their interpretive responsibilities it can be said:

> Thus righteous composers, using all their qualities for expressing every word of a text artistically in a religious composition, show sufficiently that they are not concerned only about sweetness, but also about religious matters as true Christians. And therefore a well-worded piece of church music consists not only of a melodious exterior, but even more of true holy devotion and meditation.[16]

If only this could consistently be said of the new church music coming out of the "Christian" music publishing houses and composers of our day!

Bach saw such artistic music-making as part of a preaching and teaching ministry and never merely for the entertainment of the congregation or as an adornment to the liturgy.[17] His was functional, purposeful art music; but while useful, it is far more than utilitarian. Martin Naumann has written:

> The works of other great musicians speak to us, but the works of Bach preach to us. These sermons, his cantatas, and particularly his *St. Matthew Passion*, proclaim the glory of the God of the Bible in a thousand voices in all places where men have learned to treasure the eloquence of the *Thomaskantor*. Bach had something to say by reason of his faith and by reason of his office. He said it in a language that fits the grand theme. He preached Christ and Him crucified. He extolled the Son of God as the Saviour of the world. That is why we may call him a preacher.[18]

That Bach's music has this "forth-telling" or proclamatory quality demonstrates the basic emphasis of the New Testament.[19] This emphasis is evangelical in the original and proper use of the term: pertaining to the message of the four evangelists (the gospel, or "good news" about Jesus Christ). The proclamation of the Word (Scripture) was also the proclamation of the Word (*Logos*, or Christ; John 1:1, 14).

The sermon's precedence over the Eucharist was an innovation of the Reformation, since Luther affirmed that salvation is through the Word (Christ), and that without the Word the elements of Communion are devoid of sacramental quality. The Protestant church thus made the sermon, rather than the sacrament, the focal point of the service. The Word was sterile, however, unless it was heard—true to Lutheran, Augustinian, and Pauline teaching (*fides ex auditu*—"faith from hearing" [Rom. 10:13–14, 17]).

In this sense, Bach's music not only proclaims, but also *invites.* It helps us *hear* the Word in a fuller sense. In a truly evangelical context, Bach's music invites the parishioner to be a participant, and it confronts the listener both musically and textually so that "hearing" (understanding) is enhanced. Bach does not permit retreat into the distance as a bystander; rather, he involves the listener in thought and decision on an existential level.[20] Bach shared this characteristic with Schütz, who also "had an intensely personal approach to Scripture. Like a good preacher, he [Schütz] was not content simply to declare the text but also to see himself and his hearers involved in it."[21]

Howard Adams has suggested that many of the cantata texts were selected for their emphasis on contemporaneity, that their dramatic movement gives a sense of reality and urgency, creating a genuine experience involving the congregation.[22] He believes Bach's "reverence and respect for the Bible is reflected in the librettos he chose for his cantatas, since the decisive task of the cantatas consists not in narration or dramatic presentation of the events, but in an always new relation of this event to the men of the present."[23] The worshiper is confronted and, in the closing chorale, has the opportunity to join in corporate response—if not audibly and physically (by singing), at least cognitively (through familiarity and association with the hymn).

The chorale (hymn) sometimes acts as a method of application—as a means of restating the biblical truth in the language of the people. Lutheran theologian Richard Jeske writes:

> It is this invitational character of the music of Bach that is so compellingly present in his church cantatas, and which . . . distinguishes Bach's music from the music of other great composers before him . . . This use of the biblical text to confront the hearer existentially is exactly what the Reformation exegetical and homiletical tradition has brought to the task of biblical interpretation.[24]

The preacher does not simply exposit the text but presents it as an instrument for proclaiming the saving message of Christ, available to all who believe, by grace through faith—the heart of Reformation soteriology. With this comprehensive approach to the interpretation and application of Scripture to the congregation, Bach can rightly be called a preacher—a musical, evangelical preacher who was conscious of his calling (what he called an "office") and of his role.

In Part 2 of this essay, we will discuss what Bach models for us as a church musician and what he has to teach us as a musical explicator of Scripture. From this discussion, practical ideas and application will be given to help the modern church musician.

Notes

1. *Euangelion* is a neuter noun (the good news) and *euangelizo* is the verb (the act of proclaiming the good news).

2. Don O. Franklin, "J. S. Bach and Pietism," *Pietisten* 8–12 (1993–1997), pt. 8: "Bach in Leipzig: Cantata as Text," 9.

3. Richard Jeske, "Bach as Biblical Interpreter," in *The Universal Bach* (Philadelphia: American Philosophical Society, 1986), 89.

4. Gabriel Fackre, "Evangelical, Evangelicalism," in *The Westminster Dictionary of Christian Theology*, ed. Alan Richardson and John Bowden (Philadelphia: Fortress Press, 1972), 191.

5. Bach's letter to the Church of St. Blasius, Mühlhausen, June 25, 1708, in *The New Bach Reader: A Life of Johann Sebastian Bach in Letters and Documents*, ed. Hans T. David and Arthur Mendel, rev./enlarged Christoph Wolff (New York: W. W. Norton, 1998), 56–57.

6. See George J. Buelow, "Rhetoric and Music," in *The New Grove Dictionary of Music and Musicians*, vol. 15, ed. Stanley Sadie (New York: Macmillan, 1980), 793–803.

7. George J. Buelow, "A Schütz Reader: Documents on Performance Practice," *American Choral Review* 27 (1985): 7.

8. Willem Mudde, "Heinrich Schütz, Composer of the Bible," in *Musical Heritage of the Lutheran Church*, vol. 5 (St. Louis: Concordia, 1959), 90.

9. Paul Nettl, *Luther and Music*, trans. F. Best and R. Wood (Philadelphia: Muhlenberg Press, 1948), 117.

10. For an interesting discussion of the similarities and differences in the lives and music of Schütz and Bach, see Leo Schrade, "Heinrich Schütz and Johann Sebastian Bach in the Protestant Liturgy," in *Musical Heritage of the Lutheran Church*, vol. 7, ed. T. Hoelty-Nickel (St. Louis: Concordia, 1970), 170–90.

11. Günther Stiller, *J. S. Bach and Liturgical Life in Leipzig*, trans. Herbert J. A. Bouman, Daniel F. Poellot, and Hilton C. Oswald, ed. Robin A. Leaver (St. Louis: Concordia, 1984), 150.

12. Ibid.; see also Alfred Dürr, *Die Kantaten von Johann Sebastian Bach* (Kassel: Bärenreiter, 1971), 14.

13. Eric Chafe, *Tonal Allegory in the Vocal Music of J. S. Bach* (Berkeley: University of California Press, 1991), 141–54.

14. Stiller, *J. S. Bach and Liturgical Life*, 151.

15. *Table Talk*, ed. Theodore G. Tappert, in vol. 54 of *Luther's Works*, ed. Helmut T. Lehmann (Philadelphia: Fortress Press, 1967), 129. Full statement: "God has preached the gospel through music too, as may be seen in Josquin." Josquin des Prez (ca. 1440–1521), the Burgundian church composer to whom Luther was referring, was in fact Luther's favorite composer and almost his contemporary.

16. Georg Motz, *Die vertheidigte Kirchen-Musik* . . . (Tilsit, East Prussia, 1703), 52, as quoted in Ulrich Leisinger, "Affections, Rhetoric, and Musical Expression," in *The World of the Bach Cantatas*, ed. Christoph Wolff (New York: W. W. Norton, 1997), 195.

17. Robin A. Leaver, *J. S. Bach as Preacher: His Passions and Music in Worship* (St. Louis: Concordia, 1984), 14.

18. Martin J. Naumann, "Bach the Preacher," in *The Little Bach Book*, ed. T. Hoelty-Nickel (Valparaiso, IN: Valparaiso University Press, 1950), 14, 16.

19. Leaver, *J. S. Bach as Preacher*, 42.

20. Jeske, "Bach as Biblical Interpreter," 90.

21. Robin A. Leaver, "Heinrich Schütz as a Biblical Interpreter," *BACH: The Journal of the Riemenschneider Bach Institute*, 4, no. 3 (1973): 5, referring to Roger Bray, "The *Cantiones Sacrae* of Heinrich Schütz Re-examined," *Music and Letters* 52 (1971): 299–305.

22. See Howard C. Adams, "The Contemporizing of Scripture in the Cantatas of Johann Sebastian Bach," in *Johann Sebastian: A Tercentenary Celebration*, ed. S. L. Benstock (Westport: Greenwood Press, 1992).

23. Ibid., 27. The cantata texts were not necessarily chosen by Bach. It is generally understood that the minister of the church was personally involved in their selection as well. Yet Melvin Unger also states, "Although we do not know what hand Bach had in the writing of these libretti, . . . we may assume that, at the very least, he chose them, and thereby demonstrated some of his theological and literary inclinations." "Bach's First Two Leipzig Cantatas: The Question of Meaning Revisited," *BACH: The Journal of the Riemenschneider Bach Institute*, 28, nos. 1 and 2 (1997): 107.

24. Jeske, "Bach as Biblical Interpreter," 87, 90.

26

J. S. Bach and Musical Hermeneutics—Part 2: Lessons from Bach

Oh come, let us sing to the L*ORD*;
let us make a joyful noise to the rock of our salvation! —Psalm 95:1

The music ministry of Johann Sebastian Bach serves as an excellent model for church-music leaders because he can rightly be considered the quintessential theological musician. Bach was a devout student of the Word of God (as the markings and notations in his Bible testify), and he was a great admirer of Martin Luther. One could say that studying Luther was an avocation for Bach, but it would probably be more accurate to say that Luther was Bach's hero. At the time of Bach's death, the record of his library shows that he owned two complete sets of Luther's works and part of a third edition. There is evidence that he spent a great deal of time in these as well as other theological books.

The principal purpose of the Lutheran "gospel hermeneutic" in the study of the Scriptures is the search to find Christ.[1] In other words,

Lutheran exegesis is *Christocentric*, a characteristic that it shares with preaching in the Presbyterian and Reformed traditions. According to Bach scholar-theologian Richard Jeske, J. S. Bach's desire and ability to follow this hermeneutic, by disclosing the genuine referential power of the biblical text, has earned him status as one of the most important interpreters of the Scriptures in the entire Christian tradition.[2] What one discovers in Bach is the faith of Luther reborn in the greatest German church composer since the Reformation. He understood and championed Luther's theology in musical terms. So to properly understand Bach's chief contribution to the church—the sacred cantatas—one should understand Luther and his view of music. (See chapter 1, "Sermon in Song: Sacred Music as Proclamation.") Chiefly, Bach sought to advance the message of the Bible through his music, as did Heinrich Schütz a century earlier. Günther Stiller says that

> for Bach in his entire liturgical work the life-giving and life-preserving Word of God was at stake, the *viva vox evangelii* that was to be heard in the sermon as well as in sermon music and in the church hymn. Bach's liturgical cantatas do not want to be works of music or art in their own right; they want to advance the work of Luther, the preaching of the Word and always only the Word, with their own materials.[3]

Bach's Bible

Bach also speaks for himself when it comes to purpose and goals. His thoughts about music and about what he considered the "biblical office" of church musician are written on the pages of his Bible. His creed is evident in his confessional faith, and his faith is exemplified in his musical works irrespective of genre—be it the *Orgelbüchlein*, the *Brandenburg Concerti*, or the *St. Matthew Passion*. Whether a work was sacred or secular in its text or classification, Bach often penned "J.J." (*Jesu, juva*—"Jesus, help me") or "I.N.J." (*In nomine Jesu*—"In the name of Jesus") at the beginning and "S.D.G." (*soli Deo gloria*—"to the glory of God alone") at the end. He understood the act of artistic creation itself to be a sharing in the image of his Creator, an act for which divine help was necessary. As a true disciple of Luther, he strove to compose and live according to the doctrines of confessional orthodoxy, the devotional and active faith espoused by the Pietists, and the spiritual union with Christ sought after by the mystics—worthy aspirations for any Christian musician.

A primary source of information in support of the genuine nature of Bach's faith is the *Calov Bible* he owned and in which his margin notes and markings may be found on more than 250 separate pages.[4] The 1938 discovery of Bach's commentary Bible and a careful study of it in 1969 has put to rest any credible doubts concerning the reality of Bach's faith. In the markings, four comments penned by Bach directly relate to music in worship. Bach also marked eight passages of commentary having to do with one's office. Christoph Trautmann wrote that these "reveal the conviction of Bach, the Lutheran cantor, that his office claimed the whole man and the whole artist as one indivisible unit," and that they "must be taken seriously as the expression of a mature person conscious of his responsibility, as a Christian and an artist."[5]

As mentioned in Part 1 of this essay, the cantata was performed in the Lutheran service after the gospel reading and creed, prior to the spoken sermon (sometimes it continued afterward as well). Melvin Unger, director of the Riemenschneider Bach Institute, attributes the growth of the cantata into a fully developed genre on the basis of this function "because it was regarded as a significant medium for the proclamation, amplification, and interpretation of Scripture."[6] The individual (whether singer, player, listener, or composer) becomes the active and activating element by functioning both as interpreter of the Bible and as the intermediary transmitter of the message.[7] Music thus serves, through proclamation, as a *means of grace* to the one who hears the gospel and, in faith, believes through the work of the Spirit.

Bach: The Model Church Musician

The modern church musician can learn many things from Bach. What follows are points that summarize Bach's belief. These summaries have been drawn from study of the composer's Bible, letters, and music. Each point is then briefly treated with application to the church today. It is important to examine such conclusions for veracity in light of the Word of God, something that the reader is encouraged to do as well.

Bach interpreted the Word of God with the finest art music, to the praise of God and for the enrichment of the saints. Our musical offerings in the worship service should likewise be vehicles that serve our worship of God and reflect his attributes. Musical offerings should be the best that we can bring. They should be costly, even sacrificial. Church music ought to be something extraordinary, quite distinct from popular "musics," although it should include and present the praises of the people. Its primary purpose is to bring glory to God. In so doing, it will strengthen and edify the people of God and bear witness to the lost. This implies that musicians have responsibilities—in text selection, musical setting, composition, practice, performing, and purpose.

As a devout student of the Word of God, Bach expressed his lifelong goal as desiring to compose "a well-regulated church music, to the Glory of God."[8] Churches should engage educated musicians who are committed to bringing God glory. Musicians should be students of the Word for their personal spiritual growth, but also to be equipped to teach choirs, children, and the congregation. If musicians lack theological training, they need to read, study, and ask for help. Church-music composers should have the glory of God, not financial gain, at the heart of their compositional work, in marked distinction to most compositions and composers of "church music" today and to the market-driven agencies and organizations that sell crude music to an indiscriminate Christian public. We should desire to fashion music of order and beauty that communicates biblical truth.

Bach understood his position as cantor/music director to be a biblical office instituted by King David in 1 Chronicles. Thus, he took the role very seriously and served as a dedicated, empowered leader within the church hierarchy. We tend to rely on volunteer musicians to lead in many of our churches.

This is not a biblical pattern. While lay musicians are needed and should be involved, a professional musician who understands the role of the biblical director of music/chief musician ought to be at the helm. Such musicians should have a sense of calling to this work and be deeply committed. Trust those you hire, or hire someone else; but in either case, let the person do his job. Pastors and congregations need to entrust musical details and decisions for the church to such competent persons.

Bach's cantatas functioned as the second sermon for the day in the Lutheran service. Usually, this sermon music was based on the gospel (or epistle) reading for the day and was thereby linked to the minister's sermon. The Bachian cantata has several important characteristics appropriate for music in our churches today:

- It was often newly composed or arranged (for the specific church in which he was serving) but rooted in musical and liturgical tradition.
- It was intricately tied to the liturgy and to the sermon, served as a sermon in its own right, and employed fine sacred poetry.
- It was a vital, planned element of worship in the service.
- It was artistic and complex, yet it connected with the people in that it grew out of or referred to known chorales (hymns).
- It preached, meditated on, and interpreted the Word of God.
- It was Christocentric, not anthropocentric (Christ-centered, not man-centered).
- It engaged the congregation in both contemplation and response.
- It required thought but was also full of emotion.
- It manifested good form and musical logic.
- It was art music, presented under skilled direction, involving both professional and lay musicians. It was not commercial, pop, or folk music led by amateurs.

We have considered the function of the church's chief musician and the special role of the cantata as proclamation in the Lutheran service by using Bach as an example. We have not discussed here other service music, such as the hymns sung by the congregation, settings of other liturgical music, responses, and preludes/postludes. Many of the same principles apply to these selections as well, though their role in the service may be as praise or prayer rather than as proclamation. (See chapter 2, "Sacred Music as Prayer," and chapter 8, "Service Music: What's It All About?")

Notes

1. Richard L. Jeske, "Bach as Biblical Interpreter," in *The Universal Bach* (Philadelphia: American Philosophical Society, 1986), 88.

2. Ibid., 92.

3. Günther Stiller, *Johann Sebastian Bach and Liturgical Life in Leipzig,* trans. Herbert J. A. Bouman, Daniel F. Poellot, and Hilton C. Oswald, ed. Robin A. Leaver (St. Louis: Concordia, 1984), 253.

4. For a description of the scientific study of this Bible as well as an English translation of the Bible's notations and analyses, see "The Calov Bible of J. S. Bach," in *Studies in Musicology* no. 92, ed. Howard Cox (Ann Arbor: UMI Research, 1985).

5. Christoph Trautmann, "J. S. Bach: New Light on His Faith," *Concordia Theological Monthly* 42 (1971): 93, 96.

6. Melvin P. Unger, "Bach's Cantata Texts: What Do They Mean and Did Bach Mean Them?" (lecture, Indiana University, July 1997), preceding a presentation since published as "Bach's First Two Leipzig Cantatas: The Question of Meaning Revisited," *BACH: The Journal of the Riemenschneider Bach Institute,* 28, nos. 1 and 2 (1997): 90.

7. Leo Schrade, "Heinrich Schütz and Johann Sebastian Bach in the Protestant Liturgy," in *Musical Heritage of the Lutheran Church,* vol. 7, ed. T. Hoelty-Nickel (St. Louis: Concordia, 1970), 184.

8. Bach's letter to the Church of St. Blasius, Mühlhausen, June 25, 1708, in *The New Bach Reader: A Life of Johann Sebastian Bach in Letters and Documents,* ed. Hans T. David and Arthur Mendel, rev./enlarged Christoph Wolff (New York: W. W. Norton, 1998), 56–57.

27
Heinrich Schütz: A Hermeneutical Composer

Your statutes have been my songs
in the house of my sojourning. —Psalm 119:54

Heinrich Schütz (1585–1672) was a composer of great skill whose life's goal was to honor God through the music he wrote, which was almost exclusively sacred. He is particularly recognized for his outstanding text-setting of the German language and musical interpretation of biblical texts. Some have claimed that Schütz was, in fact, the greatest musical interpreter of the Scriptures.[1] We will explore this claim by looking at some of his music and compositional procedures. In so doing, the manner in which his theological understanding of biblical texts shaped his compositions, in turn delivering his interpretation of the Bible to the listener, should become evident. This compositional style displays a kind of musical hermeneutic (hermeneutics being the art and science of interpreting literary, specifically biblical, texts).

Volumes abound concerning Schütz's life, musical training, and background, so the mention of a few key details here will suffice. Schütz received instruction in the importance of text-setting during his first period of study in Venice (1609–12) when he was a pupil of Giovanni Gabrieli (ca. 1557–1612).[2] Under Gabrieli, Schütz learned the polychoral tradition that was to inform much of his early music, most clearly seen in the Venetian style of the *Psalmen Davids* ("Psalms of David") (1619). Claudio Monteverdi (1567–1643) and the *stile concertato* ("concerto style") also influenced Schütz. Monteverdi's influence pervaded the Italian musical scene upon Schütz's return to Venice in 1628. With his wide traveling in later years, Schütz amalgamated various influences in his compositional techniques to form a truly international musical style, although his roots remained strongly North German.[3]

Schütz's Theology

Schütz's intellectual and theological training were also in the German tradition. He was born in 1585, late in the century of Martin Luther (1483–1546), who had died just forty years earlier. The Protestant Reformation and the doctrines of Lutheranism profoundly affected Schütz. Acknowledgment of this fact is crucial to an understanding of his music. The interpretation of the Bible and the truth of the Bible as the Word of God were central to this theological system. Schütz was by no means a theological bystander. He was an active participant in study and in practice. "Schütz was not only able to handle both the Latin and German translations; he also was able to cope with the Scriptural text in its original languages."[4] He had learned biblical Hebrew and Greek and exhorted his students to do likewise. This is "one evidence of Schütz's desire to represent biblical texts faithfully. He himself had excelled in Greek and especially Hebrew, and often changed even Luther's translations of the Bible for his motets."[5] This tampering with Luther was a bold step. But it was completely in line with Reformation theology, in which the individual has license to interpret the Word of God with the illuminating influence of the Holy Spirit because Christ himself is our "High Priest" (Heb. 8:1–5). If Schütz felt that Luther had erred, it was more important to be faithful to the Scriptures than to Luther.

Luther had translated the entire Bible into the German tongue; this was "his noblest achievement and for the Germans, incomparable. None of the others had the majesty of diction, the sweep of vocabulary, the native earthiness, and the religious profundity of Luther."[6] Luther wrestled in his translation to present the text accurately, and yet in a manner thoroughly German. This language dynamic is carried on in the music of Schütz. Schütz was aware that he was an interpreter of the biblical texts for others also.[7] He was not simply a student of the texts but a teacher as well.

Influences on Schütz

Luther exerted a strong influence on Schütz, but he was not the only theologian to do so. The man who would eventually preach at Schütz's funeral was also an eminent figure in Lutheran orthodoxy—Martin Geier (1614–80). Geier was professor of Hebrew at the University of Leipzig, and later the senior court preacher in Dresden (the *Oberhofprediger*). Robin Leaver, professor of church music at Westminster Choir College, notes that the Dresden post "at that time was probably the most important and influential position in the Lutheran Church in Germany" and that Geier was "a man of deep personal piety and genuine humility."[8] Geier and Schütz had much in common, not the least of which was their approach to Scripture. "His [Geier's] method was not only to elucidate the meaning of the text but also to draw out its implications within the context of a total biblical theology."[9] This is also a significant methodology and goal in the music of Schütz.

Another famous Lutheran theologian and contemporary of Schütz was Philipp Jakob Spener (1635–1705), a friend of Geier and the "father of Pietism." The Pietists were known to be opposed to art music in worship, but it was their emphasis on personal study of the Scriptures and on the experiential nature of faith that most profoundly affected Pietism's adherents. Pietism has been characterized pejoratively and to excess by orthodox Lutherans and by some others who should know better. In its genesis and essence, German Pietism was entirely Lutheran. Like many other religious groups, however, Pietists fell prey to radicals, who took the movement to an extreme and polarized it against established Lutheranism. That was unfortunate and devastating to the church, so one can understand the resentment that the word *Pietist* conjures up for some.

Pietism influenced Heinrich Schütz with regard to the texts he chose and their resulting musical settings, as it would similarly influence J. S. Bach a century later. Pietistic texts are particularly suited to Schütz's "affective" purposes, which we will discuss at greater length below. Geier's predecessor in Dresden was Jakob Weller, who was also a friend of Schütz. Weller's "great concern was that Christianity should not be presented as an intellectual system but rather as a personal response to the Biblical revelation."[10] So it is not erroneous to state that Schütz was influenced by the objectivism of Lutheran orthodoxy and the subjectivism of Lutheran Pietism, both of which helped to shape his life and work.

Schütz: A German Composer

While Schütz set numerous Italian texts to music, as did most other serious composers of the day, the majority of his work is in his native German. Words and their declamation were of primary importance to him—so important, in fact, that some musicologists claim it as the "single most important aesthetic concept of all of Schütz's music."[11] His primary motivation to compose seems to have been the setting of the Latin and German texts of the Bible. "His interest in setting text focused not only on meaning—using 'word-painting' whenever a musical figure could possibly be made to illustrate a word or idea in the text—but also on textual rhythm."[12] In other words, he personalized yet adhered to the natural rhythms of the German tongue. This function of the language may be the most striking characteristic of Schütz's music and what makes him so profoundly national. Musicologist Manfred Bukofzer suggested, "Perhaps no other German composer ever derived so much purely musical inspiration from the German speech rhythm."[13] We must note, of course, that "Germany" was not a unified nation at this time.

We refer to the language, region, and music as "German" because that is the simplest means of reference for us.

Janice Fain writes that Schütz's "musical settings often imitate the spoken gesture. That is, his melodic lines, while not often lyrical and arching, usually move up and down according to the voice's natural declamation in speaking. Too, Schütz often composed the rhythms of vocal lines to correspond with the rhythm of the spoken text."[14] This compositional trait can actually be called Schütz's "style." Basil Smallman, another musicologist, reiterates these ideas: "The most Germanic of composers, he reveals in the majority of his works his intense preoccupation not only with the meaning but also with the rhythm, inflections and cadences of his Germanic texts."[15] This linguistic allegiance was inborn, was nonmilitant, and in no way harmed or weakened Schütz's music, as is commonly suggested of nineteenth-century nationalism. Instead, this quality made his work distinct and lent it both strength and character.

Schütz's Music

The first of Schütz's great German published collections was the *Psalmen Davids* of 1619. Included here are twenty-six works of which twenty are complete psalm settings. Hans Moser wrote that "the compilation is a collection of the most beautiful, poetically most outstanding, and musically most fruitful of the psalms."[16] The compositional form and technique used in all these works is the Venetian concerto style learned from Gabrieli. The concerto style is "seen most clearly in Schütz's distinction between two types of vocal ensemble, the *coro favorito* and the *Capella*."[17] The former is the group of soloists who were highly trained and experienced, while the latter is the general chorus of less qualified singers. These groups are contrasted for their sonority, and each has its own task. The soloists carry the bulk of the composition as well as the entire psalm text, while the role of the *ripieno* group of singers or instrumentalists is more freely arranged. It was standard practice to conclude a psalm setting with the *Gloria Patri* as a doxology. Schütz does this in twelve cases, but occasionally omits this tradition if his composition is long. More often he forgoes it if the psalm itself has a grand conclusion or summary of its own. This intentional inclusion or omission demonstrates an understanding of the texts and Schütz's desire to treat them with interpretative care.

Schütz explored many styles throughout the intervening years of his career, and in 1650 he published his third and final collection of *Symphoniae Sacrae* ("Sacred Symphonies"). It has been said that the *Symphoniae Sacrae I–III* "are among the most important musical compositions of the 17th century and certainly the most significant in the composer's oeuvre."[18] The third book particularly is set apart as the greatest since the early collection of psalms. In many ways this final collection was a summation of Schütz's life's work, while in other ways it was still innovative.

The three volumes of *Symphoniae Sacrae* largely consist of pieces for solo voices with instrumental accompaniment, often two violins with basso continuo. Violins were considered extremely modern at the time, particularly in Germany.[19] But styles other than solo textures are represented in the *Symphoniae Sacrae III*. Smallman summarizes this idea in a manner worthy of restating:

> Stylistically, this final set of sacred concertos is Schütz's most advanced collection. In it the composer brings together elements from all areas of his earlier work—the polychoral and antiphonal writing of the *Psalmen Davids*, the closely wrought imitative polyphony of the *Cantiones Sacrae* and the *Geistliche Chormusik*, the monodic declamatory style (both solo and in ensemble) of the *Kleine Geistliche Konzerte*, and the idiomatic instrumental writing of the earlier sets of *Symphoniae Sacrae*. And through them he achieves a new synthesis which is grander in scale and more advanced in technique than anything he had previously attempted.[20]

An Example of Schütz's Hermeneutical Style

One of the most beautiful and characteristic works that Schütz penned in the *Symphoniae Sacrae III* was *Mein Sohn, warum hast du uns das getan,* SWV 401 ("My son, why have you made us worry?"), which we will briefly discuss. This section may be slightly more technical than the nonmusician will appreciate. If one can obtain a copy of the score or especially a good recording to listen to, however, the concepts discussed will be more apparent.[21] This musical gem is at once objective and subjective, dramatic and interpretive. It provides a good example of the hermeneutical implications obvious in the composer's work, particularly his "editing" of the text.

Mein Sohn recounts the Luke 2 story of Mary and Joseph's looking for Jesus, who has remained behind in the temple in Jerusalem. Schütz removes all narration and third-person point of view in the two verses from Luke's gospel and makes the action between the characters immediate. Next, he gives Joseph some adapted text from Mary. These alterations have the dramatic effect of producing a "scene." Schütz draws the listener into the action of the text. Leaver observes, "Schütz had an intensely personal approach to Scripture. Like a good preacher he was not content simply to declare the text but also to see himself and his hearers involved in it."[22] Schütz labels this opening to his work *In Dialogo* from the outset of its opening *Symphonia,* which employs two violins. Schütz thus musically sets the scene and mood for the biblical passage. It is sorrowful and "searching," which symbolizes the parents' plight, as the violins play motives that recur in the vocal melodies to follow. These voices represent Mary and Joseph, whose exchange of musical comment clearly shows the responsorial nature of dialogue (see fig. 27.1).

Fig. 27.1

The next outstanding choice on Schütz's part was to include verses from Psalm 84 to follow the first two-verse scene. This may have been part of an existing theological tradition, but Schütz makes it his own by choosing to include the psalm verses. For instance, in another setting of these verses from Luke (SWV 494), he does not include the psalm interpolation. Schütz's purpose is to interpret Jesus' response to his parents. They have been worriedly searching everywhere for their missing son. Upon finding him in the temple and asking him the question that titles the work, they must have been startled to hear his reply, "Did you not know that I must be in my Father's house?" (Luke 2:49). With the psalm interpolation Schütz explains for us the boy's reasoning—he exegetically claims that the purpose filling the child's life is the same as the psalmist's exclamation: "How lovely is your dwelling place, O Lord of hosts! My soul longs, yes, faints for the courts of the Lord; my heart and flesh sing for joy to the living God . . . Blessed are those who dwell in your house, ever singing your praise!" (Ps. 84:1–2, 4).

Schütz undoubtedly took a Christological view of the psalms, as Luther had done. Luther held that "the Old Testament foreshadowed the drama of redemption . . . The pre-existent Christ was working throughout the Old Testament, speaking through the mouths of the prophets and the psalmist."[23] Both Luther and Schütz were preoccupied with the Old Testament and with the book of Psalms in particular.[24] Luther, following the examples of the apostles, the first-century church, and Augustine, revived this method of interpreting a passage on the basis of an entire biblical context.

The structure of *Mein Sohn* is interpretive in its own right (fig. 27.2). Several ideas should be noted. The opening instrumental *symphonia* is evidently based on the Luke 2 passage even though no text is presented. The dialoguing violins symbolize the parents' restless search for their child.[25] The use of the full chorus and additional instruments (the *complementum*) in the same manner as the *capella* in Schütz's earlier *Psalms of David* is "to supply power and sonority at focal points in the musical structure."[26] The *complementum* was also used to introduce new sections of text, to foster antiphony, to state a refrain, or to propel a work or a section of a work to an effective conclusion.[27] For Schütz, musical structure is as important as the declamation of the text itself in the overall unified interpretation of the passage.

Fig. 27.2. The Structure of Schütz's *Mein Sohn*, SWV 401

Luke 2:48–49

MEASURES	MUSICAL MATERIAL	TEXT
1–24	Symphonia	
25–121	Dialogue	
(25–78)	A. Mary/Joseph	(The parents question Jesus)
(79–121)	B. The boy Jesus	(Jesus replies)

Psalm 84:1–2, 4

MEASURES	MUSICAL MATERIAL	TEXT
122–41	Full chorus	*How lovely is your dwelling place, O LORD of hosts!*
142–56	Trio (soloists)	*My heart and flesh sing for joy to the living God.*
157–81	Full chorus	*Blessed are those who dwell in your house . . .*

Both the presence and the absence of the *complementum* can be understood as interpretive and focal. For example, the first use of the additional vocal and instrumental forces occurs after the Lukan drama at the introduction of the psalm text. Here it shows the grandeur of the psalm verse ("How lovely are thy dwelling places, O LORD God of Hosts!") and can also be considered a representation of the heavenly host singing together. But when the text becomes more personal at the words "My heart and my flesh sing for joy to the living God," Schütz narrows to the three solo voices—the same voices that had earlier represented Jesus, Mary, and Joseph (*cantus*, *semicantus*, and *bassus*). It is likely that Schütz is suggesting that a desire to serve God and to be continually in his house was the mind-set and goal of all three God-fearing individuals—or else he might have used only a single solo voice. His setting could engender the same attitude in the engaged listener (father, mother, and children), which was undoubtedly Schütz's goal for this worship music.

Musical Rhetoric

Schütz makes use of figures of musical rhetoric that were common to other Baroque composers. Not only was he a master of such rhetorical devices, but he also employed them in interpretive ways that reveal a point of view about the text itself. Thus he expounds on the text as a preacher would, and he leads the listener toward a particular understanding of the passage. This is why Schütz's music can be called hermeneutical. Some of the rhetorical figures employed in this piece include:

1. *Interrogatio* (use of ascending intervals to act interrogatively) at the question, "*Was ist's,*" asked three times by Jesus (see fig. 27.3).

Fig. 27.3

2. *Polyptoton* (use of repetitive figures in close imitation) in the violin *symphonia.*
3. *Catabasis* (descending figure) used on the chromatic descent of *Schmerzen* ("sorrowing") in the opening dialogue between Mary and Joseph (see fig. 27.4).
4. *Auxesis/Climax* (rising sequential pattern) used at Jesus' emphatic response to his parents' concern, an answer that also pointed to his heavenly *Vater* ("Father").

Fig. 27.4

SWV 401 meas. 64-69

mit Schmer - - - - - - - - zen ge - sucht, mein Sohn

mit Schmer - zen ge - sucht, mein

5. *Suspiratio* (use of rests), fittingly employed at the setting of *verlanget und sehnet* ("longs and faints").
6. *Anabasis* (ascending motive) used with the phrase *die dich loben immerdar*, portraying continual praise of God with an ascending motive, which is repeated in other parts with different notes (*Anaphora*), and as a continuous scale cycle in thirds, sixths, or tenths (*Fauxbourdon*). Schütz further reinforces this idea of ongoing praise by making forty-four statements of the phrase within the space of twenty measures (see fig. 27.5).

Fig. 27.5

With the use of such rhetorical figures, Schütz sought to move the "affections" of his listener. George Buelow describes an "affection" in the *New Grove Dictionary of Music and Musicians* as "a rationalized emotional state or passion. Beginning in antiquity the purpose of rhetoric and subsequently, therefore, all rhetorically inspired music, was to imitate human passions."[28] In the case of Schütz, this is true both of the texts he chose and of the manner in which he personally interpreted them. So we experience at once the passions of the Bible and those of its interpreter. In his sacred music, Schütz fulfilled the Lutheran ideal of using music with the Word of God to deliver God's truth. Luther had said: "Next after theology I give to music the highest place and greatest honor. I would not exchange what little I know of music for something great. Experience proves that next to the Word of God only music deserves to be extolled as the mistress and governess of the feelings of the human heart."[29] Let us recall his words quoted earlier in chapter 1, "Sermon in Song: Sacred Music as Proclamation":

> Music and notes, which are wonderful gifts and creations of God, do help gain a better understanding of the text, especially when sung by a congregation and when sung earnestly . . . We have put this music to the living and holy Word of God in order to sing, praise and honor it. We want the beautiful art of music to be properly used to serve her dear Creator and his Christians. He is thereby praised and honored and we are made better and stronger in faith when his holy Word is impressed on our hearts by sweet music.[30]

While the use of rhetorical figures in composition is personal, it is also strongly objective. The affective purposes are planned, rational, and identifiable, not emotionally spontaneous and subjective as in the nineteenth century and following. "The Baroque composer planned the affective content of each work, or section or movement of a work, with all the devices of his craft, and he expected the response of his audience to be based on an equally rational insight into the meaning of his music."[31] The union of music and rhetoric in this manner is one of the most distinctive characteristics of Baroque music.

Musical rhetorical figures and rules, because of their origin in oration, are also closely related to preaching. Luther felt that musical composition for the church should be a *predicatio sonora* (a musical sermon).[32] Schütz followed this idea through to its practical application. His works make doctrinal statements that find their origin in a hermeneutic, an idea solemnized all the more because the texts are biblical. Leaver writes, "Schütz was probably the greatest master of the art of setting words to music, in which the content of the words is not destroyed and where the verbal form does not weaken the musical form. The center of Schütz' art is to be found in his solution of the problem of translating a text into musical terms."[33] When he combines noncontinuous biblical passages, he does so with purpose and with understanding, which we have noted to be intentionally derived from his hermeneutic.

Composer of the Word

Schütz dedicated his life to the creation and promotion of music fit for the worship of God. There was and is no greater source than the Bible from which to choose texts worthy of this function. If it is true that, for Schütz, music was entirely related to the texts with which he worked, then truly his music stemmed from a Source of divine inspiration as well as from his own humanity. It is a fitting conclusion to his lengthy career and life that his funeral text was Psalm 119:54: "Your statutes have been my songs in the house of my sojourning."

Psalm 119 served (in its entirety) as the basis for Schütz's final musical work, an eight-voice monumental piece in eleven parts (SWV 482–92). Not only is this chapter an appropriate choice in its scope as the longest of the psalms (176 verses), as the longest chapter in the entire Bible, and as a complete sectional acrostic of the Hebrew alphabet; but it is also apt in its subject matter. Virtually every verse of Psalm 119 mentions God's Word by name using various terminology (*law, testimonies, precepts, statutes, commandments, judgments, word, ordinances,* etc.). In fact, along with Psalm 1 and Psalm 19, Psalm 119 is fittingly known as a "psalm of the Word."

Schütz personally chose Psalm 119:54 in preparation for his funeral. He asked his favorite pupil, Christoph Bernhard (1627–92), to set it to music for the service, and his esteemed friend Martin Geier preached on it with careful exegesis of the Hebrew text. Therefore, it "represents not only Geier's but Schütz's understanding of the place of music in Christian life and worship."[34] Schütz found in this verse his purpose as a church-music composer: the biblical imperative and privilege of delivering the gospel to his listener. He understood the significance of his text—the Word of God—and thus the importance of his work. These truths coupled with his amazing skill set him apart as one of the greatest composers of church music in Western history.

Notes

1. Basil Smallman, *The Music of Heinrich Schütz* (Leeds: Mayflower Enterprises, ca. 1985), 8.
2. Janice M. Fain, "Text-Setting in the Music of Heinrich Schütz," *The Choral Journal* (February 1987): 5.
3. Janice Hamer, "Non-Linearity in Phrase Structure: A Stylistic Texture of the Music of Heinrich Schütz," *Sonus*, 3, no. 2 (1983): 40.
4. Robin A. Leaver, "Heinrich Schütz as a Biblical Interpreter," *BACH: The Journal of the Riemenschneider Bach Institute*, 4, no. 3 (1973): 5.
5. Fain, "Text-Setting," 7.
6. Roland Bainton, *Here I Stand: A Life of Martin Luther* (Nashville: Abingdon, 1977), 255.
7. Leo Schrade, "Heinrich Schütz and Johann Sebastian Bach in the Protestant Liturgy," in *Musical Heritage of the Lutheran Church*, vol. 7, ed. T. Hoelty-Nickel (St. Louis: Concordia, 1970), 55–57.
8. Leaver, "Heinrich Schütz," 8.
9. Ibid., 9.
10. Ibid.
11. George J. Buelow, "A Schütz Reader: Documents on Performance Practice," *American Choral Review* 27 (1985): 7.
12. Hamer, "Non-Linearity," 39.
13. Manfred Bukofzer, *Music in the Baroque Era, from Monteverdi to Bach* (New York: W. W. Norton, 1947), 90.
14. Fain, "Text-Setting," 6.
15. Smallman, *The Music of Heinrich Schütz*, 7.
16. Hans Joachim Moser, *Heinrich Schütz: His Life and Work*, trans. Carl F. Pfatteicher (St. Louis: Concordia, 1959), 296.
17. Buelow, "A Schütz Reader," 6.
18. Wolfram Steinbeck, *Translations and Commentary on the* Symphoniae Sacrae III, Deutsche Harmonia Mundi label, 7910-2-RC (New York: BMG Music, 1989), 8.
19. Ibid., 9.
20. Smallman, *The Music of Heinrich Schütz*, 87.

21. I recommend the complete two-disc recording of *Symphoniae Sacrae III* (1650) by Musica Fiata/Kammerchor Stuttgart/Frieder Bernius on the Deutsche Harmonia Mundi label, 7910-2-RC.

22. Leaver, "Heinrich Schütz," 5, referring to Roger Bray, "The *Cantiones Sacrae* of Heinrich Schütz Re-examined," *Music and Letters* 52 (1971): 299–305.

23. Bainton, *Here I Stand*, 261.

24. Leaver, "Heinrich Schütz," 6.

25. Moser, *Heinrich Schütz*, 609.

26. Smallman, *The Music of Heinrich Schütz*, 88.

27. Joshua Rifkin, "Heinrich Schütz," in *The New Grove North European Baroque Masters* (New York: W. W. Norton, 1985), 102.

28. George J. Buelow, "Rhetoric and Music," in *The New Grove Dictionary of Music and Musicians*, vol. 15, ed. Stanley Sadie (New York: Macmillan, 1980), 793–803.

29. Bainton, *Here I Stand*, 267.

30. Walter Buszin, *Luther on Music* (Saint Paul: North Central, 1958), 14, quoting Luther, "Treatise on the Last Words of David," in vol. 15 of *Luther's Works*, ed. Jeroslav Pelikan; and Martin Luther, "Preface to the Burial Hymns (1542)," in *Liturgy and Hymns*, ed. Ulrich S. Leupold, vol. 53 of *Luther's Works*, ed. Helmut T. Lehmann (Philadelphia: Fortress Press, 1965), 327.

31. Buelow, "Rhetoric and Music" (*New Grove*), 800.

32. Moser, *Heinrich Schütz*, 181.

33. Leaver, "Heinrich Schütz," 3.

34. Robin Leaver, "The Funeral Service for Heinrich Schütz," in BACH: The Journal of the Riemenschneider Bach Institute, 4, no. 4 (1973): 11.

28
Felix Mendelssohn's Psalm Settings

Sing aloud to God our strength;
shout for joy to the God of Jacob!
Raise a song; sound the tambourine,
the sweet lyre with the harp. —*Psalm 81:1–2*

Jakob Ludwig Felix Mendelssohn-Bartholdy (1809–47), known to his family, friends, and present-day musicologists simply as "Felix," wrote nine substantial choral settings of psalms. Along with his oratorios, *St. Paul* and *Elijah*, these psalm settings are among his greatest and most mature compositions, although they have been largely overshadowed in the public forum by his symphonic works. In fact, most of Mendelssohn's religious music is neglected today despite the fact that it makes up a considerable percentage of his output. While the psalms have been an important textual source for many composers, they may have had special meaning for Mendelssohn—personal and spiritual meaning, and possibly social and political as well. Mendelssohn's family history provides the context for this thinking.

Background

Moses Mendelssohn (1729–86) was Felix's paternal grandfather. Moses was a German-Jewish philosopher and a leader in the movement for cultural assimilation and religious tolerance in Germany. His philosophical writings, such as *Philosophische Gespräche* (*Philosophic Conversations,* 1755), *Philosophische Schriften* (*Philosophic Writings,* 1761), *Phädon* (*Phaedo,* 1767), and *Jerusalem: oder, Über religiöse Macht und Judentum* (*Jerusalem: or, On Religious Power and Judaism,* 1783), anticipated the aesthetics of Immanuel Kant and Friedrich Schiller. Moses Mendelssohn also translated Psalms and the Pentateuch into German. He worked as a partner in a Berlin silk-merchant firm to support his family. His son Abraham, Felix's father and a banker, converted from Judaism to Christianity and changed the family name to Mendelssohn-Bartholdy. Felix thus grew up in a wealthy, highly cultured, Protestant Christian home. He was baptized in the Lutheran church in 1816.

Felix lived to be only 38 years of age, but he enjoyed a tremendously successful career. A child prodigy, he wrote his first symphony (in C minor, Op. 11) at the age of 15, and what some have considered his first mature work, *Overture to A Midsummer Night's Dream,* Op. 61, at the age of 17. Certainly the *Octet for Strings* (age 16) is among his brilliant early work. But even earlier, by age 13, he had composed a *Gloria,* a *Magnificat,* a *Kyrie,* and settings of Psalm 19 and Psalm 66. In addition to playing violin, viola, piano, and organ, he composed chamber music, songs, choral music, organ sonatas, the violin concerto, eight sets of *Songs without Words* for piano, five symphonies, and the *Hebrides Overture,* Op. 26 (*Fingal's Cave*), among other pieces.

He served as choirmaster of the Berlin *Singakademie* and later as music director at Düsseldorf, two posts that provided him with great insight into choral writing. In his choral works, Felix paid homage to the styles of J. S. Bach and George Frideric Handel while delivering to the world his own musical language, particularly his sense of orchestral color. Friends with Robert Schumann, Clara Wieck (later Clara Schumann), Franz Liszt, Frédéric Chopin, Ignaz Moscheles, and many other well-known musicians of the day (including his own very talented sister, Fanny), Mendelssohn enjoyed immense popularity in the musical world and wielded a lot of clout in Leipzig, where he conducted the Leipzig Gewandhaus Orchestra and helped to found the Leipzig Conservatory.

So why might Mendelssohn write large choral/orchestral settings of the psalms rather than setting other universal texts to music? He could have chosen other "librettists" for choral works, such as the poet laureate Goethe (the septuagenarian with whom Felix stayed for two weeks while traveling with Carl Friedrich Zelter, who was his teacher and a good friend of Goethe), Shakespeare, or others. After all, Goethe was the inspiration of songs by both Felix and his sister Fanny, as well as Felix's *Meeresstille und glückliche Fahrt*, Op. 27 ("Calm Sea and Prosperous Voyage") overture of 1828.

First, it seems clear that he chose psalm texts because he was a Christian, and the psalms as musical prayers of God's people are eminently fitting for a Christian, particularly a Jewish Christian, composer.[1] Second, Mendelssohn's Jewish heritage may have drawn him toward the Psalter, especially because his grandfather had translated the book of Psalms. Third, he may have purposely used his position and influence as a celebrated composer to further the work of the gospel by providing concert music that was biblical in nature and thus perfectly suited to church contexts. Musicologists have criticized Mendelssohn for this, saying that the Romantic combining of concepts from Handelian oratorio and Bachian passions errantly mixed the idea of religious/nationalistic edification with Protestant liturgical form. On the other hand, one might suggest that Mendelssohn was not only entirely conscious of his actions, but purposely attempting to spiritually influence a broader public through musical means. Fourth, his keen interest in the renaissance of music from earlier times may also have spawned in him a desire to compose music for some of the earliest known musical texts, as Heinrich Schütz and others had done generations before him with the psalms. To some degree, all of these factors probably come into play.

Connections with Bach

In 1829 at the age of twenty, near the completion of his terms as a student at the University of Berlin, Felix conducted a performance of Johann Sebastian Bach's *St. Matthew Passion*, BWV 244, which helped to launch a rebirth of that composer's music. This performance of what many considered the "greatest Christian musical work" or the "ideal German artwork" was a Romantic vision and an altered version of the earlier composer's work, to be sure. Bach had composed the passion for the Lutheran church and liturgical ceremony, but it was now, according to Alfred Einstein (the musicologist brother of more famous Albert):

> transplanted to the concert hall; shortened, mutilated, completely modernized in sound, and—as Zelter expressed it—"rendered practical for the abilities of the performers"! Not merely for the abilities of the performers, but also for the mental capacity of the public. It was no longer the Bach of the Bible, of the Lutheran faith, of the magnificent simplicity, but a Romanticized Bach, reduced to Mendelssohnian formulae. But precisely these Romanticized details were what made the greatest impression on the public.[2]

While there is understandable negativity on the part of purists, Mendelssohn's efforts were quite evidently the impetus that Berlin and the rest of Germany needed to revive the music of Bach. For Felix personally, this was both a statement of faith and a performance that established him in the musical world of the time. The performance was sold out, and more than a thousand Berliners were turned away. In attendance were the king and his retinue, Friedrich Schleiermacher, G. W. F. Hegel, Heinrich Heine, Gaspare Spontini, Carl Friedrich Zelter, and other persons of note, possibly even Nicolò Paganini.[3]

This rediscovery of the early masters by the composers of the Romantic period included the study and parody of music by Palestrina, Schütz, Handel, Bach, and many others. Mendelssohn continued these labors in the one city in which Bach should surely have never been forgotten—Leipzig. For much of his professional life Mendelssohn lived in Leipzig, the place where Bach had held his final and lengthy twenty-seven-year post at the *Thomaskirche* a century earlier. Felix took it upon himself to learn much of the music of Bach, and throughout his performing career he reacquainted the public with various works of the master, from the *Chromatic Fantasy and Fugue* (for keyboard) and the *Triple Concerto* (for three harpsichords/pianos) to the church cantatas and works for organ.

Many great composers have been weaned on the music of Bach and have deepened their skills by studying it. But Mendelssohn had additional profound connections, both in terms of musical intelligence and ability and in terms of a sense of place. While Mendelssohn was not a church musician in the Bachian sense, he valued and understood Bach's calling and work. Felix's father, Abraham, once wrote to him, "Every room in which Sebastian Bach is sung is transformed into a church."[4] This kind of veneration of the *Thomaskantor* must have been a formative influence in the young musician's life. At times the power of Bach's music may have imposed itself upon his own writing and opened him to the criticism of others. To his friend Ferdinand Hiller, Mendelssohn wrote, "That my compositions have some resemblance with those of Sebastian Bach, I can do nothing about. For I wrote them, line by line, at a moment's impulse. And if the words impressed me in the same manner as old Bach, I can only be happy."[5]

Like Bach, Mendelssohn was a Lutheran. Yet it is interesting to note that he married Cécile, the daughter of a French Huguenot pastor, Auguste Jeanrenaud. They were married in a Reformed church on the Goetheplatz in Frankfurt. He even wrote one hymn for the Reformed church, at the request of the minister who married them, published in the Huguenot hymnbook, *Recueil de cantiques chrétiens* (1849).

The Oratorios

While we will not discuss the oratorios in detail, it is important to mention at least a few concepts related to them. First, the two major works, *St. Paul* (1836) and *Elijah* (1846), occupied much of Mendelssohn's mature compositional energy and stand as two pillars toward the middle and at the end, respectively, of his abbreviated career. Of *St. Paul* it has been said that Felix "seems to have regarded it as confirming his own Protestant faith."[6] In 1831, he announced to Karl Klingemann that the work would form a sermon (*Predigt*). Its completion and reception by the public also achieved his father Abraham's cherished agenda—assimilation of his family into Prussian society.[7] The theme of the oratorio—Saul's conversion, name change, and missionary journeys—was mirrored in the life of Mendelssohn's own family to an extent. In some ways the oratorio could be considered a personal statement. This would be particularly true if the choice of biblical texts and Christian themes in Felix's music was intentionally evangelistic, which is possible. He also assimilated aspects of the English oratorio (after Handel) and the German passion in this work. He included five chorales in the oratorio (after the manner of Bach), ending with Luther's 1525 hymn form of the Nicene Creed, *Wir glauben all* ("We All Believe"). With this appearance of the Creed, Mendelssohn suggests the Pauline doctrine of justification in the complex chorale fugue finale—a definite statement of faith not otherwise essential to an oratorio setting of the life of Paul.[8]

Elijah, by contrast, is a dramatic rendering of the Old Testament prophet's life and ministry, particularly his face-off versus the prophets of Baal. Yet even here, other biblical texts are interpolated so that the result is a pan-scriptural statement of faith. While it does not end with an explicit New Testament reference, as its German librettist, the theologian Julius Schubring, felt was essential (although the tenor solo following Elijah's ascension cites Matthew 13), Mendelssohn employed a chorale and other devotional biblical texts, including messianic texts from Isaiah. Those who said the work was neither Jewish nor Christian and did not remain true to the Old Testament story criticized him for this. Others, though, have suggested that if the libretto for *Elijah* is viewed from a Christological perspective, its weaknesses dissipate and an overarching Christian worldview becomes evident. The libretto may well have been shaped to highlight the typological parallels between Elijah and Christ, in various ways picturing the transformation of the Old Covenant into the New.

At the time of his death, Mendelssohn was working on a third oratorio, *Christus.* Some scholars have suggested that this was to be the New Testament complement to *Elijah.* The thirteen surviving movements handle the birth and passion of Christ. It is believed that these constitute the first of three intended sections and that the latter two would have been concerned with the resurrection and the final judgment. One of the surviving movements is a setting of the chorale *O Welt, sieh' hier dein Leben* ("O World, See Here Your Life") also used by J. S. Bach in the *St. Matthew Passion.*

The Psalms

Throughout his life, Mendelssohn set to music at least seventeen of the psalms or parts of them. Some of this music is from his student days with Zelter, but the nine published psalms (with opus numbers) are part of his mature work as a composer of renown. They take various forms, often resembling the cantatas or motets of Bach or even earlier polychoral writing of the Venetian composers. A full listing of Mendelssohn's setting of the psalms may be seen in figure 28.1 (major works in bold).

Fig. 28.1

PSALM		YEAR	FORCES
2	**Op. 78, no. 1**	**rev. 1845**	**Double chorus, *a cappella***
5		1839	(hymn setting)
19		1821	Chorus
22	**Op. 78, no. 3**	**1844**	**Tenor, double chorus, *a cappella***
24		1843	(harmonization)
31		1839	(hymn setting)
42	**Op. 42**	**1837**	**Soloists, chorus, orchestra**
43	**Op. 78, no. 2**	**1844**	**Double chorus, *a cappella***
55		1844	Soprano, chorus, organ (later orchestrated)
66		1822	Women's chorus, continuo (verses)
90	**Op. 79, no. 2**	**1845**	**Chorus, *a cappella***
95	**Op. 46**	**1839/41**	**Soloists, chorus, orchestra**
98	**Op. 91**	**1845**	**Soloists, double chorus, orchestra**
100		1844	Chorus, *a cappella*
114	**Op. 51**	**1839/41**	**Soloists, double chorus, orchestra**
115	**Op. 31**	**1830**	**Soloists, chorus, orchestra**
119		1821	Two choral fugues (verses)

It may be helpful for us to look a little more closely at one of these. *Psalm 42* was important to Mendelssohn personally and thus makes a good choice.

Psalm 42, Op. 42

Felix himself is reputed to have favored *Psalm 42* above all his previous works (at least up until its completion in 1837). In November of that year he sent the manuscript to his publisher, claiming that it was "the best I have composed of the kind" and that it was "dearer" to him than all his other compositions. He penned the bulk of the work during his honeymoon in Switzerland in 1837, a particularly happy period in his life. Robert Schumann agreed with Mendelssohn's assessment of the piece, writing that it was "at the highest summit he has ever reached as a church musician, and that church music as a whole has ever attained."[9]

Some twentieth-century critics have found the piece too "sentimental," a word often used of Mendelssohn's music, particularly when it is characterized by sweet melodies and chromaticism, as in the *Songs without Words* for piano. One reason that it may be used of *Psalm 42* is the very personal nature of the piece, which could be considered more nostalgic or melancholy than sentimental. Felix chose to represent the Soul as calling out to God for help in trouble, but still assured of the answer—God is present through my song (v. 8); he is my salvation (v. 5); I shall again praise him (vv. 5, 11), etc. In other words, this is not a bitter, tragic cry of anguish, but the song of a hurting child aware of his heavenly Father's love and desiring the fullest experience of that relationship once again.

The entire work functions in a manner akin to the dialogue cantatas of Bach in which the Soul (always represented by a soprano) and Jesus (often represented by a bass) converse with each other. Mendelssohn's setting also employs a soprano to represent the Soul. The men's chorus first asks the pervading question, "Why are you troubled, O my soul?" while the full chorus provides the answer. Roles and questions are shifted throughout the work (and there is no direct personification of Christ); nevertheless, the assurance of God's help and presence is presented through the other psalm verses.

Much of Mendelssohn's music can be categorized as "classicist" notwithstanding the fact that he is a composer of the Romantic period. Einstein titled him the "Romantic Classicist." This designation has to do with Felix's formal procedures and choices for his music, which maintain structural integrity in the classic manner. Perhaps this is as evident in *Psalm 42* as in any of his other music, for here one discovers a chiastic or "arch-like" form (found often in Bach), symmetrical in every respect (see fig. 28.2). A clearer way of viewing the structure might be figure 28.3.

Fig. 28.2

General structure of Mendelssohn's *Psalm 42*, Op. 42

MOVEMENT	FORM	VOCAL FORCES EMPLOYED	KEY
1	Chorus	Choir	F major
2	Aria	Soprano	D minor
3	Recit./Aria	Soprano/Female chorus	A minor
4	Chorus	Choir	F major
5	Recitative	Soprano	transitory/G minor
6	Aria	Soprano/Male quartet	B-flat major
7	Fugue	Choir	F major

Fig. 28.3

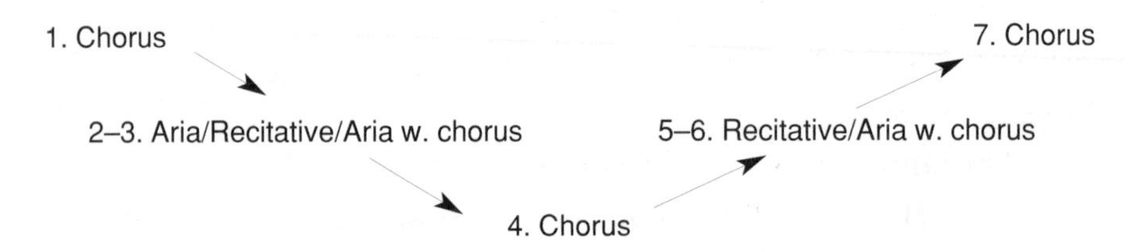

In most chiastic structures, the *crux* or central, middle section is the most significant. This is true not only in musical settings but also in literary works, including many psalms and other wisdom literature of the Old Testament. In *Psalm 42* the chorus of Movement 4 (*Harre auf*

Gott!) takes this position. This movement provides the reassuring answer to the disquieted soul: "Hope in God!" (Ps. 42:5b). Verse 5 reappears verbatim as verse 11, so it makes perfect sense for this music to be revisited at the end of the setting. Here the *Schlusschor* (closing chorus), Movement 7, restates the themes of Movements 1 and 4 before commencing the fugue that closes out the psalm setting in a manner characteristic of the great choral works of Handel, Bach, Mozart, Beethoven, and other of Mendelssohn's forebears. The thematic material of the primary choruses is similar in that the themes of Movements 4 and 7 are manipulated versions of Movement 1. This makes sense and provides musical unity to the work that well matches the overall spirit of the psalm. The "thirsting after God" of the first verse (Mvt. 1—"A") is musically reworked for the setting of verse 5 (Mvt. 4—"B") and then altered again for verse 11 (Mvt. 7—"C").

Fig. 28.4

Fig. 28.5

Fig. 28.6

Notice, as well, the manner in which the opening melodic figure of the entire psalm ("A" below, fig. 28.7) becomes the germ motive for many of the work's primary melodies, and acts as the opening measures of the closing fugal theme ("D"). Comprising a rising major second (M2) and minor third (m3) (seen in "A" and "B"), or the inversion of this interval set ("C" and "D"), this figure provides melodic unity throughout the work.

Fig. 28.7

Fig. 28.8

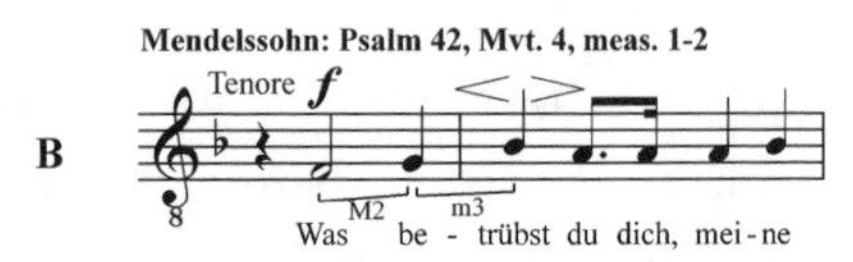

Fig. 28.9

Fig. 28.10

Other Sacred Choral Works

While the psalms were his most significant contribution to sacred music, Mendelssohn also composed a cantata, *Lauda Sion* (Op. 73), on that particular sacred Latin text.[10] He set to music the words of Christ to Peter from Matthew 16:18–19, *Tu es Petrus* (Op. 111) for chorus and orchestra, and wrote a number of smaller works, including six *a cappella* miniatures for high-feast days—Advent, Christmas, New Year's Day, Holy Week, Good Friday, and Ascension Day. He completed an entire version of the *Deutsche Liturgie* in 1846, although this was not published in its entirety as a collected edition until 1998. Other short works for chorus *a cappella* include a *Nunc dimittis*, a *Jubilate Deo*, and a *Magnificat*. Works for chorus and organ include quite a number of Latin pieces for women's chorus, men's chorus, or mixed chorus, a *Te Deum* and works he titled *Geistliches Lied* ("Sacred Song"), *Choral*, and *Hymne*. In short, Mendelssohn composed a great deal of church music and concert music with sacred text—a repertoire that should be championed again in the evangelical church. Let us begin to do for Mendelssohn's sacred music what Mendelssohn did for Bach's.

Notes

1. On the matter of Mendelssohn's conversion and the level to which he retained his Jewish identity while living as a Protestant Christian, there has been some debate among Mendelssohn scholars. In his review of two books on Mendelssohn by R. Larry Todd and Clive Brown, published in *The New York Review* (Nov. 4, 2004, pp. 44–46), Lewis Lockwood asks the question, "Which Is the Real Mendelssohn?" Lockwood refers to arguments made by Eric Werner, Leon Botstein, Michael P. Steinberg, Jeffrey Sposato, and others.

Werner, a Jewish musicologist of Austrian background who escaped the Nazis, posited that Mendelssohn retained deep feelings for his Jewish roots and felt strong solidarity with the Jewish people. Botstein accepts that Mendelssohn's conversion was sincere but argues that the choral works and other evidence point to the idea that Mendelssohn viewed Christianity as a logical, modern, moral equivalent of Judaism. Steinberg suggests that the dualistic nature of Mendelssohn's religious outlook is his primary strength. Sposato points out weaknesses in Werner's ideas and wrote a doctoral dissertation on the Mendelssohn oratorios and nineteenth-century anti-Semitism (now published as *The Price of Assimilation: Felix Mendelssohn and the Nineteenth-Century Anti-Semitic Tradition* [New York: Oxford], 2005).

Do any of these, however, represent a strong argument against Mendelssohn's genuine Christianity? Even if Mendelssohn retained strong links with his roots, that would not mean that his faith was suspect because many Christians (Jewish Christians especially) similarly identify with the Jewish people. Embracing the Christian faith does not necessitate the complete rejection of one's cultural heritage even when that heritage is intertwined with a religion; certainly one cannot change one's own genetic makeup or lineage. Christ was himself a Jew, so there is no place to argue that Christianity and Judaism do not share a close relationship that would be strongly evidenced in a Jewish Christian. In a sense, Botstein is also correct because Christ perfectly fulfilled the law, sacrifices, and prophecies of Judaism. Morally, even, nations of the West claim a Judeo-Christian basis for their laws and practices.

2. Alfred Einstein, *Music in the Romantic Era* (New York: W. W. Norton, 1947), 49–50.

3. R. Larry Todd, *Mendelssohn: A Life in Music* (New York: Oxford, 2003), 196.

4. Abraham to Felix, March 10, 1835, in Paul Mendelssohn Bartholdy, *Letters of Felix Mendelssohn Bartholdy from 1833 to 1847*, trans. Lady Wallace (London, 1868), 67, as quoted in Todd, *Mendelssohn: A Life in Music*, 343.

5. Liner notes by Pierre Michot, trans. Michelle Bulloch, CD-635 (Lausanne: VDE-GALLO, 1992), 18.

6. Todd, *Mendelssohn: A Life in Music*, 338.

7. Ibid. This religious and racial assimilation was undoubtedly part of the impetus for Abraham Mendelssohn's change of religion and name. Some have sought to dis-

credit the true Christianity of Felix on these grounds, but there is sufficient evidence in his music and letters to counter such thinking.

8. Ibid., 339.

9. Michot (trans. Bulloch), CD-635, 22. See also Robert Schumann, *On Music and Musicians,* ed. Konrad Wolf, trans. Paul Rosenfield (New York: W. W. Norton, ca. 1946), 206.

10. *Lauda Sion Salvatorem* ("Praise, O Zion, Praise Your Savior") was composed c. 1264 by Thomas Aquinas. It was one of the five sequences retained in the Roman Missal.

29

Evidence of Igor Stravinsky's Faith: The *Symphony of Psalms*

Let everything that has breath praise the L*ORD*!
Praise the L*ORD*! *—Psalm 150:6*

There are authors who attempt to find an active Christian faith or spiritual life in every great composer of sacred music. This assumption is based on their musical compositions. For example, reading a Christian faith and worldview into the music of Johannes Brahms is possible, but Brahms was not a believer. Wolfgang Amadeus Mozart wrote a lot of church music, but he was no evangelical—he was a Roman Catholic by heritage and a Freemason by practice. Other writers have attempted to discredit the genuine faith of committed Christian composers such as J. S. Bach and Felix Mendelssohn by arguing that they composed sacred music solely according to employment (the former) or out of political expediency (the latter).

Igor Stravinsky (1882–1971), one of the most celebrated composers of the twentieth century, is a musician that people relegate entirely to the secular world. This may be due to his choice of subject matter in certain works or as a consequence of his serial/atonal period. Throughout his various "periods" of composition he proved to be a composer of the highest rank, and one whom others had to emulate, admire, or despise. He is a force with which a modern classical musician must be engaged at some level. Closer study also reveals that he was a committed Christian who wrote music *à la gloire de Dieu* ("to the glory of God").

Who was this international twentieth-century composer who presumed to compose classical art music intended for the public stage "to the glory of God"? Why did such a successful composer of ballet scores on mythological themes turn to sacred texts and biblical subjects in the latter decades of his life? While a few sentences in print hint at his "religious tendencies," why has so little been written about his spiritual life and beliefs? These are questions that we will attempt to answer, though not thoroughly in so limited a space.

Stravinsky, it seems, is a composer whom secularists are not inclined to give over to Christianity and one whom Christians are queasy about embracing. This much is certain: Stravinsky demonstrated his faith time and time again in his words and compositions. And without careful attention to his faith, one can be accused, as his son Theodore insisted was possible, of distorting "the true message of his music."[1] Theodore insisted that the essence of his father's work would always escape the minds of those for whom religious ideas had become "incomprehensible, or foreign, or chimerical."[2] I intend to quote Stravinsky and others close to him extensively throughout this essay so that firsthand evidence of his faith is substantiated. Such evidence is further verified by careful study of his *Symphony of Psalms.* The musical discussion included here will be more detailed than in other chapters in this volume. (I apologize to the reader who may not be familiar with some of the musical terminology.) A *Symphony of Psalms* score in hand will prove helpful when the piece is discussed.

Stravinsky's Conversion

Several sources point to 1923 as a watershed year of religious crisis in Stravinsky's life. Stravinsky had been born in 1882, baptized and raised in the Russian Orthodox church. As a youth, he rebelled against this religion but officially returned to it in 1926. Apparently the rebirth of his faith in 1923, at the age of 31, even approached semi-fanatical proportions. At that time he renounced ballet as "l'anathème du Christ" (accursed by Christ).[3] Within a few years his rhetoric and manner became more tempered, and he returned to composing ballet. In 1924, Stravinsky became friends with a Russian priest, Father Nicolas, with whom he spent a great deal of time during the next five years. There is also the famous incident when his abscessed forefinger was suddenly healed at the beginning of a piano performance in Venice. Stravinsky considered this to be a miracle in response to his prayers. He also claimed to have had a profoundly moving religious experience while attending the seven-hundredth-anniversary celebrations of St. Anthony in the Basilica of Padua, which in turn affected his compositional life.[4]

Commenting later in life on his conversion, Stravinsky said, "I cannot now evaluate the events that, at the end of those thirty years, made me discover the necessity of religious belief. I was not reasoned into my disposition . . . I can say, however, that for some years before my actual 'conversion,' a mood of acceptance had been cultivated in me by a reading of the Gospels and by other religious literature."[5] This explanation harmonizes well with Russian Orthodox theology, as we will see. At the time of his conversion, Stravinsky wrote to his colleague Sergei Diaghilev, the famous ballet impresario, commenting on the experience and requesting forgiveness for any wrong that he may have ever committed against him.[6]

During the rest of his long life, Stravinsky gave many evidences to his friends and associates of a deep Christian faith.[7] Yet some respected musicians and writers have spoken out against such an assertion. For example, the musicologist Paul Henry Lang wrote, "Of late he [Stravinsky] has turned to religious subjects—is he a genuinely religious composer of 'sacred' music? No, he could not be, for his ideal world is too little concerned with the final inwardness of life . . . His spiritual center lies somewhere between dream and make-believe."[8] Lang felt that Wilfrid Mellers had penetrating insight when he wrote that Stravinsky seemed to be "in love with the idea of God rather than with God himself."[9] But these are severe judgments rendered against a man whose integrity and discipline in both work and faith demonstrate otherwise. Statements by the composer and others close to him outweigh such criticisms:

- His disciple and personal assistant, Robert Craft, wrote, "He believed that God created the world; he believed literally in all of the events in the Bible."[10]
- Stravinsky said, "I regard my talents as God-given, and I have always prayed to Him for strength to use them. When in early childhood I discovered that I had been made the custodian of musical aptitudes, I pledged myself to God to be worthy of their development, though, of course, I have broken the pledge and received uncovenanted mercies all my life, and though the custodian has too often kept faith on his own all-too-worldly terms."[11]
- Stravinsky also said, "The more that one separates oneself from the canons of the Christian Church, the further one distances oneself from the truth. These canons are as true for musical composition as they are for the life of an individual . . . Art is made of itself, and one cannot create upon a creation, even though we are ourselves graftings of Jesus Christ."[12]
- "Stravinsky had a natural predilection for texts of supplication, invocation, and praise. Like the psalmist, he had a very personal relationship with the Divine."[13]
- "During the time of the composition of the *Symphony of Psalms* there are two things that are certain. Principally, Stravinsky had a profound belief in God; and secondly, he felt a tremendous affinity between his God and his Art."[14]
- "One fact stands beyond question—that religious consciousness was firmly rooted in Stravinsky, manifesting itself less strongly at some times and then asserting itself with a new strength, and predominating in his final creative phases, when it found expression in works based for the most part on biblical or gospel themes."[15]
- Edmund Wilson said, "I'm not in the least religious, but I think it's significant and admirable that Stravinsky should begin every day with a prayer."[16]

- It is known that Stravinsky prayed daily, every morning, before and after composing, and when facing difficulty.[17]
- In his lectures at Harvard University, Stravinsky said that music comes to reveal itself "as a form of communion with our fellow man—and with the Supreme Being," and that, "I myself having been created, I cannot help having the desire to create."[18]

Stravinsky's Russian Orthodox Faith

As aforementioned, Stravinsky's faith is rooted in the Russian Orthodox tradition. Some of what will be discussed here may seem foreign to Western Christians. Like his intensely religious sister, Catherine, Stravinsky was familiar with the *Dobrotolyubiye,* which Craft felt was an essential book for anyone interested in Stravinsky's theological beliefs. This is the Russian version of the Greek *Philokalia,* a collection of the writings of the early church fathers.[19] The texts in it act as guides to the practice of the contemplative life, of a "mystical school of inward prayer," with the goal of illuminating the consciousness and achieving purity of heart.[20] An advanced state in the pursuit of this mystical path is known as *hesychia,* a word describing tranquility and silence or "stillness," but also the Greek root idea of being seated, fixed, or in a state of concentration. This search for peace through prayer is similar to the German mystics' quest for "detachment" or the desire of monks everywhere for separation from the world. An awareness of the spiritual world and spiritual struggle comes to the fore, while the goal is a spiritual union with Christ through denial of the physical. This may not fit the modern American evangelical understanding of spirituality, but for some of the Christian world it is closer to the Pauline concept of "prayer without ceasing" than most of us attempt or experience. One would need to avoid a works-related asceticism of which Paul warns us in Colossians 2, however.

When asked whether one must be a believer to compose sacred music, Stravinsky replied, "Certainly, and not merely a believer in 'symbolic figures,' but in the Person of the Lord, the Person of the Devil, and the miracles of the Church."[21] We will return to this idea of "symbolic figures" momentarily. The science of the soul and emphasis on faith (along with the acceptance of a dark, demonic reality) are traits identifiable in Stravinsky's words and works. Certainly the idea of the demonic and eternal damnation is seen in *The Rite of Spring, The Flood, Anthem: The Dove Descending Breaks the Air*, the *Cantata on the Lyke-Wake Dirge, The Rake's Progress*, and *Orpheus*, among others. The concept of *hesychia* "stillness" appears in Stravinskian works that end with the Greek/Byzantine *epithalamium* (*Les Noces, Symphony of Psalms* third mvt., etc.). An *epithalamium* is a slow, formal religious procession characterized by the ringing of bells. In such musical compositions, a sense of timelessness is achieved by the repeated overlapping of "layers" of musical material as a means of distancing the listener from metrical norms and temporal boundaries.

Stravinsky's Philosophy of Music

The Russian Orthodox emphasis on the importance of constant prayer, tied in with liturgy and ritual, also harmonizes with Stravinsky's compositional practices and musical works. Prayer and praise are the central themes of the *Symphony of Psalms*. Stravinsky wrote in August 1930, "It is not a symphony in which I have included Psalms to be sung. On the contrary, it is the singing of the Psalms that I am symphonizing."[22] The psalms, while being hymns of the Hebrew people, were also prayers. This is attested to at the end of the "second book" of psalms (Ps. 72:20), where we read, "The prayers of David, the son of Jesse, are ended." Since the Scriptures relate music and prayer unequivocally, not only in the psalms but also in several New Testament passages, how appropriate it is, then, for a musician as great as Stravinsky also to be a man of prayer.

Stravinsky's personal comments and writings confirm his understanding of music's purpose. He wrote:

> The Church knew what the Psalmist knew: music praises God. Music is as well or better able to praise Him than the building of the church and all its decoration; it is the Church's greatest

> ornament. "Glory, glory, glory"; the music of Orlando Lassus' motet praises God, and this particular "glory" does not exist in secular music. And not only the glory . . . but prayer and penitence and many other [actions] cannot be secularized. The spirit disappears with the form.[23]

Stravinsky also said: "Religious music without religion is almost always vulgar . . . I hope, too, that my sacred music is a protest against the Platonic tradition . . . of music as anti-moral."[24] And with regard to his choice of psalm texts for a major work, he wrote:

> Apparently people have lost all capacity to treat the Holy Scriptures otherwise than from the point of view of ethnography, history, or picturesqueness. That anyone should take his inspiration from the Psalms without giving a thought to these side issues appears to be incredible to them . . .[25]

The ideas of the moral nature of music, contemplation, and art music in praise of God correlate with Stravinsky's now-famous lectures given at Harvard University during the 1939–40 academic year. He articulated in these essays that the limits, control, and discipline imposed on a composition—indeed, on the process of composing itself—simultaneously represent aspects of liberty and freedom: that the more art is controlled, limited, and worked over, the more it is free. One cannot help but notice the parallels between these concepts and basic tenets of the Christian faith. One is free in Christ's perfect law of liberty only when one is his disciple and captive to him. Whereas with anarchy a certain terror and fantasy is inherent, since everything is permissible (free), in reality all is enslaved to chaos and ultimately to death. Stravinsky believed freedom was greater the more narrowly limited the field of action. In composition it was essential for him to proceed by elimination in order to select those parameters that the work demanded of him (i.e., differentiation permits unification). He also stated in these lectures that "art is by essence constructive" and that chaos and art oppose each other.[26] While daring is necessary, arbitrariness is undesirable and does not contribute to the formation of art.

The Theological Background of the *Symphony of Psalms*

The Russian Orthodox doctrine of *theosis* (the process of being united with God, of having soul and body transformed by his grace throughout one's life) is also echoed in the *Symphony of Psalms.* Justification and sanctification are understood as one ongoing process rather than as separate acts. Stravinsky's faith has been described as intensely personal and mystical. One writer has suggested, "The doctrine of theosis can shed light on why Stravinsky did not write of 'salvation' in the Western Evangelical manner, and why his Christian devotion was expressed in prayer, worship and work (composition)."[27]

An aspect of the *Philokalia* (or *Dobrotolyubiye*) that is significant to the *Symphony of Psalms* is the relationship between Orthodox prayer and gematriology. This includes some of the "symbolic figures" referred to earlier. One discovers interpretive relationships between prayer and certain numbers outlined in the "One Hundred and Fifty-Three Texts" on prayer by Evagrios the Solitary.[28] Stravinsky would have been familiar with passages such as this one:

> The triangle can signify knowledge of the Holy Trinity. Or you can regard the total sum, one hundred and fifty-three, as triangular and so signifying respectively the practices of the virtues, contemplation of the divine in nature, and theology or spiritual knowledge of God; faith, hope and love (cf. 1 Cor. 13:13); or gold, silver and precious stones (cf. 1 Cor. 3:12).[29]

Stravinsky must have known this text. The evidence is strong enough to posit that he was in some way attempting to express this teaching on prayer in music. The "sermon" of his *Canticum sacrum* is a "triptych of choral exhortations to the theological virtues: faith, hope, and charity" (the central, longest movement is divided into three sections, which are exhortations to "Caritas," "Spes," and "Fides").[30] The themes of faith and fire appear many times in the later works, including (in addition to *Canticum sacrum*) *A Sermon, a Narrative, and a Prayer; Anthem: The Dove Descending Breaks the Air;* and of course the *Symphony of Psalms.* The emphasis on the number three (3), especially, is evident in the *Symphony of Psalms,* and in later works of the composer.[31] (See endnote for a longer discussion of these "third relationships.")

The *Symphony of Psalms*: A Brief Discussion

While a detailed discussion of the *Symphony of Psalms* itself is more appropriate to another forum, a few noteworthy details demonstrate Stravinsky's concern with the spirituality of the work. First, he chose Latin as the language for the psalms. Stravinsky felt that Latin was appropriate for sublime subjects. He carefully avoided sentimentality as well as trite effects or rhetorical temptations in which other composers who set Psalm 150 so often indulge. William Austin says it is characteristic of Stravinsky to put "his most poignant, chromatic chord progressions at points where the words protect them from sentimentality . . . To a listener alert to the paradox, these are sublime."[32] A certain degree of cerebrality and austerity is present, as one would expect, since Stravinsky was acutely aware of the transcendent and metaphysical nature of his subject matter. This in no way diminishes the genuine offering of prayer and praise that Stravinsky writes to the glory of God despite its dissonant sounds even to the trained ear.

Rhetorical ideas are prevalent in the *Symphony of Psalms,* Stravinsky's avoidance of the overused notwithstanding. Walter Piston suggested that Stravinsky achieved here "expressive power and an astonishing fitness of music for words and underlying idea."[33] The only device about which Stravinsky speaks blatantly is the "Elijah chariot" music in the third movement—referring to the vision given to the prophet Elisha as Elijah was transported into heaven via the fiery horses and chariot of God. The relationship here is clearly that of the awesome power, fire, and miraculous nature of God that Stravinsky believes should be praised by all possible musical means, but not without distance and a holy fear. Stravinsky begins his text-setting in the first movement with the psalmist's prayerful lament "*exaudi orationem meam*" ("Hear my prayer"). This lament is, according to renowned choral conductor Margaret Hillis, a "theme of bondage" bound to two oscillating pitches a half step apart (see fig. 29.1).

Fig. 29.1

At the text "*ne sileas*" or "Be not silent!" Stravinsky ingeniously leaves a quarter-note rest (a moment of silence) before the punctuation of the two appearances of the "psalms chord" that set this text apart. This chord begins the movement and returns throughout as a sort of structural pillar (see fig. 29.2). The "psalms chord" occurs one before 9.

Fig. 29.2

The second movement, which Stravinsky said was the most symbolic of the three, symbolizes God and man, respectively, in its instrumental and choral fugues. The polarity of these concepts is heightened by their association with the work's two tonal centers, themselves a third apart (C and E-flat).[34] What is most convincing about this interpretation is the blending of the two fugues together in the third section of the movement. At least three plausible explanations for this symbolism emerge:

1. The fugues' conjunction symbolizes the mystic idea of the blending of the soul with God (*theosis*).
2. The fugues' merger occurs in the third part of the movement—the first section being the Creator's theme, the second being the creation's theme. One can see the two reconciled in the person of the Holy Spirit, as the third person of the Trinity indwells the believer and unites man with God.
3. The two fugues and key areas (God and man) are perfectly united in the person of Jesus Christ, which may account for the neo-Baroque French Overture effect of this closing section.[35] This is my favorite hypothesis.

In the final movement, the use of triads in opening ostinati, metrically offset, and in keys related by thirds (C major, C minor, E-flat major) creates a sense of stasis, otherworldliness, distance, timelessness, euphoria, and awe. As has been previously mentioned, the "Elijah's chariot climbing the Heavens" music (3rd mvt., rehearsals 5, 17, and 18) refers to one of the Old Testament's most stirring and visual examples of God's power (through horses and fire).[36] This immediately follows the text "Praise Him in the firmament of His power."

Stravinsky avoids the temptation to use the literal instruments called upon by the text at the micro level, but on a larger scale he interprets the text. For example, at "Praise Him for the multitude of His mighty acts" there is a steady growth in range, dynamic, and use of wind instruments, as well as the addition of more vocal lines. At the text "Praise Him with the sound of the trumpet," the trumpets are already playing, but all four horns are added while most of the winds and both pianos are pulsing *forte* in eighth notes (not "un-trumpet-like"). The final chord of the work is held over three measures, and includes five "C" octaves. Wilfrid Mellers wrote that this "super C" chord is "unlike anything we have ever heard, including C major triads."[37] It may represent both the realization of absolute stability (an inherent musical quest of the work) and eternal union with God (see fig. 29.3).

Summary

Although this short essay has at best only approached the subject at hand, clearly Stravinsky's faith has significant bearing on his compositional output. That this has not been understood was noted by the composer himself with regard to the *Symphony of Psalms*: "I noticed a certain perplexity, not by the music as such, but by the inability of listeners to understand the reason which had led me to compose a symphony in a spirit which found no echo in their mentality."[38] His religious music is not a synthesis of earlier works, but an outworking of a thoughtful, committed Christian composer whose "religious music reflects another side of his musical and spiritual sensibility, one hidden but powerfully present in his earlier works."[39] Stravinsky felt he

Fig. 29.3

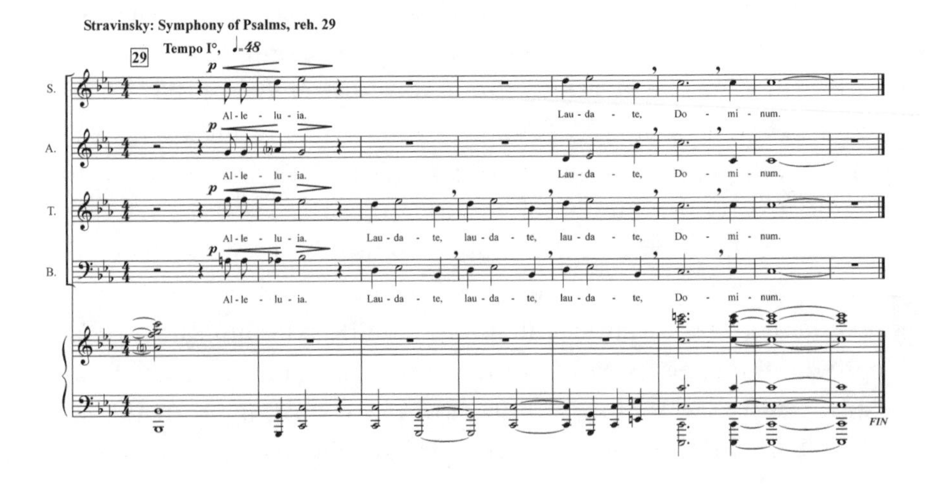

was born out of time, in the sense that "by temperament and talent" he "would have been more suited for the life of a small Bach, living in anonymity and composing regularly for an established service and for God."[40] While in some senses the two composers could not have been further apart, in other ways Stravinsky was like the legendary German composer. For like Bach, "Stravinsky firmly believes; his praying and adoring are functions of his deepest self."[41] And also like the great Bach, he wrote music to the glory of God alone: *soli Deo gloria—à la gloire de Dieu.*

Notes

1. Theodore Stravinsky, *The Message of Igor Stravinsky*, trans. Robert Craft and André Marion (London: n.p., 1953), as quoted in William Austin, *Music in the 20th Century* (New York: W. W. Norton, 1966), 534.

2. Ibid.

3. Robert Copeland, "The Christian Message of Igor Stravinsky," *The Musical Quarterly* 68 (1982): 563–79. See also Serge Lifar, *Diaghilev* (London, 1940), and Eric Walter White, *Stravinsky: The Composer and His Works*, 2nd ed. (London, 1979), 85.

4. Eric Walter White and Jeremy Noble, "Stravinsky," in *The New Grove Modern Masters* (New York: W. W. Norton, 1984), 148, and Glenn Watkins, *Soundings: Music in the Twentieth Century* (New York: Schirmer Books, 1988), 466.

5. Igor Stravinsky and Robert Craft, *Expositions and Developments* (Garden City, NJ: Doubleday, 1962), 63–64.

6. See Igor Stravinsky and Robert Craft, *Memories and Commentaries* (New York, 1960), 51.

7. Copeland, "The Christian Message," 565.

8. Paul Henry Lang, "Editorial" (on Stravinsky), *The Musical Quarterly* 48 (1962): 371.

9. Ibid.

10. Robert Craft, "Stravinsky the Man," National Public Radio, July 2, 1979, as quoted in Copeland, "The Christian Message," 566.

11. Igor Stravinsky and Robert Craft, *Dialogues and a Diary* (London: Faber, 1968), 26.

12. Igor Stravinsky, in an interview in *Le Vingtième Siècle*, Brussels, May 22, 1930, as quoted in Vera Stravinsky and Robert Craft, *Stravinsky in Pictures and Documents* (New York: Simon and Schuster, 1978), 295.

13. Amy Gilbert, "Aspects of the Religious Music of Igor Stravinsky," in *Confronting Stravinsky*, ed. Jann Pasler (Berkeley: University of California Press, 1986), 195.

14. Bruce Chamberlain, "Igor Stravinsky's *Symphony of Psalms*: An Analysis for Performance" (doctoral diss., Indiana University, 1979), 10.

15. Mikhail Druskin, *Igor Stravinsky: His Life, Works and Views*, trans. Martin Cooper (Cambridge: Cambridge University Press, 1983), 111.

16. Austin, *Music in the 20th Century*, 535.

17. Igor Stravinsky and Robert Craft, *Themes and Episodes* (New York: Alfred A. Knopf, 1967), 172–75, and also Copeland, "The Christian Message," 565.

18. Igor Stravinsky, *Poetics of Music* (Cambridge, MA: Harvard University Press), 21, 50, 146.

19. Published in English as *The Philokalia*, comp. St. Nikodimos of the Holy Mountain and St. Makarios of Corinth (Venice, 1782), English trans. G. E. H. Palmer, Philip Sherrard, and Kallistos Ware (London: Faber & Faber, Ltd., 1983). The *Philokalia* is a collection of texts written between the fourth and the fifteenth centuries by spiritual masters in the Orthodox Christian tradition. The Russian monk Paisii Velichkovskii (1722–94), who visited Mount Athos and later settled in Moldavia, translated a selection of the texts into Slavonic (Moscow, 1793). A translation into Russian was made by Ignatii Brianchaninov (1807–67), published in 1857. Another Russian translation was made by Bishop Theophan the Recluse (1815–94) in 1877 (reprinted in 1883, 1885, 1905, and 1913). This is probably the version that the Stravinskys owned.

20. See the introduction to the *Philokalia*, 11–18.

21. Igor Stravinsky and Robert Craft, *Conversations with Igor Stravinsky* (Garden City, NY: Doubleday, 1959), 125.

22. Vera Stravinsky and Robert Craft, *Stravinsky in Pictures and Documents*, 297.

23. Stravinsky and Craft, *Conversations*, 124.

24. Ibid.

25. Igor Stravinsky, *An Autobiography* (New York: M. & J. Steuer, 1958), 162.

26. Stravinsky, *Poetics of Music*, 12.

27. Copeland, "The Christian Message," 570.

28. Evagrios outlines the way of prayer as twofold: "It comprises practice of the virtues and contemplation. The same applies to numbers: literally they are quantities, but they can also signify qualities. I have divided this discourse on prayer into one hundred and fifty-three texts. In this way I send you an evangelical feast, so that you may delight in a symbolical number that combines a triangular with a hexagonal figure. The triangle indicates spiritual knowledge of the Trinity, the hexagon indicates the ordered creation of the world in six days." See *Philokalia*, 55–57.

29. Ibid., 57.

30. Austin, *Music in the 20th Century*, 532. Moreover, the antithesis to the Christian's "gold, silver and precious stones" is his "wood, hay and stubble"—all of which are to be tested by divine fire. This appears to be the theme of Stravinsky's twelve-tone *a cappella* anthem, "The Dove Descending Breaks the Air" (T. S. Eliot), where we are "consumed

by pyre or pyre, fire or fire"—possibly, the fire of God's testing of our works for eternal reward, and the fire of eternal damnation.

31. First of all, the symphony is in three movements from three psalms. It is interesting that the written tempos beginning all three movements are divisible by three, and that with only one exception (half note = 80), even interior tempos are divisible by three. Next the *Grundgestalt* motive, which Stravinsky called the root idea of the whole work, is built of two minor thirds and a major third (or three sets of thirds) [0134]. Most of the pitches of this interval collection are third-related (E, G, B-flat, C-sharp) with the most commonly occurring being the E and B-flat, which constitute a tritone. The principal key centers or poles of the work (E, C) have a third relationship. The first entrance of the choir, interestingly, is at measure 33. The distinctive "Psalms" chord (which occurs six times in the first movement in a total area of nine beats [chord+rests]) recalls the "number of creation" and is built from two triads at opposing ends of the pitch spectrum (high/low and four octaves apart) with a doubled G (their third) occurring in the middle. The last section of the three-part first movement ends in a meter of 3/2, the same tempo of the extensive *epithalamium* in movement 3. The three-measure climax of this movement occurs at 12, measures 65–67.

The second movement is a fugue with three expositions, which Stravinsky claimed was in the form of an upside-down, three-part pyramid. The numerological design of Evagrios' prayer texts comes into play even more here. Geometric patterns emerge from the combination of various numbers to form triangles (when triangular like 3) and so forth. This movement has the key signature of three flats, and the phrase groupings of five and then four gradually diminish so that the movement concludes with groups of three measures from 15 (m. 75) on. The text comprises three verses from Psalm 39. Even more significant is the statement by Stravinsky that " 'The Waiting for the Lord' Psalm [second movement] makes the most overt use of musical symbolism in any of my music before *The Flood* [1962]." In the opening fugal subject of this movement it is possible to see the interlinked thirds of the *Grundgestalt* motive displaced by an octave.

The third movement contains many examples of tertian construction. Textually, the "Alleluia" that opens the movement appears three times at structural points. After each of these, the "laudate" motive of three notes is heard three times (near rehearsal 1, 13, and 29). The stasis-infused "Dominum" also occurs in three places (four after 1, three before 3, and the last three measures of the movement). The last time, for the final chord of the movement, no fifth is heard, which places more emphasis on the third of the chord. From rehearsals 9–12 and 24–26, "laudate" is set three times each time this text appears. At rehearsal 20, there is a descent by thirds (C-sharp, A-sharp, F-sharp, D) from the "Elijah" music into the D major–centered "organ" section, which has a triadic melody outlined in D, G, e, a, and g. One should recall Stravinsky's identification of the "Elijah" section, which he was almost embarrassed about being so "literal" in its display of fanfare and gallop, as a section in which triplets forming triads are the predominant texture. The first notes he wrote down occur at rehearsal 3, where one finds music on three of the four beats in the measure, built in thirds. The triad is an all-important building block in the movement, occurring, for example, as chords at measures 100 and 110 in the woodwinds, in the English horn melody; at the three measures of flute elaboration (147–49); and in all the *laudate Dominum* appearances of rehearsals 14–17. The "inner" music (the "organ" section) begins at measure 150, interesting primarily because this is a setting of Psalm 150—the final psalm in the fifth book of the Psalms. At measure 163 we arrive at the true start of "stasis" in a key signature of three flats, where there are three pitches in the ostinato (E-flat, B-flat, F), these pitches representing tonic keys for each of the three flats and occurring a fifth apart (5 being a circular or spherical number that embodies the idea of the eternal, reminiscent of Ezekiel's vision of spheres/wheels as representational of God).

32. Austin, *Music in the 20th Century*, 334–35.

33. Walter Piston, "Stravinsky as Psalmist—1931," *Modern Music* 8, no. 2 (1931): 44.

34. For a complete discussion of these God/man relationships, see Wilfrid Mellers, "1930: Symphony of Psalms," *Tempo* 97 [Stravinsky issue] (1971): 19–27.

35. The dotted rhythms reminiscent of a French overture remind us that we are in the presence of royalty, in this case not the "Sun-King" (Louis XIV) but the Son-King, Jesus Christ. A more familiar example to the reader may be Handel's *Messiah*, which begins with similar dotted rhythm. Another interesting observation: at the mention of the "new song" in the mouth of God's children, causing many to "fear," we encounter the tritone, which in this context cannot represent its usual function as a diabolical interval (the *diabolus in musica*). Rather, the interval in this case can represent the "fear" and sense of awe inspired by the experience of approaching the triune, transcendent God.

36. Stravinsky and Craft, *Dialogues and a Diary*, 46.

37. Mellers, "1930: Symphony of Psalms," 27.

38. Stravinsky, *An Autobiography*, 163–64.

39. Gilbert, "Aspects of the Religious Music," 196.

40. Stravinsky and Craft, *Dialogues and a Diary*, 26.

41. Theodore Stravinsky, "The Message of Igor Stravinsky," trans. Robert Craft and André Marion (London, n.p., 1953), 19 as quoted in Copeland, "The Christian Message," 579.

30
The Anatomy of a Hymn Tune

Praise the Lord*! Sing to the* Lord *a new song,*
his praise in the assembly of the godly! —*Psalm 149:1*

Many "hymn stories" are associated with famous hymns. These stories often give us helpful insight into the meaning behind the text or at least a better picture of the author's state of mind. At times we encounter tales that have grown beyond reality into the realm of legend and lore. But as interesting and informative as these hymn accounts are, rarely do they trace the interior thinking of the author or the composer as it relates to the creation, composition, or construction of the work itself. This chapter presents an opportunity for the reader who has not personally had such an experience, or contact with someone who has, to take a brief journey into this world.

This journey represents only one composer's perspective, and only one of many different experiences at that. It may, however, reveal something of what goes into writing a hymn and thereby encourage one to take hymn study and hymn singing more seriously. To that end, we will explore together the composer's view of what went into writing St. Andrews, the tune for "Almighty God, We Come to You" by Eric J. Alexander.

The Text

The music for the hymn was completed in July 2001. The text had been finished some months earlier. While visiting the Rev. Alexander in Scotland in June, I worked on the tune with him at his home in St. Andrews—thus the hymn-tune name. He had written this hymn with the intention of having it sung before the preaching of the Word of God. The hymn is a prayer for the Holy Spirit to illumine our hearts and minds and to empower the one delivering the sermon. Rather than being based on a specific passage of Scripture, this prayer hymn incorporates Trinitarian and other doctrinal truths from numerous books of the Bible. It teaches about the origin and the power of the Word of God (stanzas 1–2), the gospel of Christ (stanza 4), and the work of the Holy Spirit (stanzas 3, 5 and refrain).

One of the most obvious biblical references is the refrain's hearkening back to Isaiah 6, in which the prophet had a vision of the glory of God. In this experience of God's holiness, Isaiah was smitten with a realization of the depth of his own sin and the sin of his people. One of the seraphim touched Isaiah's lips with a burning coal from the altar, removing his guilt and atoning for his sin (Isa. 6:7). Isaiah was then called by God to prophesy. The parallel is that a true minister of the Word serves as a vessel for the communication of God's truth. He is a sinner, saved by grace, chosen to utter the revealed Word of God to others, and in need of the Spirit's calling and anointing.

With that message in mind, let us look at the music more closely for a few minutes. It may be helpful to refer to the picture of the manuscript pages for some of the technical discussion. I am not an expert hymn-tune writer but have become more intimately involved with the art in recent years (see fig. 30.1). The process I undertake goes something like this.

First I spend a good deal of time with the text—reading it, thinking about it, feeling its rhythm, attempting to grasp its theological meaning and its poetry. I mark down initial thoughts, words that are important, the strongest point in a stanza, and so forth. Before much time passes, I start to think about possible musical time signatures for the tune prompted by the poetry's scansion. I thought two options could work well for this particular hymn on the basis of its textual meter, and I scribbled these in the top right-hand corner of the page. I noted the stress of the text and exceptions to the pattern. Alexander had been consistent overall, but at certain points in the course of the stanzas he wrote more freely. This meant that the composer would need to consider whether the time signature would allow for these permutations or whether it would make them feel awkward.

In my experience, newly composed hymn texts are frequently still in a draft form when musical work commences. One can see from the manuscript that certain words were missing capitalization or contraction. At first I thought "the anointing" would need to be elided to "th'anointing" in order to maintain the meter, but this was not necessary after the author amended the line from nine syllables to eight by removing the word "O." I also thought (along with the author) that the text was a bit lengthy and that the refrain might need to occur only at the beginning and end of the hymn instead of after each stanza. Time and further work proved this assumption to be faulty as well, since the refrain very much focuses each stanza on the prayer for the Spirit's help. Without its repetition, the hymn would be weaker.

Meter

The text employs "long meter" [L.M.] 8.8.8.8. (a standard meter of many hymns, and a variation of "common meter" [C.M.] 8.6.8.6.). In this instance, it is also extended by a two-line refrain (8.8.). For those unfamiliar with hymnic meter and metrical indexes, the numbers simply mean that each line of the text (the four stanza lines and the two of the refrain) comprises eight syllables. A 6 would indicate six syllables, and so forth.[1] The opening syllable for this hymn should logically be set as an upbeat, since the second syllable's stress is stronger: "Al-*might*-y God." I did not choose to do this, however.

At first glance (and completely within the realm of possibility), the obvious way to set this text would be in duple time (a time signature divisible by two, thus 2/2, 2/4, 4/4, or something similar). The first syllable would be an upbeat (as an incomplete bar before the first full measure). But I chose a triple time signature for a few reasons:

1. The strong downbeat (in three) matches most of the textual stresses.
2. These stresses change occasionally, so using the 3/4 meter helps to avoid long stresses on unstressed syllables. It minimizes time in such places and has a greater sense of forward motion than 4/4, probably because the downbeats are more frequent and also because the time can be felt in one as well as in three.
3. A 3/4 meter suits a hymn dealing with the Trinity, and with the Holy Spirit as its third member especially.

Rhythm/Pacing

The length of notes also helps to determine the weight or emphasis placed on certain syllables. With two exceptions, the white notes on the page (half notes and dotted half notes) all fall on stressed syllables in our hymn. This pattern is altered in the third line of the tune and in the third measure of the refrain on the word *Spirit* (see fig. 30.3). Why? One would not have to do so, but I elected to change here for one reason—momentum. The rhythmic pattern, particularly in a fast triple meter, is always in danger of becoming too regular at best, or dancelike and trivial at worst. Changing it on the third line seems to help propel the piece into the fourth line of the stanza; and from there, the harmony leads the music into the refrain. You might notice that the first two phrases of each stanza come to rest musically, while the third pushes into the fourth because of this change in rhythm. This musical progression matches the text. If you look at the poem for a minute (fig. 30.1), you can see that during the planning stages of writing the tune, a small arrow was penned after the third line to show the text's continuing motion and the need to move forward into the fourth line.

Fig. 30.1

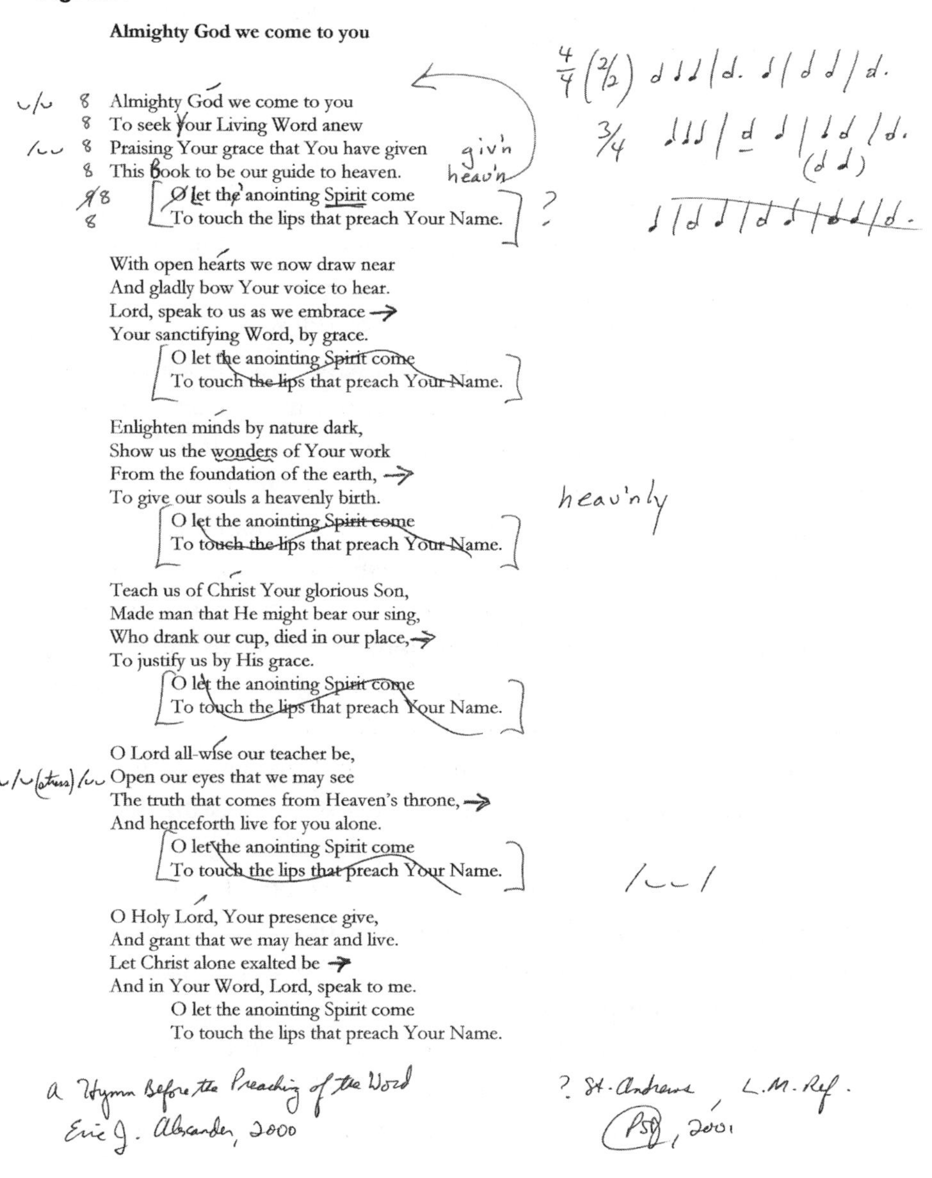

Almighty God we come to you

Almighty God we come to you
To seek Your Living Word anew
Praising Your grace that You have given
This Book to be our guide to heaven.
O let the anointing Spirit come
To touch the lips that preach Your Name.

With open hearts we now draw near
And gladly bow Your voice to hear.
Lord, speak to us as we embrace
Your sanctifying Word, by grace.
O let the anointing Spirit come
To touch the lips that preach Your Name.

Enlighten minds by nature dark,
Show us the wonders of Your work
From the foundation of the earth,
To give our souls a heavenly birth.
O let the anointing Spirit come
To touch the lips that preach Your Name.

Teach us of Christ Your glorious Son,
Made man that He might bear our sing,
Who drank our cup, died in our place,
To justify us by His grace.
O let the anointing Spirit come
To touch the lips that preach Your Name.

O Lord all-wise our teacher be,
Open our eyes that we may see
The truth that comes from Heaven's throne,
And henceforth live for you alone.
O let the anointing Spirit come
To touch the lips that preach Your Name.

O Holy Lord, Your presence give,
And grant that we may hear and live.
Let Christ alone exalted be
And in Your Word, Lord, speak to me.
O let the anointing Spirit come
To touch the lips that preach Your Name.

A Hymn Before the Preaching of the Word
Eric J. Alexander, 2000

? St. Andrews, L.M. Ref.
PSG, 2001

As for the refrain, I felt that changing the pattern would draw attention to the word *Spirit*, but more significantly, it would underscore the emphasis on the next word, *come*, since the coming of the Spirit is the action that we are seeking and anticipating as we sing the hymn. Like most other elements of composition, this was a subjective decision and could be legitimately argued against. In fact, the hymn's author graciously questioned this choice—a welcome inquiry from an astute collaborator.

Melody

The melodic range was held to an octave (D to D), with one exception. This is a very singable range, accessible to the majority of congregational singers. A few patterns unify the melody and make it easier to learn. For example, the use of the ascending interval of a fifth occurs several times (measure 1, fourth measure of the second line, third to fourth measures of the third line). Four melody notes are also repeated as a group: the first four notes of the hymn and the fourth measure of the second line into the fifth (see fig. 30.3).

Two aspects of the refrain's melody merit explanation. Both of these choices were intentional, but the reasoning may not be immediately apparent. First, I set the words *anointing Spirit* in a first-inversion triad with the highest note (which, incidentally, is also the highest note of the piece) ending the word *Spirit* on the third of the chord. This is symbolic. It also affects the singing of the piece and the delivery of the text. It focuses attention on this moment and makes the anointing work of the Holy Spirit—the textual emphasis—align with the musical climax.

Second, I chose an unusual interval between the fourth and fifth measures of the refrain. The melody drops from a D down to an E at the words "to touch." This descending interval of a seventh is used to help illustrate the condescension of the Spirit to indwell believers and to empower them to preach the gospel of grace in the same way that the angel from on high stooped to touch the lips of Isaiah. Further, the number seven is an important biblical number when it comes to the

Spirit. This is not the first time the interval appears in the piece, but it is the first time that it appears in the melody. Actually, the seventh as a chordal interval occurs seven times in the hymn.

Harmony

Such intervallic relationships between voices other than the melodic one (i.e., the alto, tenor, and bass) have to do with harmonic choices. The harmony throughout the hymn tune is functional, yet colorful, with numerous intentional dissonances. Some of these dissonances are what theorists designate as "passing tones" and "suspensions": nonchord notes added for the purpose of contributing motion both through actual movement and through the heightening and resolving of harmonic tension. Such notes were added between the third and fourth lines, and especially in the fourth to help move the singer into the refrain. The phrases of each stanza end on the harmonies shown in figure 30.2 (see also the hymn itself, fig. 30.3).

Fig. 30.2

PHRASE	ENDING KEY	CHORD IN G	FUNCTION IN RELATION TO MODE
1	C major	IV	Subdominant
2	D major	V	Dominant
3	B major	V of vi	Dominant of the relative minor
4	D major	V	Dominant
5	G major	I	Tonic
6	G major	I	Tonic

Form

The hymn takes a form that matches the text's meter and scansion. There are six lines of eight syllables in each stanza forming three couplets—an excellent choice on the part of the author for a hymn invoking the help of our triune God, specifically through the work of the third person, the Holy Spirit.

Fig. 30.3

Almighty God, We Come to You

We have not received the spirit of the world but the Spirit who is from God, that we may understand what God has freely given us. 1 Co.2:12

A Hymn before the Preaching of the Word
Eric J. Alexander, 2000

ST. ANDREWS L.M.ref.
Paul S. Jones, 2001

Stanza:

A   Almighty God, we come to you
A1   To seek your Living Word *anew*,

B   Praising your grace that you have giv'n
B1   This Book to be our guide to *heav'n*.

Refrain:

C   Let the anointing Spirit come
C1   To touch the lips that preach your name.

Musically there are formal patterns also. The first "A" line and the first "B" line begin with the same four melody notes. This links them as initiating elements of the couplets. The italicized final words of "A1" (*anew*) and of "B1" (*heav'n*) are linked by virtue of harmony. Each is set to a dominant (V) harmony, which means that they are cadentially and harmonically incomplete. In other words, "the song must go on!" It is obviously not over yet because a musical conclusion has not yet been reached. This moves the tune forward. The refrain provides a unifying element in the text because it is repeated after each stanza. It also summarizes the thoughts of the various stanzas into one action—a prayer or call for help to God: "Let the anointing Spirit come to touch the lips that preach your name."

More technical things could be said and explained, but I hope this brief look inside the world of the hymn composer will provide an unusual vantage point—one that might lead to thoughtful consideration of other hymns and thereby enrich the singer's experience.

Notes

1. Use of a metrical index (typically found in the back of a hymnal) has little to do with composing (other than that a composer can survey other hymns written in a similar meter to see how a certain meter has been handled in the past). But metrical indexes can serve to point one toward existing alternate tunes that will fit a text. This can be helpful if a tune is not well suited to a text, or if the tune is unfamiliar to the congregation and using a familiar one would serve better. In the index, each meter serves as a header and all the hymns with that particular meter are listed below it.

31
Criteria for Good Church Music

Sing to him a new song; play skillfully on the strings, with loud shouts. —*Psalm 33:3*

Many people are on the lookout for a short list of acceptable pieces or composers of church music. Some authors have penned articles or books in which they attempt to guide others with such a list. These are compiled with the best of intentions, no doubt, but are not adequate because of their subjectivity. So other questions arise. What composers write well for the modern church? What pieces from previous generations are still valid for our services? What publishing companies should we trust? What is good church music? Who should decide?

The two difficulties in providing answers to these questions are: (1) doing so objectively, and (2) doing so knowledgeably. Music is a very personal matter to most people. In fact, it has been said, "When it comes to music, everybody's an expert." Naturally, this is not the case; but each individual will know what he or she likes. Liking a piece or style of music, however, does not mean that it is appropriate music for church. Sacred text alone does not make a piece of music worthy of use, either. When an attempt is made to please everyone by doing a little of this and that, or by trying to select music enjoyed by all, we of necessity degenerate toward the lowest commonality. Yet biblically we are called to give our best in worship, and this requires effort and choice. Change for the better does not come easily, but education assists in achieving positive results. So let us consider some criteria to help discern *what is good church music.*

Textual Considerations

Considering a text is a first avenue of critique. It almost goes without saying that any text sung in worship should harmonize with biblical principles. I say "almost" because this basic principle is increasingly being forgotten or missed. Pastors should be involved at this point if the church's musicians lack sufficient theological training to select appropriate texts or if they have questions. This consideration does not apply to new music alone. Some hymns, anthems, and solo songs, particularly those with sentimental texts, may distort or contradict basic doctrines of the faith. Everything sung in worship should be examined in light of Scripture, and only what passes the test should be employed.

When a song quotes the Bible, the setting should take contextual meaning into account. In other words, Scripture should not be taken out of context in music any more than in a sermon or in prayer. This is an issue with many modern worship songs. It is fine to praise God and to say that we are praising God, but the example from the psalms and biblical canticles is to say *why* one is praising God—always for his acts or attributes. Songs in the Bible about the acts of God continually strike two main themes: his acts of *creation* and his acts of *redemption.* His attributes (holiness, justice, mercy, love, faithfulness, omnipotence, etc.) are many and make wonderful subject matter for worship music.

Worshipers should always be pointed to God, who is both the subject and the object of worship. Songs or hymns of encouragement that relate personal experiences are fine to include in worship, as long as they can be considered the common experience of the general body of believers. The testimony of John Newton's "Amazing Grace," for example, is true for every Christian. Songs or hymns of personal experience should always point one to Christ. Sentimental Christian folk narratives that describe someone's Sunday-school teacher, old stringed instruments, or some other human-interest story should be kept out of worship services. Their place is elsewhere.

Appropriateness is another textual test. One must determine whether the text is appropriate to the service itself, to a particular place in the service, and to the congregation. Finally, the text must be able to be understood in terms of both language and delivery. Strongly metaphoric poetry or anthem texts with Victorian English may require explanation to assist the congregation. Some language may need to be updated, although great care and consideration should be given before altering known texts, and such alteration should be a rare rather than a regular activity. Many hymnal editorial committees change texts without giving any notation or attribution—an omission that should cease.

Musical Considerations

Musical considerations include level of difficulty, melody, harmony, rhythm, form, and required forces. The acceptable level of difficulty will vary according to who will sing or play. A choir will be capable of singing more challenging music than the congregation. In this vein, it is preferable to sing something simple well rather than to attempt a complex work with poor results. At the same time, congregations, choirs, and other ensembles need to grow and to be stretched. In general, melodies for a congregation should be singable and memorable without being monotonous or overly predictable. Harmony should be interesting and should follow rules of good counterpoint and voice-leading. These are perhaps the most commonly missing elements of much new church music. Rhythm should match the text, placing strong syllables on strong beats, and should invigorate the singing. None of these musical features can be permitted to obscure the meaning of the text. In the case of contrapuntal music with multiple layers of text, printing words in the bulletin will help the listener follow the message.

Many of these basic musical features are found wanting in much Contemporary Christian Music (CCM). Melodies tend to be monotonous or to move in extreme ranges. Harmony often is simplistic and consists of repeated standard chords that have little direction or contrapuntal logic. Rhythm, especially, is often much different in "performance practice" from the way it is notated. And since the congregation will rarely have access to printed music or know how to read it (much less follow the particular rendition by the praise team of the morning), the soloistic nature and rhythmic complexity of most CCM pieces will elude the congregation, rendering successful unison singing difficult. Many "gospel hymns" (which should really be called "gospel songs" because they do not regularly manifest the characteristics of hymns) also exhibit trite harmony and melody and repetitive rhythm. Inclusion in a hymnal does not make a piece a hymn, nor does it make it worthy of use.

The fourth musical parameter by which music is judged is form. A piece of music, like any other type of art or literature, must have form. Form determines the overall structure, and phrasing defines the inner structure. Some pieces have lovely melodic/harmonic elements or a strong rhythm, but they lack good form. Judgments about musical parameters such as these require the insight of trained musicians. There is not one ideal form: many types are acceptable. But the ideal is for the musical form always to be well wedded to the text, so that what it communicates will reinforce, rather than contradict, the message of the text. Form, like melody, harmony, and rhythm, communicates musical meaning.

The performing forces available to present the music also factor in to determining its usage. If the necessary instruments, solo singers, or choral musicians are not available, certain music should be avoided. Aesthetic considerations are significant, although we will not discuss them here. Variety comes into play, as does association as an including or excluding parameter. For instance, if certain music is associated with the shopping mall, a baseball game, or a nightclub, its appropriateness for the church service should be questioned even though there may be nothing intrinsically wrong with the music in and of itself. Music that predisposes one to lightheartedness, frivolity, rebellion, or sensuality does not befit the worship of our great and holy God.

General Considerations

General considerations include musical function, marriage of text/tune, and style. How is the music to function within the service (prelude, postlude, prayer, praise, or proclamation)? Will the selection precede a prayer of confession or follow the sermon? Such placement has bearing on the choice of repertoire. Text and music should be well matched. At times one will encounter a solid, doctrinal text set to a trivial tune—this can be true of contemporary music or of a favorite hymn. Familiarity is a strength in worship; sentimentality is not. Fresh, new music is needed; but cheap, lackluster music should be avoided.

While musical style can be a subjective matter, trained church musicians will have insight to offer here that ordinary laymen will not normally possess. Church musicians should make these decisions for the people of God. This is the biblical model. Music directors are entrusted with the responsibility to guard and to teach the church's musical heritage. If the musical leader has sufficient musical and theological training (and people skills), he should have the respect of the pastor, church leaders, and congregation, and should determine what music is best for the body. Verbal and written explanation to accompany the introduction of new music or the reintroduction of great music of the past will go a long way in aiding the congregation and in raising its level of music appreciation.

Association and appropriateness to the text/occasion are factors that will help to determine how fitting a certain style may be. The corporate worship of God should be somehow set apart from the mundane tasks of everyday life (though it should be a regular activity). Thus, one may conclude that music used to worship God should be meaningful and other than ordinary (in other words, *extraordinary*). May the Spirit help us to write it, find it, rehearse it, and offer it for the glory of God.

Conclusion: Three Principles That Would Change Church Music Today

Although this book has espoused ideas that may differ from modern practice in many evangelical churches, none are more significant or powerful than the three concepts that will be reiterated here. These three ideas, examined in light of Scripture, found to be biblical (as I submit they are), and adopted as the philosophical and practical underpinning of ecclesiastical music-making and musical worship, would transform the church. This is not an overstatement, because that is precisely what happens when worship is accomplished according to Scripture.

1. We must measure our worship practices by the Word of God.

Scriptural principles should inform all our thinking, traditions, and practices in worship. Evaluating our actions and thinking by the Bible implies several things. First, we must believe that the Bible delivers God's will to us and that it is authoritative. Second, there must be the desire to live according to God's will through the work of the Holy Spirit. Third, knowing God's will and doing it are different things—but obviously one cannot do it without knowing it, and will be judged for knowing it but not doing it. Therefore, when we discover that our practices are in conflict with biblical teaching and principles, we must change. Change can be difficult. As creatures of habit we do not like it; yet we need to explain it to our congregations and embrace it even when doing so is costly. Such decisions may cost us personally, corporately, and financially. We may need to release certain things that we like or to which we have grown accustomed; but we will also gain the blessing of God. God blesses those who honor his Word.

2. We need to comprehend the pastoral nature of music ministry.

Music is not in competition with pastoral work. It *is* pastoral work in the sense that it can provide many of the same kinds of spiritual care and leadership that pastoral ministry provides. Music can comfort, encourage, exhort, teach, proclaim the gospel, and reach the spirit. Musical ministry also requires the work of the Holy Spirit. Therefore, when and where there are parallels, the parameters that one applies to ministerial staff should be applied to church musical staff, and those applied to sermons and prayers should be applied to church music. Pastoral musicians, irrespective of title, should be qualified, trained, spiritual, mature, humble, accountable, and aware of their role. They should be afforded honor, respect, authority, and sufficient, even generous, remuneration. The music presented in worship should be excellent, the best the congregation can offer, spiritual, joyful, thoughtful, intelligible, fitting, God-honoring, theocentric, properly rehearsed, live, instructive, functional, and artistic. Musicians other than the director should be skilled, devoted, prepared, service-oriented, and aware of their roles. What a difference it would make if every person involved—congregation, musicians, pastors—came to think about church music this way.

3. We should ensure that budgets and practices are informed by these truths.

Music in worship cannot be truly conformed to biblical standards and examples of excellence unless it is actively supported by the church leadership in word and deed and is adequately funded. Church musicians, too, like pastors, need this support in a world where there are no more Levitical cities to care for ministerial staff. Priorities in our churches need to demonstrate our care for people, even when a temporary focus may be placed on programs or buildings. Our practices and priorities need to be informed by our knowledge of what God has revealed to be important—rather than by the status quo, common opinion, or "the way it has always been." Our evaluation of what is good and appropriate in worship must be conformed to scriptural principle, not to popular taste or acceptance of unsubstantiated practice by assumption. We must ask three questions: (1) "*Why* do we do *what* we do in the *way* that we do it?" (2) "*How* should we be doing it according to Scripture?" and (3) "*What* will it take to make it so?"

Appendix 1: Thoughts about Music

This book has asserted ideas about music on the basis of Scripture. Other concepts have been proposed on the basis of inference from biblical truths, while a few were drawn from experience and were thus practical in nature. Perhaps some of these ideas have been convincing, while others have not. Undoubtedly some concepts would be clearer if the reader and I could have a conversation wherein both overarching ideas and subtle distinctions about music could be explored. Since such conversations are rare, I concluded that it might be helpful to express some general thoughts about music that inform my point of view. The reader can choose to critique, endorse, reject, or otherwise alter such statements in the process of articulating his or her own thoughts, but at least it is a place to begin. The ideas that follow, then, are the philosophical underpinnings of my approach to music.

Music as Language

Music is much like language. Some have called it a language, in fact. If this supposition is true, it implies that one must learn to speak the language of music in order to achieve fluency, and that those who speak it well will know when others likewise do and when they do not. Even if music cannot be fully accorded the status of a language, it certainly is analogous to language. As in language there can be good and bad writing, there can be good and bad musical composition. Those who "speak" the language of Western music have been schooled in it; they understand how a musical sentence, paragraph, or masterwork is constructed, and can "read" it intelligently. They have the skills and knowledge to evaluate a work's vocabulary, syntax, and form. This is why the supposition that "everyone is an expert" when it comes to music is insupportable. People may know that they *like* the sound of a certain musical group or a particular song, and they can have some degree of rapport with it, but one does not *know* music simply because one likes it. The declaration of a piece of music as "good" on such a basis does not make it so.

Musical quality is more than a matter of taste. Judgments about a piece of music based on personal pleasure or interest say little about the quality of the work itself, although this does not negate the pleasure or experience of the one offering them. Decisions of musical worth or value, however, do not hinge on popular opinion, although the financial recompense to a composer or company invariably does. Our society regularly judges "success" by commercial demand and fiscal gain. An educated, professional musician, however, should be able to proffer judgments about the quality of music apart from its appeal to the masses. Much as an insightful, trained editor can improve an essay, a good musician with a "highly developed, self-critical awareness of how well something is played or made" can evaluate a piece of music.[1]

One must have even greater insight to judge how something is *made* than is necessary to judge how it is *played.* A bad performance of good music is troubling to many, but probably more so to a trained musician. This pain is multiplied, however, if the music itself is already poor. As one professor has put it, "For a musician, listening to badly written music is like taking part in an inane or even nonsensical conversation."[2] Unfortunately, more and more such "conversations" have been occurring in evangelical worship, although (and perhaps because) fewer educated musicians remain in our churches to hear them—an equally troubling phenomenon, but a discussion for another place. It is also possible that one can lose perspective or miss the opportunity to gain a discerning ear with respect to musical judgment. As Johann Sebastian Bach's first biographer, Johann Nikolaus Forkel, put it, "The critical sense, which permits a man to distinguish good from bad, develops later than the aesthetic faculty and may be blunted and even destroyed by frequent contact with bad music."[3] He was right.

Art music, while sharing important characteristics with other categories of music (such as folk, patriotic, or pop, realizing that these genres are all difficult to define and are of necessity generalizations), exists for purposes different from those of other "musics." While all good music exists to express truth about creation, humanity, or divinity, the true value of art music, like all other art, resides in the experience or encounter with truth beyond us—something transcendent, something *Other*. Christians should recognize the latter as an encounter with God and his truth, even though art's reflections of his glory are still seen "through a glass darkly." This is not saying that art is somehow Art, but that great art music reflects the glory of God in ways that more common forms do not and cannot.

Modern pop music, in general (here I would exclude much jazz and blues, which are more artistic genres), does not accomplish this reflecting of God's glory; for only rarely does it set forth man's best or purposely attempt to enlighten, teach, or display truth for the betterment of society. It is not transcendent. The occasional pop song may point to some noble aspiration or quality, and many call attention to injustice or disparity; but overall this is music written for mass distribution and mass appeal, produced by big business to make money and to entertain. In short, it is commercial. While nothing is essentially wrong with making money or entertaining, these two purposes do not belong in worship or in worship music.

Music in Worship

Strictly utilitarian approaches to music do not engender the right spirit or valuing of music, either, although music has function and properly serves in worship in a functional as well as an aesthetic manner. The uses of church music as an "audience draw" and for the satisfaction of felt needs are not proper functions and wear the cloak of *means toward ends.* As Samuel Hsu put it, "We have some who are interested in music only for its usefulness in evangelism. Any style that does not effectively serve the purpose is discouraged. This too does not harmonize with the biblical teaching on music. It is a form of aesthetic utilitarianism. Such people do not so much despise music as abuse it."[4] Church music, of course, has a function; in fact, it has the highest function—to serve our worship of God, and even to be itself a form of worshiping God. The manner in which art music in church or other church music manifests its greatest good has to do with transcendence. Church music involves us, but it should help us move beyond ourselves, as the proper worship of God will do. Much church music today falls far short of this purpose even in its basic construction, let alone in its performance.

Worship is not about us, but about the Almighty. Worship music may reveal or communicate truth about us, but it must also cause us to sense something greater. Such music obviously involves us, yet we are neither its subject nor its object. We must give God what is excellent, and that for which he asks, not simply what we prefer or desire to give. The sacrifices of Cain and Abel are an enlightening example. Is our best too good for God? Hardly. Even our finest is like dust to the infinite Creator. Yet he delights in sacrificial music of devotion or praise from his children when our hearts are yielded to him. We should offer our personal best, simultaneously realizing that what we offer is flawed and that the grace and work of the Holy Spirit is necessary for any good to come of it. Confidence and humility should be the twin companions of this perspective—qualities that should balance each other and be present in the Christian musician or artist.

Real art music requires humility on the part of the listener and the musician, and it requires patience, too; it makes demands of us, rather than the other way around. This does not characterize an appreciator of fine music as an elitist, as the allegation sometimes goes. Rather, the systemic exclusion of classical art music from the education of the masses (by the state and by the church) constructs and fosters the very perception of exclusivity that cultural pluralists reject in the name of diversity and inclusiveness. When we (as the church) reclaim our right and privilege to educate ourselves, especially our children, in great music, we can then embrace our collective musical heritage, which will, in turn, help us bear new fruit. Prevalent influences in postmodern society sometimes mar the clarity of this truth.

For example, we must not permit our consumer culture to influence our approach to church music so that it is analogous to a record store where people move from aisle to aisle until they find that for which they are shopping. "Blended" services rarely seem to succeed for this reason. Such services do not evidence enough of any one style to appeal to a clear majority—so churches split into services of various music styles to satisfy their "customers." But why would either worship or worship music be patterned after what a majority or minority of people (supposedly) want? Why would the accomplishment of such a feat be considered "good"? And why do we equate worship style with musical style?

The worship of God is not all about young people, or any other demographic, or about attracting unbelievers to worship. If our music, by virtue of its grandeur, beauty, and nonworldly subject matter, causes unbelievers to become interested in Christianity or our God, that is a wonderful result. Christian worship is a sign to unbelievers; it is not about them. Neither is it about giving each age group, or other culturally identifiable group, a taste of its own musical dialect in the context of a comprehensive worship service. Again, such an approach puts an undue emphasis on people, who are significant participants in worship but are not its subject or object. Variety and diversity in musical expression are useful parameters that will inform a good music director, but neither should be our highest goal. Thus, the music employed in our worship, despite music's potential power to allure, is not about drawing any particular group into the church or enticing them to stay. A great question that Hsu asked his readers, and that we can ask ourselves, is: "Can the world know how much we care about God by our music? More importantly, can God?"[5]

Musical Meaning

In discussing the power of music itself, I do not intend to downplay the usefulness and power of words; but music can and does say something meaningful without them. Music engages us emotionally, physically, intellectually, and spiritually; and at times, it communicates something quite different from the text that accompanies it. This does not imply that music is direct in such communication, or that one can necessarily articulate or decipher its wordless "message." More often music communicates at a spiritual or emotional level, beyond words, in broad strokes at some times and in fine nuances at others. This metaphysical element is precisely what makes music so powerful and what makes a discussion about it considerably complex.

The metaphysics of music, however, cannot be ignored simply because it is difficult to understand. In this area, is it possible that many pastors, churches, and musicians err regarding the choice of music employed in worship? If engagement with music at the level of text or personal taste is the extent of our selection process, the "screening" and value determinations about a song end prematurely. Is it true that as long as the text is passable or the style feels familiar, the piece is acceptable? What about the music itself? Does it not strike us as ironic that decisions about church *music* (i.e., the arrangement of sound, the thing that distinguishes song from other verbal communication, the force analogous to a powerful language) are often based strictly on the merits of text? Music is not devoid of meaning—intrinsic or extrinsic. People may disagree about what is meant, or may not even be aware of it, but music itself is still a powerful communicative force.

Music consists of sounds and rests; yet the definition of "music" is not sound itself or the lack of it, but the arrangement or organization of those sounds and silences. The best "texted" music (assuming that the text itself is legitimate) is music whose text and its musical setting agree in tone, quality, and character—ultimately, then, in meaning. When this agreement occurs, "texted" music is fully authentic. Music contains subtext, just like language, where meaning is implied. Any spoken conversation or written communication has the capacity to convey more than it appears to be saying on the surface. The giver and receiver of this information may be conscious of such subtext or may remain unaware of it. Cognizance of verbal subtext does not affect its existence, although it may affect its rendering. So it is with music. The instruments, performers, style, tempo, dynamics, form, associative connections, historical context—all of these musical parameters, and more, inform the subtext. And a performer who is aware of what a piece of music "says" is logically better situated to further such meaning than one who is not.

Other things can also affect what music "says." The temporal and physical spaces in which music unfolds, and the gesture and nuance that accompany and shape it, inform musical meaning to some degree. So it follows that the order of the organized sounds has purpose, logic, and meaning, as does the delivery or performance (though the "reading" or performance of the music is also separate from its construction). Art music, as a discursive form of human interaction, communicates something beyond words, and this "something" must be either true or false. It must either better our souls and minds or harm them. It must point us either toward God or away from him. Music cannot remain neutral, although it will not affect all people in the same way.

Music, Morality, and Memory

Some have suggested that music is amoral—that there is no "musical meaning" except that which is attached to music. Therefore, it is argued, the good or bad resides in the association, not in the music itself, and thus all styles are legitimate. But is not the identification of something as "legitimate" tantamount to calling it "good" (in both a moral and a qualitative sense), whereas something illegitimate would be "bad"? In other words, the determination *not* to make a judgment about music actually *makes* one—albeit a pluralistic and relativistic one. The concept of extrinsic (associative, attached) meaning has credibility, of course. But using such reasoning as a basis for the amorality of music is a non sequitur because music is *never* devoid of attached meaning—whether this is cultural, personal, or the collective consciousness of those familiar enough with it to extrapolate a normative interpretation (for instance, a subculture of appreciators who, in some sense, agree). So even if music were essentially amoral, which I do not concede, it would necessarily exist in physical (aural) reality as a moral force. William Edgar put it this way: "Music is not neutral. It has a 'message.' This message is not always easy to discern, but, like architecture, it conveys a world-view."[6] Throughout the centuries, other writers and thinkers have argued for the moral nature of music, as we will momentarily see.

Usually, the *memories* of feelings are evoked as one listens to music, more than feelings themselves. This explains the nostalgia we attach to certain pieces, and it speaks to the power that music has to help us, even to force us, to recollect. Paul Hindemith, the celebrated German twentieth-century composer who immigrated to America and taught at Yale University, wrote:

> We cannot keep music from uncovering the memory of former feelings, and it is not in our power to avoid them, because the only way to "have"—to *possess*—music, is to connect it with those images, shadows, dreamy reproductions of actual feelings, no matter how realistic and crude or, on the contrary, how denatured, stylized, and sublimated they may be.[7]

Here again, the attached associations that inform our perception of musical truth are mentioned. Augustine evidently believed the same thing, for he wrote in the *Confessions*, "The several affections of our spirit have their proper moods answerable to their variety in the voice and singing, and by some secret association they be stirred up."[8] Augustine and others have also stated or implied that music must have moral consequence. For example, John Calvin, in the preface to the 1543 edition of Marot's *Psalter*, claimed:

> There is hardly anything in the world with more power to turn or bend, this way and that, *the morals of men* . . . It [music] has a secret power to move our hearts in one way or another. Wherefore we must be the more diligent in ruling it in such a manner that it may be useful to us and in no way pernicious.[9]

Plato said something similar to Calvin's observation centuries earlier, in the *Republic*. In discussing the need to guard education and tradition in music and poetry, Plato pinpointed an insidious danger that is verifiably true of our culture and time:

> Then it seems, I said, that it is in music and poetry that our guardians must build their bulwark. At any rate, lawlessness easily creeps in there unnoticed. Yes, *as if music and poetry were only play and did no harm at all.* It is harmless—except, of course, that when lawlessness has established itself there, it flows over little by little *into characters and ways of life.* Then, greatly increased, it steps out into private contracts, Socrates, it makes its insolent way into the laws and government, until in the end it overthrows everything, public and private.[10]

Calvin also classed music among the "excellent gifts of the Holy Spirit."[11] Martin Luther loved music and wrote much about it, including this excerpt from a letter written in 1530 to his contemporary, the composer Ludwig (Louis) Senfl, in which he discusses the effects of music:

> Indeed I plainly judge, and do not hesitate to affirm, that except for theology there is no art that could be put on the same level with music, since except for theology [music] alone produces what otherwise only theology can do, namely, a calm and joyful disposition. Manifest proof [of this is the fact] that the devil, the creator of saddening cares and disquieting worries, takes flight at the sound of music almost as he takes flight at the word of theology.[12]

Obviously, on the basis of such statements, Luther would not and could not state that either music or theology is amoral. Frank Gaebelein noted that with respect to the writings of Augustine and Boethius on music, "the two views . . . differ in their estimate of the inherent moral and spiritual influence of music; but in respect to the tie between music and the moral side of man they are at one. Both imply that music cannot be morally neutral."[13] Julian Johnson, in his brilliant book *Who Needs Classical Music?* states that art music "has an ethical dimension, and our use of music and the musical choices we make involve us in ethical decisions."[14] Aristotle held that the kind of music that one listens to will affect his inner self, that music, "in reflecting character, molds and influences it."[15] In this respect, one must take to heart the words of King Solomon: "Keep your heart with all vigilance, for from it flow the springs of life" (Prov. 4:23), and the words of the apostle Paul: "So flee youthful passions and pursue righteousness, faith, love, and peace, along with those who call on the Lord from a pure heart" (2 Tim. 2:22).

Music and the Church

Gaebelein asked the question in 1954: "Can it be that we evangelicals are not only aesthetically immature but that we also insist upon remaining so?"[16] At times, one must come to this conclusion; and yet, some go too far in the opposite direction. To become aesthetically more mature does not mean that aesthetics must be elevated to the point where it becomes sacramental. Music is not to be worshiped, nor can we somehow rest in the idea that great music in church means that genuine worship is taking place.

The idea that "higher" thoughts are appropriate to the church is not a new one, and the postmodern church's struggle with excellence and mediocrity is not new, either. C. S. Lewis, in his essay "On Church Music," wrote:

> I do not think it can be the business of the Church greatly to co-operate with the modern State in appeasing inferiority complexes and encouraging the natural man's instinctive hatred of excellence. Democracy is all very well as a political device. It must not intrude into the spiritual, or even the aesthetic, world.[17]

Johnson speaks similarly in his assessment of the present:

> We live in a digest culture in which an unwillingness to engage in sustained thought rapidly becomes a hostility toward it. Before long, the hostility masks an incapacity to do so . . . This is glaringly obvious in the case of music . . . Our culture is not just ignorant; it is stubbornly and arrogantly so.[18]

Need this be said of the church? I believe it need not be so. Our churches should be centers of biblical and musical education. They should be preservers of our rich musical history and promoters of excellent new music. We should be the intellectually aware and emotionally engaged appreciators and artisans of all that is fine, noble, and lovely in God's great world. We should anticipate the glories of heaven in a musical language that is as close as we can get to that glorious place and Presence, even while we are physically and temporally earthbound. So let us think and dialogue about music; let us carefully evaluate it, consider its roles in worship, and reflect on how we engage in this spiritual activity.

Notes

1. Julian Johnson, *Who Needs Classical Music? Cultural Choice and Musical Value* (New York: Oxford, 2002), 97.

2. Ibid.

3. Johann Nikolaus Forkel, *Johann Sebastian Bach: His Life, Art, and Work* (1802; repr., New York: Vienna House, 1974), 99.

4. Samuel Hsu, "Sacred Music," in *Toward a Harmony of Faith and Learning: Essays on Bible College Curriculum*, ed. Kenneth O. Gangel (Farmington Hills, MI: William Tyndale College Press, 1983), 142–43.

5. Ibid., 139.

6. William Edgar, professor of apologetics, Westminster Theological Seminary, e-mail correspondence with author, February 6, 2005.

7. Paul Hindemith, *A Composer's World* (1952), in *Composers on Music*, ed. Josiah Fisk (Boston: Northeastern University Press, 1997), 314.

8. Oliver Strunk, *Source Readings in Music History* (New York: W. W. Norton, 1950), 65.

9. Ibid., 347 (italics added).

10. Plato, *Republic*, trans. G. M. A. Grube, rev. C. D. C. Reeve (Indianapolis: Hackett Publishing, 1992), 99–11 (424 b–e) (italics added).

11. Frank E. Gaebelein, *The Pattern of God's Truth* (New York: Oxford, 1954), 72.

12. Martin Luther, in *Letters II*, ed. Gottfried G. Krodel, vol. 49 of *Luther's Works*, ed. Helmut T. Lehmann (Philadelphia: Fortress Press, 1972), 427–29.

13. Gaebelein, *Pattern of God's Truth*, 73, quoting Augustine's *De Musica*, Book VI, and Boethius' *De Institutione Musica*.

14. Johnson, *Who Needs Classical Music?* 115.

15. S. H. Butcher, *Aristotle's Theory of Poetry and Fine Art* (London: n.p., 1920), 130.

16. Gaebelein, *Pattern of God's Truth*, 78.

17. C. S. Lewis, "On Church Music," in *Christian Reflections in the Collected Works of C. S. Lewis* (New York: Inspirational Press, 1996), 241.

18. Johnson, *Who Needs Classical Music?* 89.

Appendix 2: A Philosophy–Theology of Music for Tenth Presbyterian Church

The following philosophy–theology of music statement is not offered as a standard, norm, or rule for all churches and assemblies of believers. It merely serves as an example of what one church asserts is a biblical view of music with application to its specific context. The document is offered here, by its author, with the hope that it may be of some help to others who may wish to make a similar statement, and to all who seek to glorify God in their musical worship and work.

Our Philosophy–Theology of Music
Tenth Presbyterian Church Philadelphia, Pennsylvania

The philosophy–theology of music at Tenth Presbyterian Church is based on four considerations. The first is that every aspect of music in the church must be submitted to the lordship of Christ. The second consideration is that music in the church serves various functions, and while they should all be biblical, these functions imply and result in different parameters and guidelines. Most notably, musical activity outside corporate worship will have some different parameters from music within worship services. Third, as Christians we recognize that our lives are to be characterized by the continuous worship of God and that in this respect all musical activities for the individual Christian should be, in some sense, acts of worship. Further, the Tenth Mission/Purpose Statement, in accordance with Scripture, declares that our music is to be thoughtful and excellent—so these qualities should pervade all areas of musical activity in the church. What follows is a theological and philosophical statement on music in the church with application to our congregation, including aspects of specific function and responsibility.

Praise the Lord!
I will give thanks to the Lord with my whole heart,
in the company of the upright, in the congregation. (Ps. 111:1)

Worship Music

We believe that all music employed in gathered worship (including wedding ceremonies, memorial services, and other types of worship services) should be:

1. *Biblical*—As our rule of faith and practice, the Word of God is our authority. It contains sufficient principles, examples, and directives to inform our concept of worship music. Music serves in worship as praise, prayer, and proclamation (1 Chron. 25:1; Ps. 51; 96). Although there are distinctions, in these ways the music ministry shares similar roles and goals with the pulpit ministry. Music may carry our thanksgiving as well as our lament and cries for mercy (Ps. 95; 102). It should include psalms, hymns, spiritual songs, voices, and instruments (Ps. 150; Eph. 5:19; Col. 3:16–17). Sung texts must not conflict with the teachings of Scripture, and the Scriptures themselves are the best texts for worship (Ps. 119:54; 2 Tim. 3:16).
2. *God-centered*—Texts and hearts should be focused on God who is both the subject and object of worship (Ps. 22:22; 100). The

music is offered principally to him, rather than to each other, and it is for his glory, not for our own. Yet it should also edify, admonish, and teach the body of Christ (1 Cor. 14:26; Col. 3:16). It is a communal activity. Applause for musicians in the context of worship is therefore unnecessary and unbiblical. We present most noncongregational service music from the rear choir loft, so as not to draw undue attention to the vessel through which the music is offered (Matt. 6:1; Rom. 12:1; Phil. 2:5–7). Although clapping one's hands to God is mentioned in the psalms, in our cultural context applause is overwhelmingly associated with the entertainment industry, and so it is best avoided as a worship response.

3. *Excellent*—Excellence is, first of all, an attribute of God (Gen. 1:31; Ps. 8:1). We should offer him the best we can and nothing less. Our best has to do with the intrinsic and extrinsic qualities of our music—its melody, harmony, rhythm, form, and texts—which will be judged according to musical standards of excellence, as will its appropriateness for a worship context and its delivery by the musicians offering it. Decisions about the quality and type of music offered in worship are entrusted to the music director, who will consider musical, theological, cultural, and other informing aspects when making such decisions for the congregation. Excellence should never become a goal in and of itself, however, and it does not substitute for offering music with the proper spirit.
4. *Of the Spirit*—Without the work of the Holy Spirit, our efforts are meaningless (John 4:24; 6:63; 1 Cor. 2:13). Music is not worship in and of itself. Without due caution, one can actually be guilty of worshiping the music that one enjoys. It is important to be mindful of the distinction between spiritual truth and musical pleasure. Worship directed anywhere but to God is idolatry.
5. *In truth*—Truthfulness in worship refers to the actions we take, the attitudes of our hearts, and the intentions of our minds. These should align with biblical teaching on worship (John

4:24). Musical offerings should be genuine and offered to the best of one's ability. The congregation and its leaders should sing psalms and hymns with understanding and with conviction—with the mind and the spirit (1 Cor. 14:15).

6. *Skillfully led*—According to Psalm 33:1–3, we are to compose, sing, and play skillfully to the Lord. This demands that those leading in public worship music should be skillful, trained musicians. For musical leadership we draw on proficient amateur, semi-professional, and professional musicians from within the congregation and Christian brothers and sisters from other fellowships. In keeping with biblical practice (Neh. 12:46–47a; 1 Chron. 23) and in order to support musicians who are dedicated to music as a calling, we customarily provide salaries for church musicians who are full- or part-time members of the staff (including interns) and offer honoraria for vocalists, instrumentalists, and choristers (section leaders of the choir) who participate in public worship.
7. *Prepared*—Because our music should be excellent and skillful, it follows that it must be carefully chosen, adequately rehearsed, and presented by musicians who have prepared themselves before God (1 Chron. 25:6–7). Choirs (adult and children) and soloists should be well prepared for the significant roles they will play in corporate worship. Worship is not an opportunity to "try out" one's ability or to showcase anyone or anything.
8. *Meaningful*—Our musical offerings must be intentional and have purpose. They should never be trite or perfunctory (Matt. 6:7; 15:8–9). The ministers carefully select the psalms and hymns sung in worship with the input of the music director. All other music is selected or approved by the music director, who by biblical example is to be the guardian of the people's praise (1 Chron. 15:22). An attempt is made, whenever possible, to make service music meaningful by suiting it to a particular element of the service and/or to the theme of the sermon.
9. *Of the people*—Largely this means that our music will find its basis in congregational song, the most important kind of worship

music. It also means that the congregation should be fully involved in singing, listening, and learning (Ps. 111:1; 149:1). This characteristic also informs our musical choices—that our music should be generally accessible to the people (or made accessible/taught by communicating information about it), although it is directed principally to God. This does not mean, however, that music selected will not require thought or that it will be "popular" in nature or immediately accessible to all who hear it.

10. *Joyful/emotional*—One of the most significant aspects of music in worship is that it should reflect the joy of being a Christian (Ps. 47:1), and a thankful, grateful spirit (Eph. 5:19–20). Many other emotions are inherent in music-making, and the book of Psalms provides examples of the musical expression of many of them within the context of worship.
11. *Intelligible*—This parameter has ramifications for sung language, which on most occasions should be English. Language used in worship should be comprehensible, and texts for noncongregational, sung music will appear in the order of service. When other languages are utilized, a translation will be given so that worshipers can fully interact with the textual and musical meaning (1 Cor. 14:7–10, 19).
12. *Authentic*—Authenticity in worship is related to truthfulness, but here refers to the realm of aesthetics. We utilize live musicians for worship-service music and believe that it is important to do so. The Bible models this practice in many places. We do not use prerecorded music or accompaniment tracks both because this precludes other participants from the body and because such recordings are historical rather than organic. The use of live musicians affords flexibility in tempo, nuance, time, pitch, and all the other living aspects of music. Instrumentalists will play on acoustic instruments. The argument can be made that something real is better than something that is not real. We avoid electronic instruments that require amplification and function as recording devices because they are aesthetically inau-

thentic.[1] Truthfulness should characterize all that we offer God (John 4:24), and this extends to music, musicians, and musical instruments.

Concert Music

Concert music, by definition, is music performed in programs called "concerts" or "recitals" that are outside the context of regular worship services. Concerts are not worship services, although one is certainly capable of worshiping in a concert context, and the performers' work can be a musical offering to God. Some of the parameters such as theme, language, applause, and other protocol for a concert, however, will be different from those in force in the context of worship. Challenging art music and other music that primarily exists to display the virtuosity of the performer are welcome in this context.

We believe that music performed in concert programs at Tenth should be:

1. *To the glory of God*—All music is offered *soli Deo gloria* irrespective of its origin, its compositional language, or the composer's intention. Applause on the part of the concert audience is culturally appropriate recognition for the effort and skill of the performers. At the same time, both audience and performers should internally acknowledge that it is all "from him and through him and to him" (Rom. 11:36).
2. *Excellent*—This has to do with the level of performer/performance as well as with the music selected and how it is presented. (See "Worship Music," above, for more on this subject.)
3. *Artistic*—Most music performed in concert contexts will be art music or sacred music. Art music is music that exists for purposes beyond function, though it may be functional. This is different from popular music, commercial music, patriotic music, or other idioms. Art music primarily includes the genre of "classical" music, although some jazz and sacred music fits here as well. The amount of repertoire and variety of styles and forms

that fit these classifications are incredibly large, spanning more than a thousand years.

4. *Edifying to the saints*—We hold that concerts presented at Tenth, or other places where ensembles from Tenth perform, should be a means of bolstering both the spirit and the mind. Concerts should encourage believers in their faith, musical understanding, and artistic experience. Thus, in addition to the qualities listed above, verbal or written notes will be regular facets of such programs to aid the audience.
5. *An outreach to the community*—Concert programs draw some into the church buildings who do not attend our regular worship services. All programs are open to everyone without charge. We also aim to give some verbal witness to Christ and the Christian faith in our concert programs.
6. *A venue for professional Christian musicians*—Tenth concerts also exist to provide an opportunity for Christian musicians of the highest order to offer back to God what he has called them to do and to be as artists. The music director invites the soloists, who may be from Tenth but will often be Christian brothers and sisters from other fellowships. Other musicians may play a supporting role as accompanists or orchestral/choral musicians.

Music in Settings Outside the Worship Service

Music is included in activities ranging from Bible study, to men's or women's groups, to banquets, meetings, coffeehouses, retreats, conferences, and other church functions. All music for these activities should be God-honoring and biblical with regard to text and music, in keeping with the principles outlined in this document. The church's music director, in partnership with pastoral staff and ministry leaders, will oversee music and musical events occurring within the church buildings outside the context of regular worship services or Sunday school. This is primarily to safeguard the church and to ensure a level of quality by having an educated musician guide in such decisions. Any Tenth group desirous of engaging guest musicians, soloists, or instrumentalists for Tenth events should consult with the music director as a first step. Though musical style will be more broadly defined outside the context of worship services, standards of excellence will be upheld for all events.

Music Education

The church has a responsibility to educate its people in the music of the church and, indeed, to teach Christian doctrine through music. Church-music education takes place in many forms.

Some of the ways we seek to provide such education at Tenth Church are through:

1. *Hymn singing*—Congregational hymnody and psalmody teach and propagate our faith even as we sing to God. These bear witness to the lost and help the Christian recall biblical teaching. They are also a means for every Christian present to be a musical participant in worship and to join the heavenly choirs that praise God without ceasing (Eph. 5:19–20; Col. 3:16–17; Rev. 4, 5).
2. Schola Cantorum—(*Schola Cantorum* means "Singing School" and is the name of our children's music education program, taken from historical models in the church.) Of particular importance is the training of children to sing and to be musically literate (Ps. 8:2; 78:1–8; Matt. 21:15–16). The example of Scripture is for parents to teach children, who will in turn teach their own children (1 Chron. 25:6–8). Since many adults today do not have sufficient musical literacy or education to do this, we provide general musical education for our covenant children. This education is grounded in tonal and rhythmic foundations and is expanded on in choral experiences as well as hymn study and memorization. *Schola* is taught by a faculty of professional music educators and musicians from within the congregation.
3. *Choral ensembles*—The choral groups at Tenth (Tenth Church Choir, Men's Choir, ACTS Choral Ensemble, and *Schola Cantorum* choirs), in addition to their primary function in worship services, provide opportunity for many to learn more

about vocal technique and music in general, to have fellowship with other believers, and to exercise and develop their musical abilities.

4. *Bible School weekly opening exercises*—The music director or members of the music staff teach aspects of church music to the Bible School children (Grades 1–6) briefly each Sunday morning. The focus is hymnody, often the opening hymn for morning worship that day.
5. *Hymn services*—Approximately once a month the congregation is led in a brief hymn service preceding evening worship. Generally, the hymns are linked by theme. This forum provides contextual information and teaching about psalmody/hymnody so that the congregation is intellectually engaged with what it sings.
6. *Hymns of the month*—Each month a new or less familiar hymn is sung during evening worship throughout the month, with the goal of expanding the congregation's hymn repertoire.
7. *Tenth Concert Series*—The Concert Series provides opportunity for Tenth members and guests to experience many different types of art music performed by a wide array of musicians. The musical mediums include solo and ensemble, vocal and instrumental, old and new, classical and sacred, chamber and symphonic. Performers offer verbal commentary about the music being played or sung, thereby providing a link for the audience to both music and performer.
8. Tenth Press *articles*—Several times annually the music director writes articles for the congregation that describe the repertoire for an upcoming musical event, issue a call for involvement, explain a facet of musical worship, or relay a need or opportunity having to do with the music ministry.
9. *Community-school instruction*—We believe that music lessons on various instruments as well as voice should be available to church members and members of the community through the auspices of the church. This extends to basic music skills, such as reading and theory, as well as to hymnody and the history of Christian worship. Although plans are still being developed, in time we

hope to offer music lessons and classes for all ages taught by Christian musicians. This will be another means of musical outreach.

Music Internships

As a church we have a responsibility before God to help young church musicians prepare for music leadership positions in other churches (in the same way that seminarians preparing for pulpit ministry apprentice with pastoral staff). Thus, the music director has two or three college-age interns/assistants working with him each year. These younger musicians are selected by the music director and interviewed by the music committee. They give reports to the music committee at scheduled meetings. They serve nine-month terms (September through May) in part-time, salaried positions. The interns/assistants selected are assigned varying responsibilities according to their abilities and need whereby they gain experience and firsthand knowledge in virtually all aspects of church-music ministry. Also emphasized is the development of their overall musicianship. These younger musicians contribute to the ministry of music in the church in valuable ways during their year or years on staff.

Music and the Individual

The church has no specific authority over the music that individuals choose to purchase, or that to which they listen or in which they participate. Nor does the church seek to make such decisions or determine what is good or bad music for its members with respect to their private lives. But the following concepts and Scripture passages are offered for consideration when choosing music for oneself or for one's household:

1. Music is an integral part of the Christian life and should be encouraged in the home, particularly in family worship. Martin Luther (with hymnody) and John Calvin (with psalmody) both encouraged singing in the home. Singing and learning to play instruments is consistent with biblical teaching (Ps. 92:1–3; 98; Eph. 5:15–21; Col. 3:16). Singing is, in fact, one of those few

activities that we know is eternal (Rev. 4; 5). It also gives opportunities to glorify God inside and outside the church.

2. Music is a powerful medium that teaches and communicates things in deep ways. It can overpower other verbal or written teaching with ease. There is good and bad music. Music is not neutral—it will affect those who listen either positively or negatively. Thus, musical choice is essentially an ethical choice. Texts that are anti-God, anti-authority, or humanistic (and these can appear in any musical style) will have a negative effect. Styles that are associated with baser things will not usually be edifying and would best be avoided. It is left up to the individual under the guidance of the Holy Spirit to determine what is God-honoring or destructive in this regard.
3. Most people identify with a certain style of music or several styles as a means of defining themselves (sociologically, intellectually, and in other ways). The music to which we listen shapes our character, personality, and mind. Music is not without moral substance or consequence. Parents especially should be mindful of this on behalf of their children and be cognizant of aesthetic concerns as well.

Finally, brothers, whatever is true, whatever is honorable, whatever is just, whatever is pure, whatever is lovely, whatever is commendable—if there is any excellence, if there is anything worthy of praise—think about these things. (Phil. 4:8)

Notes

1. A current exception to this standard is our digital organ. The session has approved the concept of a new pipe organ and intends to ask the congregation to replace our current instrument when the Lord provides the means.

Index of Subjects and Names

Paul S. Jones is Organist and Music Director at historic Tenth Presbyterian Church, Philadelphia, where he conducts the choirs and chamber orchestra and oversees the music program. He served five other churches before being called to Tenth in 1997.

He holds undergraduate degrees in performance, composition, and Bible from Philadelphia Biblical University, where he served on the faculty for eight years; a master's degree in piano performance; and the Doctor of Music degree in choral conducting from Indiana University. As a conductor or pianist he has collaborated with internationally renowned artists such as David Kim, Anne Martindale Williams, Sharon Sweet, Jerome Hines, and Menahem Pressler and has led the Mendelssohn Club of Philadelphia, the Chamber Orchestra of Philadelphia, the PBU Symphony, and other ensembles in major venues, including the Kimmel Center in Philadelphia.

Dr. Jones is president of Paul Jones Music Inc., a corporation distributing the music of Christian composers who seek to provide new artistic and functional music for the church. He has composed/arranged more than seventy sacred works and has recorded six compact discs as pianist, organist, conductor, or composer/arranger. He also serves on the Council of the Alliance of Confessing Evangelicals, and speaks at universities, seminaries, and conferences for pastors and musicians around the country.